The Great Rebalancing

How our debt-driven economy turns scarce assets into the ultimate investment

JEROEN BLOKLAND

The Great Rebalancing

How our debt-driven economy turns scarce assets into the ultimate investment

The Great Rebalancing

Published by Jeroen Blokland Uitgeverij, Rotterdam, Netherlands

First Edition, December 2025
ISBN: 9789083598826 (paperback)
Category: Business & Economics / Macroeconomics
Design and Layout: Bruggn Design, Armando van Bruggen
Cover Photography: Sander Nagel Photography
For permission requests, contact: jeroen@bloklandfund.com
Website: greatrebalancing.com | bloklandfund.com

For Jonah and Elin, forever the most important people in my life and the ultimate proof that the most valuable asset needs no cash flow.

Table of contents

Introduction

It's 9:30 a.m. on Friday, September 23, 2022, an early autumn morning, when the newly appointed Chancellor of the Exchequer, Kwasi Kwarteng, stands ready in the House of Commons to present his so-called "mini-budget." Just hours earlier, the clock had ticked mercilessly past midnight as he and his boss, Prime Minister Liz Truss, put the final touches on their reckless gamble, the launch of their "Trussonomics" stimulus plan.

Within hours of Kwarteng's appearance, the United Kingdom is in turmoil. The £45 billion in unfunded tax cuts for the wealthy hits Britain's financial system like a hammer. Markets shudder as panic strikes without mercy. The pound plunges to a historic low and interest rates surge.

But what comes next is even worse. Still oblivious to the coming fallout, Kwarteng defends his plan and even hints at more tax cuts during the BBC talk show *Sunday with Laura Kuenssberg.* By Sunday evening, it's clear that when markets reopen the next morning, an unprecedented financial carnage will unfold.

By Monday, the fragility of Britain's bond-dependent financial system becomes brutally clear. Phone lines light up at pension funds and insurers that, often with leverage, have piled into long-dated government bonds to hedge their risks. They are forced to post collateral as the value of those bonds plunges. But pension funds and insurers are out of cash, forcing them to sell their bonds at steep losses. This vicious spiral pushes Britain's supposedly safe pension system to the brink of collapse.

It's now Wednesday, September 28. Outside, the weather has turned grim, gray, and wet. While Truss and Kwarteng stay silent, the Bank of England snaps and finally decides that enough is enough. Even with inflation running at a staggering 8.6 percent, the central bank does the unthinkable: It abandons its price stability target and steps in with an extraordinary emergency operation, injecting as much as £65 billion into the system. The Bank of England ends up spending more to keep the system afloat than the government would spend on Kwarteng's unfunded tax cuts. Britain's financial system, and the fragile pension pots of hard-working Britons, narrowly escape disaster. Kwarteng and Truss do not.

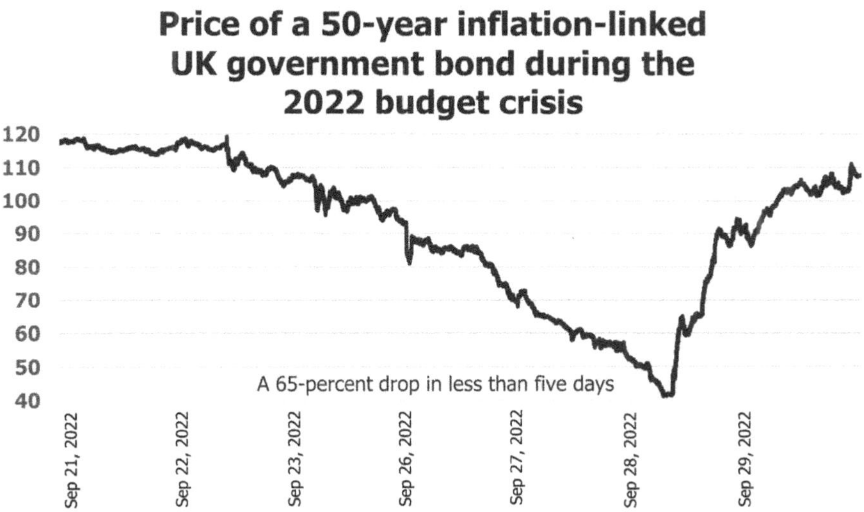

Source: The Great Rebalancing

A Nonfiction Investment Book

If you're wondering whether you've just opened a financial thriller, this introduction has done its job. Yet what you're holding in your hands will be labeled an "investment book" instead of a non-fiction thriller. The central message of this book is straightforward: In today's debt-driven economy, your investment portfolio must be built radically different.

The 60/40 portfolio (60 percent equities, 40 percent bonds), which traditional wealth managers still impose on their clients, is hopelessly outdated. Bonds are anything but safe, as the chaos in the United Kingdom a few years ago made abundantly clear. In fact, bonds have become steady killers of purchasing power. That these same wealth managers continue to claim otherwise, proudly advertising bonds as "low risk" on their websites, remains bewildering.

Beyond the price swings and potential losses, investing in debt does nothing to preserve the value of your wealth or pension. With bonds, you're almost guaranteed to lose purchasing power over time as inflation quietly eats away at it. The same is true, even more so, for savings accounts. This book explains that inflation will stay far above the levels central banks "promise."

I'm fairly sure nobody sets out to lose purchasing power. So if bonds aren't the answer, what should you invest in? The short answer is assets that are intrinsically scarce, things that cannot be printed or created at will. These have consistently proven to protect against the corrosive effects of inflation and to shield investors from the ever-expanding policies of governments and central banks determined to finance endless deficits.

If you've followed me for some time or know my investment fund, you'll know that gold ranks among my favorite scarce assets. With a history stretching back thousands of years, gold has proven, time and again, to be "good money." It offers unmatched protection against inflation and serves as the anchor beneath nearly every financial system. These qualities ensure that gold inevitably stages a comeback whenever the system comes under strain. And it always will, sooner or later. Humanity's relentless hunger for growth keeps pushing us to the edge, and often beyond it.

But this book is far from being just about gold. Other scarce assets also offer answers in a debt-driven world marked by artificially low interest rates, rising inflation, and governments playing an ever-larger role. A key advantage is that scarce assets complement each other remarkably well within a diversified portfolio. And let's be clear: You don't need to be an eternal pessimist to invest in scarce assets. On the contrary, as this book will show, scarce assets are part of the solution. They help prevent systemic collapse.

Astonishingly, scarce assets almost never make it into the portfolios of traditional wealth managers, not even in tiny allocations. Their outdated belief is built entirely on stocks and bonds, to the detriment of their clients, all while their models for deriving portfolio allocations are crying out for a broader investment mix.

The combination of soaring debt, low interest rates, high inflation, outdated portfolio models, and shifting investor needs will trigger the most profound transformation of investment portfolios in modern history. That's why this book is called *The Great Rebalancing*, with scarce assets at its very core. I am convinced that within a decade, perhaps even five years, our portfolios will look entirely different from today's. This book gives you the tools, and the timing, to start your rebalancing today.

A Book About "Everything"

Calling it merely an "investment book" would sell it short. To truly grasp how our financial system works, and what it means for the average portfolio, we need to embark on a wide-ranging journey. This book spans economics, history, society, politics, and even science. From Roman emperors debasing their coins, to our primal instinct for growth and the unsustainability of the welfare state; from wealthy Norwegians fleeing to Switzerland to the rise of artificial intelligence, the fragmentation of economic thought, the consequences of polarization, bitcoin as a safe haven, and the catalyst of the largest wealth transfer the world has ever witnessed.

I could go on, but this book will guide you, sometimes in broad strokes, through all the reasons why we must rethink the value of saving and radically reshape how we invest. To give all this some structure, here's a brief overview of what to expect in the five parts of this book:

Part I shows how deeply ingrained our desire for growth is. Not out of luxury, but out of necessity. We grow to survive, and economic growth is no different. Unfortunately, the original sources of economic growth are running dry. With rapid demographic aging, labor is becoming scarce, and productivity gains cannot make up for the shortfall. In an effort to satisfy our insatiable desire for growth, policymakers increasingly turn to a magic solution: debt.

Part II makes clear that the discipline required to sustain a debt-driven economy has disappeared entirely. Governments can no longer rely on higher revenues or lower spending to close their huge deficits. On the contrary, aging populations are driving an explosive increase in public spending on welfare and healthcare. What remains is a vast fiscal gap that cannot be bridged, putting welfare states everywhere under strain.

Part III describes what happens when traditional solutions to ensure debt sustainability evaporate. In a regime of fiscal dominance, monetary policy is subordinated to the policies of governments. Central banks are forced to finance government debt and abandon their inflation targets. The combination of structurally low interest rates and high inflation makes debt more sustainable, but it is disastrous for the purchasing power of savers and bondholders. The evidence of this happening can be found everywhere.

Part IV provides the solution to escaping the corrosive effects of low interest rates and high inflation: scarcity. In a world where money and debt are ever more abundant, value lies in assets that cannot be endlessly created or issued. Bitcoin, physical gold, and shares of exceptional companies are the three most important examples. They combine protection against fiscal dominance, geopolitical turmoil, and inflation with attractive risk-return characteristics. They offer the best of both worlds, while still being largely ignored by traditional wealth managers.

Part V brings all the previous parts together. *The Great Rebalancing* is not a vision of the future but a process already underway. The classic 60/40 portfolio cannot survive in a world of rising debt, geopolitical risk, and currency debasement. The financial system must search for a new foundation. That requires a radical change in how we construct portfolios, a process that will be accelerated by the largest wealth transfer in history. Those who recognize this in time will have a decisive advantage, preserving the true value of their wealth.

Part I

An Unrelenting Desire for Growth

CHAPTER 1
Growth as Survival

Introduction

Most investing books get straight to the point. How to read a balance sheet, draw the right lines to reveal price patterns, build profitable trading strategies, and so on. This book does not. Instead, it is a fusion of economics, history, philosophy, and psychology, enriched with hard data and charts. No quick fixes or gimmicks, but a quest to uncover the deeper forces behind our financial system. If you truly want to understand how to protect and grow your wealth, you do not start with a spreadsheet, you start with a fundamental analysis of reality.

A key premise underlying this book is that economies, nations, and societies are trapped in a vicious cycle, driven on one side by an unrelenting desire for growth, and on the other by an acute shortage of it. The yawning divide between what we desire and what is scarce keeps pushing us toward ever more extreme means of chasing growth.

Economic growth is no exception. In fact, it is where the imbalance between demand and supply manifests itself most clearly. An increasing number of countries grapple with a chronic growth deficit, prompting drastic and, at times, bizarre attempts to engineer artificial "progress." The result: profound consequences for our financial system, our wealth, our money, and ultimately for how we should invest. That last point is the central focus of this book. But before we get there, we have a long road ahead.

Survival Instinct

To understand where our drive for growth comes from, we need only look in the mirror. Open a book on economics, history, or psychology and it quickly becomes clear that growth is embedded in the very core of our being. The reason is simple: since growth is directly tied to the most basic element of our existence: survival.

Many people do not realize that growth is often not an end in itself. On the contrary, it is a necessary strategy for endurance. Every form of growth pursued throughout history in the end traces back to just one principle: increasing the chance of survival. Growth is existential, which is why our hunger for it never fades. Growth is an all-encompassing phenomenon that reaches into every corner of life. If you do not grow, you do not survive.

To illustrate this, the following pages outline six types of growth and their corresponding forms of survival.

1. Biological Growth, Physical Survival

The most basic example of growth as a prerequisite for survival is, of course, biological growth. Whether a single cell or a complex organism, for everything alive, growth is essential to survival. Babies eat, sleep, soil their diapers, and deprive their parents of sleep for a single purpose: growth.

Growth is also decisive for the survival of any species. Those that fail to embrace a smart growth strategy cease to exist. I'm endlessly fascinated by the ingenious survival tactics of animals and plants that, for instance, David Attenborough brings to life in his BBC documentaries. Biological growth determines who lives on and who disappears.

2. Growth Through Struggle, Survival by Force

Conflict, in the broadest sense, has always been a path to growth and survival throughout civilizations. No society or faith has ever grown without confronting struggle. Libraries overflow with often-romanticized tales of how the Romans expanded their empire through conquest, and how Genghis Khan's Mongols built the largest contiguous empire in history through discipline, mobility, and psychology.

Today, physical power struggles no longer always play out on battlefields. They often take the form of contests over "who is the bigger one." The Cold War was a psychological standoff in which two military giants held each other in check through fear that the other might one day press the button.

The war in Ukraine, conflicts in the Democratic Republic of Congo, Yemen, and Sudan, persistent tensions in the Middle East, and sudden flare-ups between India and Pakistan or Cambodia and Thailand all show that physical conflict remains a driver of survival today.

3. Technological and Scientific Growth, Survival Through Knowledge

As the legendary military strategist General Sun Tzu once wrote, "To subdue the enemy without fighting is the acme of skill." Though written some 2,500 years ago, that insight is more relevant than ever. It is no coincidence that many of today's geopolitical tensions revolve around intellectual property and access to the most advanced knowledge and technology. In recent years, the United States restricted exports of NVIDIA's most advanced microprocessors to China. It also successfully pressured the Dutch government to curb exports of ASML's chipmaking machines. The goal was clear: to choke off China's technological capabilities, and with them its growth.

4. Economic Growth, Material Survival

The bigger you are, the better your chances of survival. To borrow again from Attenborough: Among lion cubs, eagle chicks, or polar bears, the largest offspring are the most likely to survive. Economies work the same way. Nations and regions that control the most resources, employ the largest workforce, and sell the most to others grow the fastest. In other words, the nations that, by force or by innovation, manage to claim the scarcest resources and outcompete the rest are the ones that endure. Those that fail to grow eventually disappear from the global stage.

Economic growth, like biological growth, has become an existential condition for the survival of nations and their populations. That makes it highly unlikely that our drive for economic growth will ever disappear. As the traditional engines of growth run dry, our relentless pursuit of it creates deep friction, the very tension that runs through every page of this book.

5. Personal Growth, Emotional Survival

Before diving deeper, let's look at two other forms of growth that are directly linked to survival. Today, we are constantly, and I mean 24/7, bombarded with stimuli. The sheer amount of (mostly useless) information, data, and (social) media hurled at us is beyond comprehension.

Coping with it requires perpetual updates to our knowledge, skills, and networks, alongside other essentials such as relationships, family, work, exercise, social contacts, and, not to forget, writing a book. In that light, it is no surprise that in 2024 more than $45 billion worth of self-help books were sold. And frankly, this book would not be out of place in that category.

In his brilliant book *Sapiens*, Yuval Noah Harari shows how we, Homo Sapiens, outpaced the Neanderthals by building better networks, learning faster, and sharing knowledge more effectively. That we now, wrongly, see Neanderthals as crude cave dwellers is explained by just one thing: growth. Those who don't grow get left behind. It's as simple as that.

6. Sustainable Growth, Survival Through Balance

Based on the types of growth discussed above, it is hard to escape the conclusion that our desire for growth will never end. Abandoning it would mean giving up our instinct to survive. Which immediately raises the question of how that growth can be made sustainable. In a world bounded by ecological limits (resources, energy, climate) and social limits (inequality, housing, labor), we face crucial choices to keep growth in balance.

It's no coincidence that I describe sustainable growth as survival through balance. This is the opposite of an ideological, and often misinformed, pursuit of sustainability at the expense of all other forms of growth. Yet it is this ideological pursuit of sustainability, most notably in Europe, that has taken on a life of its own. But when other forms of growth are subordinated to sustainability, you invite a backlash that fuels instability and polarization, because the element of survival is inextricably embedded in every form of growth. In addition, instability and polarization strongly influence government policy and are a major catalyst for why investors worldwide must prepare for a sweeping transformation of their portfolios.

Economic Growth = All-Encompassing Growth

My focus is primarily on economic growth. Building a robust investment portfolio grounded in a fundamental understanding of the financial system is, after all, central to this book. But if I had written a book about technological or personal growth, it would almost certainly have been largely about economic growth as well. Economic growth is the primary ingredient of other forms of growth.

Two crucial forces explain why economic growth increasingly plays the role of all-encompassing growth. The first is the evolution of economic growth into the benchmark for progress and success. The second is that economic growth is the most quantifiable form of growth, or at least, that is what we believe.

From Enlightenment to Capitalism

In *The Infinite Desire for Growth* (2018), Daniel Cohen explains why economic growth has become increasingly important. The transition from agrarian societies to industrial and later capitalist economies heightened the desire for growth. During the Enlightenment, people realized that through science and technology they could shape their own destiny. They were no longer at the mercy of the gods, nature, or chance.

It is no surprise, then, that during the Industrial Revolution the foundation was laid for growth as a system: capitalism. In *The Wealth of Nations* (1776), Adam Smith described a market economy in which goods and services are traded in free markets, prices are set by supply and demand rather than by governments, and companies compete for profit. Corporate profits, rising household wealth, and, sequentially, the speed of economic growth became the benchmark and the clearest evidence of success. In capitalism, it's less about shaping the world and more about producing ever more within it.

The Need for Measurable Growth

Although capitalism, where firms expanded their competitive strength to produce more and maximize profits, was widely embraced, the overall economic growth of a nation or region remained an abstract idea for decades. That changed in June 1934, when American economist and future Nobel laureate Simon Kuznets presented his landmark report *National Income 1929–1932*. It was a response to a request from the US Senate for an estimate of the nation's "national income." His straightforward idea would reshape the world.

Kuznets defined national income as follows: "If the value of all goods produced and all direct services rendered during the year are added up at their market value, and from this total we subtract the value of that part of the nation's stock of goods consumed (both raw materials and capital equipment) in producing this total, the remainder is the net product of the national economy for the year."

This elaborate definition instantly reveals Kuznets as a traditional economist. Economists have a habit of defining things as broadly, and often as abstractly, as possible, ideally with every imaginable uncertainty attached. Hence their tendency to anchor estimates in scenarios and probability distributions.

Fortunately, Kuznets's calculations offered a simpler definition of national income: the total monetary value of goods and services produced by a country over the course of a year. Although he never used the term himself, Kuznets's 1934 estimate of national income laid the groundwork for what later became known as Gross National

Product, or GNP. (This differs slightly from Gross Domestic Product, or GDP, as we know it today.) Kuznets interpreted the Senate's request as an instruction to measure the added value generated by all US citizens and companies, wherever they were in the world.

Less than a decade later, Kuznets's concept of national income became fully entrenched in the global financial system. At the 1944 Bretton Woods Conference, named after the small hamlet in New Hampshire, the postwar global financial order was established, and both the International Monetary Fund (IMF) and the World Bank were founded. These newly created institutions were tasked primarily with restoring monetary stability after World War II and revitalizing global economic activity.

To help these fledgling institutions measure such activity, there was a need for a benchmark that would allow the economic performance of nations and regions to be easily compared, and just as importantly, one that could serve as a guide for government policy. Thus, the chosen benchmark was not Kuznets's Gross National Product but a variant: the total value added by all citizens and companies operating *within* a nation's borders, regardless of where they come from. The politicians and central bankers from the forty-four nations at Bretton Woods clearly recognized that it is far easier to craft policy around a growth figure confined neatly within national borders. Still, it took another ten years before GDP, which exactly measures that value added within borders became popular.

Over the past 80 years, as capitalism evolved into the dominant economic system, GDP has remained the undisputed measure of growth, success, and prosperity. In the spirit of the Enlightenment, which taught that people's faith could be shaped and directed, the production of GDP became the central economic focus of policymakers.

Today, most major economies represent a form of *modern capitalism*, with their roots tracing back to the ideas of Adam Smith. In this economic regime, GDP continues now plays an all-defining role. Whether it will remain so for another 80 years is far from certain.

Later in this book, I will examine a crucial side effect of today's financial system: the ever-expanding dominance of governments, which has made markets far less free than capitalism once intended.

Why GDP?

It is unlikely that Simon Kuznets could have foreseen how GDP growth would come to shape, and even dominate, the modern economic world. The irony is that Kuznets himself warned of GDP's limitations as a measure of progress and success: "The welfare of a nation can scarcely be inferred from a measure of national income," he cautioned. Yet GDP remains the holy grail of measuring economic growth. Aside from the occasional jab, its status has remained virtually unchallenged for the past eight decades. Still, those critiques produced some timeless aphorisms worth pondering. Two of those, coincidentally, emerged in the same year.

In 1968, Senator Robert F. Kennedy, in his searing critique of society's obsession with GDP growth, famously remarked: "The gross national product measures everything, except that which makes life worthwhile." That same year, during the French student protests, a graffiti slogan declared: "You can't fall in love with a growth rate."

Economists themselves also voiced substantive criticism of GDP as a measure of success. In 1974, economist Richard Easterlin showed that in wealthy nations, despite steady GDP growth, people's happiness levels hardly rose. This finding became known as the *Easterlin Paradox*, which shows that greater prosperity does not automatically translate into greater well-being, underscoring once more the limits of GDP.

Yet to this day, only one country in the world has officially adopted an alternative measure of economic growth. In the 1970s, Bhutan introduced the concept of *Gross National Happiness*, focusing on physical, social, and spiritual well-being. While other nations have sought to place more emphasis on well-being than on wealth, GDP remains unchallenged even there.

The Endless Desire for Economic Growth

At the beginning of this chapter, I argued that our longing for growth stems from our instinct to survive. Those who grow less, survive less, whether we are speaking of species, of individuals in today's whirlwind of a world, or of access to knowledge and technology.

Even so, economic growth appears to play an ever more dominant role. Its presumed measurability is decisive. It is not so much the growth number itself, but the prestige, the prosperity, and ultimately the power that accompany it. The measurability of GDP also gives policymakers and politicians an instrument to prove how successful their policies are, or how disastrous those of their opponents. GDP also largely determines how much tax revenue governments can generate, especially once tax rates have hit their ceiling. More taxes mean more resources for governments to fund policies and to survive politically by catering to voters.

Economists, whose discipline thrives on comparisons, love benchmarks that let them measure and contrast the performance of economies and nations. Politicians, in turn, are eager to enlist economists to validate their policies.

Central banks base their decisions almost entirely on estimates of GDP growth (and the inflation derived from it) that are far from perfect. These estimates have enormous effects on the financial position and confidence of businesses and households. When GDP projections are favorable, companies expect higher profits, hire more workers, and raise wages. This, in turn, boosts consumer confidence and spending.

The dominance of economic growth has become so pervasive that it underpins all other forms of growth. The country with the largest GDP has the resources to build weapons stockpiles, strengthen its military, and project force. Even as survival is less often a literal matter of life and death on the battlefield, economic success largely dictates physical and military growth.

The reason my home country, the Netherlands, no longer has a voice in geopolitics is that it has slipped to seventeenth place in global GDP rankings. That list shows, at a glance, who holds sway.

The same applies to science and technology. The country with the most resources and the most competitive companies can invest the most in innovation and attract top talent from around the world, reinforcing its GDP. Likewise, countries with high GDP typically have better education systems that enhance economic opportunities for their citizens.

This, in turn, translates into more personal growth. People can work longer and healthier lives and retire with pensions, reducing financial worries. Everything suggests that our endless desire for growth is, in reality, a desire for economic growth.

Economic growth has outgrown capitalism itself, permeating almost every aspect of our lives and societies. And here lies the root of an immense problem with colossal consequences: that growth simply isn't there.

In the coming chapters, I will show you exactly why this is the case.

CHAPTER 2

A World Without Workers

Introduction

The conclusion of the previous chapter is clear: The likelihood that we will resist our urge for growth is virtually zero. Because growth is directly tied to our chances of survival, there will always be a deep-rooted, instinctive drive for more.

I also demonstrated that, thanks to its scope and measurability, economic growth has, for better or worse, become the defining form of growth.

This translates into an insatiable demand for an ever-expanding gross domestic product (GDP). It may sound trivial on paper, but that doesn't make it any less real. On the eve of the 2025 German elections, numerous media headlines warned that it was now truly "2 minutes to midnight" for Germany after years of economic stagnation. If Germany still wants to matter on the world stage, it faces the bitter necessity of returning to growth.

Yet the harsh reality is that Germany, like nearly every major economy in the world, faces a structural, worsening, and ultimately irreversible shortage of growth.

Sources of Economic Growth

An unrelenting demand for economic growth amid a structural shortage inevitably raises the question: How much growth is truly available? What is the actual available supply of growth (or GDP), knowing it will never be enough to feed our endless appetite for more?

Although economists debate every model and theory within their field, there are, in short, two common ways to determine the supply of economic growth: the Solow growth model and the growth accounting model.

Solow: A Theoretical Growth Model

The first, the Solow growth model, was introduced in 1956. Robert Solow, an American economist, argued that economic growth and GDP depend on three key factors of production:

- Labor: The number of people employed within an economy.
- Capital: The stock of physical means of production, such as buildings, machinery, and infrastructure.
- Productivity: How much (more) workers can produce per hour, driven primarily, though not exclusively, by technological progress.

The core idea behind the Solow growth model is simple: add up the three production factors, and their sum determines the (potential) growth of an economy.

The Solow growth model comes with a rather charming anecdote. Australian economist Trevor Swan, working at the Australian National University, independently and in the exact same year, developed a nearly identical economic growth model.

Yet it was Solow who took the spotlight, and the credit. He published his model slightly earlier than Swan, and crucially, in a prestigious international journal, *The Quarterly Journal of Economics,* while Swan published his work in *Economic Record*, a far less influential outlet.

Backed by his publication in a top financial journal and his position at the Massachusetts Institute of Technology (MIT), arguably the world's most influential university, Solow remained prominent. That visibility eventually earned him the 1987 Nobel Prize in economics. Swan, by contrast, remains quoted at times, but by no means comparable to Solow, unmistakable proof that timing, place, and luck often shape success.

Growth as Arithmetic

Despite taking home a Nobel Prize, the Solow growth model has its limitations. It serves primarily as a theoretical framework for explaining economic growth, but its practical application is far more challenging. Measuring capital, as a factor of production, turns out to be especially tricky. How do you determine how many machines and factories truly contribute to growth? Moreover, distinguishing between capital and productivity is close to impossible. New technologies designed to improve production processes, products, and services are often embedded in capital goods, machinery, factories, robots, and transportation systems. Capital and productivity are intertwined; you cannot cleanly isolate one without the other.

Solow rightly argued that the capital factor cannot be a sustainable source of growth. The law of diminishing returns applies, each additional unit of capital yields less incremental GDP growth than the one before. According to Solow, lasting economic growth can arise from only one source: technological progress.

As policymakers, central bankers, and institutions such as the IMF and World Bank increasingly adopted GDP (rather than Kuznets's GNP) as the primary measure of economic performance, they also began searching for a simpler, more uniform alternative to Solow's model, one that avoided the complexities of capital and was easy to measure.

They opted for an empirical model, a model into which you could simply plug numbers to produce a growth estimate, without the burden of heavy theoretical assumptions. For most policymakers, I would argue, the Solow model was not only too abstract but simply too complex. When your political fate hinges on GDP, it helps if you can calculate it quickly and sell it even faster to voters.

Because economists and politicians opted for a simple calculation model, it was not named after its creator, nor given a catchy title. American economist Edward Denison helped bring the model to prominence, yet we are still left with the somewhat hazy construct known as the "growth accounting model."

The Growth Accounting Model

In the growth accounting model, there are two key sources of economic growth, instead of Solow's three:

- Labor. Usually defined as growth in the working-age population and the amount of labor supplied. The more people work and the more hours they put in, the more output can be produced.
- Productivity growth. Technological progress, education, and organizational improvements that enable more efficient use of labor and capital, leading to higher output.

For noneconomists, this model will probably look much like Solow's, except that the capital factor has been absorbed into productivity growth, conveniently sidestepping Solow's measurement issues. More importantly, this intuitive model is perfectly suited to show that the world is now facing a structural and unprecedented shortage of economic growth.

GDP per Capita

Before diving into that, a quick side note. Both the Solow and growth accounting models primarily focus on GDP per capita, which makes perfect sense at first. When a nation's workforce expands and more people are employed, a country's total GDP rises, but not GDP per capita. If the aim is to raise living standards and improve prosperity for every individual, then productivity growth is imperative.

Hence, the bar for growth, success, and progress is set higher for GDP per capita, which requires productivity growth, than for total GDP. However, central bankers, politicians, and other policymakers prefer not to set that bar too high. That's why they almost always choose GDP, rather than GDP per capita, as the measure of their "success."

Moreover, when it comes to geopolitical power, total GDP is what matters, not GDP per capita. China, the world's second-largest economy, ranks only ninety-second on the World Bank's list of countries ranked by GDP per capita (2023 data), yet wields far more power than Monaco, which tops that list. The United States, undisputedly the world's most powerful nation, holds only ninth place in GDP per capita.

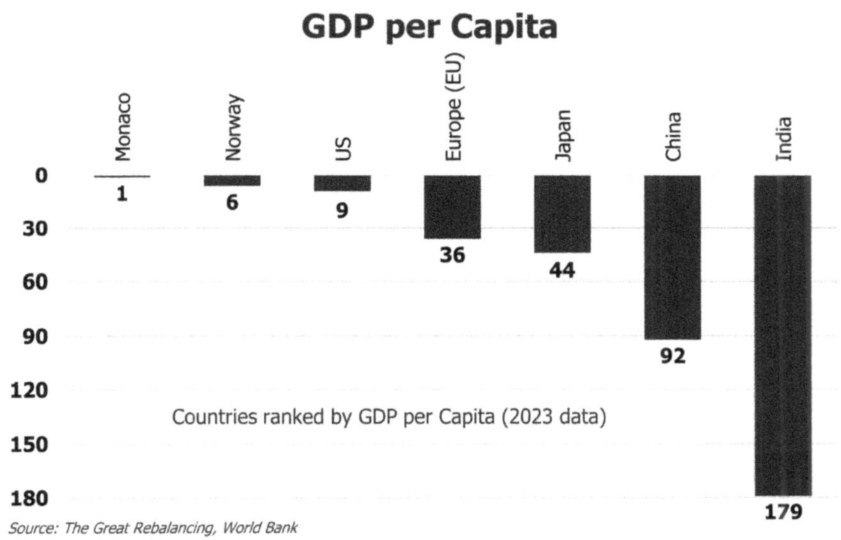

The fact that most large and powerful economies rank far from the top in GDP per capita underscores that total GDP is what ultimately matters.

Countries with the largest GDPs tend to wield the greatest diplomatic influence, attract the most innovation, and dominate international trade. And crucially, history shows that the world's largest economy almost always ends up issuing the world's reserve currency: Spain in the sixteenth and seventeenth centuries with the silver real, the Netherlands in the seventeenth and eighteenth centuries with the guilder, Britain in the eighteenth and nineteenth centuries with the pound sterling, and now the United States with the dollar.

Despite all the turmoil surrounding President Trump's trade wars in 2025, the global financial system still revolves predominantly around the US dollar. Yet plenty of nations are eager to break the grip of US and dollar dominance, an ambition with far-reaching consequences for global markets and for the core theme of this book: investing in scarcity.

The Original Source of Growth: Labor

History is full of technological breakthroughs that have dramatically improved living standards. More than that, they have made economic growth an ever more dominant force in our very survival.

That labor is often seen as the original source of growth likely won't surprise you. Labor, the engine of economic expansion, is simply the application of human effort, both physically and mentally, to produce goods and services.

The supply of labor in an economy or country depends on three population-based factors:

- Demographics: The age distribution of a population, which determines the size of its labor force.
- Participation rate: The share of the population that is in the labor force.
- Hours worked: The total number of hours people work in a given country.

Of these three, you're probably most familiar with demographics. And for good reason: Every day we're flooded with headlines about the rapid pace of aging. It's hard to miss that fewer people are working, while the ranks of the elderly keep swelling.

Too Few Children

Demographics, covering the size, structure, and changes in a population's composition, are largely determined by fertility rates and life expectancy. A high fertility rate, measured by the average number of children per woman, implies a larger future workforce, while a low fertility rate signals the opposite.

The chart below shows fertility rate trends in the world's five largest economies: the United States (black, solid line), China (black, dashed line), Europe (dark gray, dashed line), Japan (black, dotted line), and India (light gray, solid line). This line-style scheme will be used consistently throughout the book for charts comparing these major economies.

The first thing that jumps off the chart is that fertility rates across the globe have been falling for decades. Women are having fewer children, and that's taking a toll on the global workforce. The supply of people, including those of working age, is shrinking across the world.

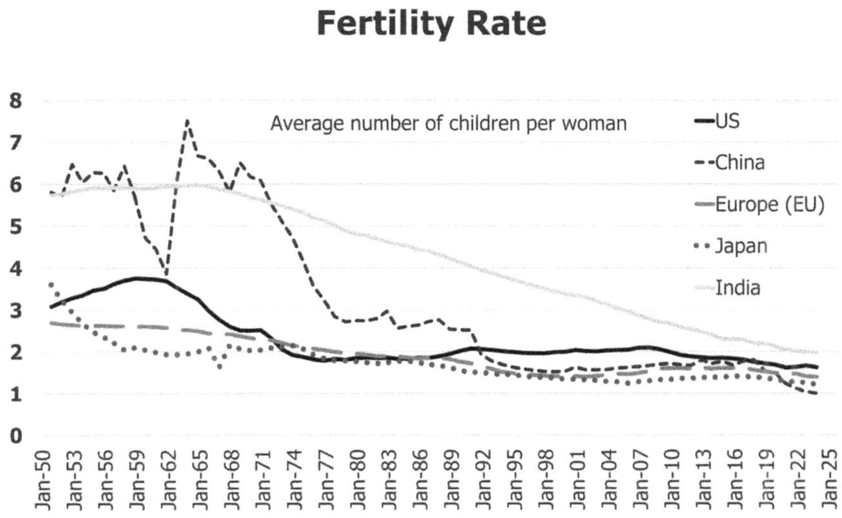

Source: The Great Rebalancing, OECD

In fact, in nearly all major economies, populations are already shrinking or on the verge of doing so. To keep a population stable, apart from immigration, a fertility rate of roughly 2.1 children per woman, called the replacement level, is required to keep a population stable over the long term. This is because not all children live to the age at which they have children of their own, and not all women can or want to have children, slightly more than two children per woman are required to prevent populations from shrinking.

Yet in none of the economies shown in the chart does the fertility rate exceed the replacement rate. In China, fertility has dropped below one child per woman. In Europe, Japan, and the United States, the rates stand at 1.4, 1.2, and 1.6, respectively, nowhere near the 2.1 required to sustain population levels without migration. Even in India, long praised for its favorable demographics, the fertility rate has dropped below two.

Globally, the fertility rate currently averages around 2.3 children per woman and continues to fall. Just thirty years ago, women around the world had an average of more than three children, fueling explosive population growth. Now the rate is nearing the tipping point where the global population will start to shrink.

Shrinking Populations

It takes little imagination to see what happens when women have fewer than two children. But the effect on future economic growth becomes strikingly clear once you look at some actual population data.

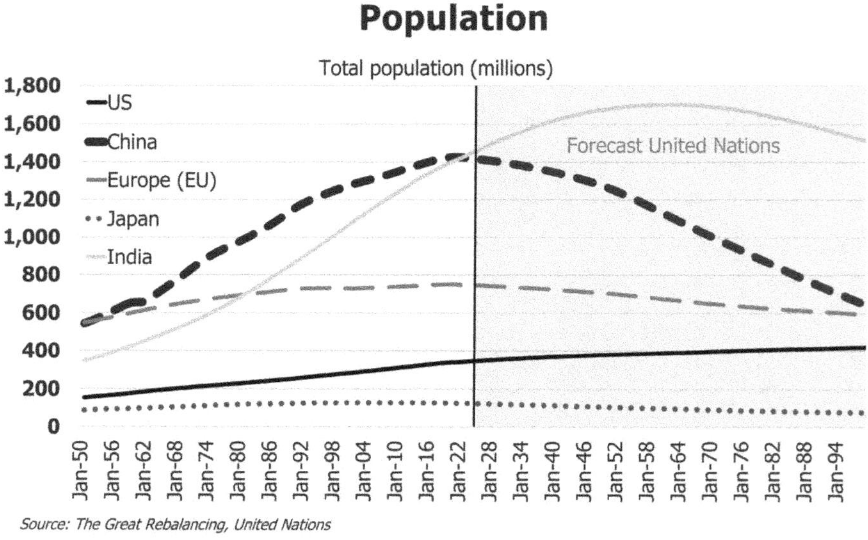

Source: The Great Rebalancing, United Nations

The chart shows officially reported population sizes (white area, left of the black vertical line) and projections (gray area, right of the black vertical line) for the five largest economies. The black vertical line marks the latest actual figure, with the population displayed in millions.

To illustrate the scale of low fertility's impact, China's black, dashed line is bolded. China's population will shrink dramatically in the decades ahead, and the shift is already well underway. In 2021, China's population peaked at 1.43 billion. The UN now projects a fall to just 633 million by 2100, a staggering 56 percent decline. China's share of the global population will collapse from 18 to 6 percent in the next 75 years, in stark contrast to India, whose population is expected to peak in 2061 at 1.7 billion.

One of the most frequently cited claims among economists is that China is on track to become the world's largest economy, and therefore, at least on paper, the dominant global power. Yet China's population trajectory makes that assumption deeply questionable. Although India's economy is currently much smaller than China's, the possibility that it will eventually overtake the United States as the world's largest economy is far from negligible. Still, the more plausible outcome is that the United States will stay right where it is, remaining the world's largest economy.

Who Will Be Working?

When a country's population shrinks by more than half before the end of this century, it is hardly surprising that its workforce, too, will contract dramatically. And this trend has been unfolding for quite a while now. The next chart tracks annual changes in the working-age populations of the five largest economies, again the United States, China, Europe (EU), Japan, and India, using a ten-year moving average to smooth long-term trends (the average annual growth of the labor force between 2011 and 2020, then between 2012 and 2021, and so on).

Similar to the population, the left side of the black vertical line (the white area) shows the realized labor-force figures, while the right side (the gray area) shows the projections. Along the black vertical line, you can see that the growth of China's working-age population (black, dashed line) has slipped below zero, meaning it is already shrinking. As the line shows, that decline will accelerate in the decades ahead. Before 2040, China's labor force will be shrinking by about 1 percent a year. Later, that pace will accelerate to more than 2 percent. To put that into perspective, today, nearly a billion Chinese are of working age; by 2050, that number will collapse to about 745 million, a staggering quarter fewer than today.

Labor Force Growth

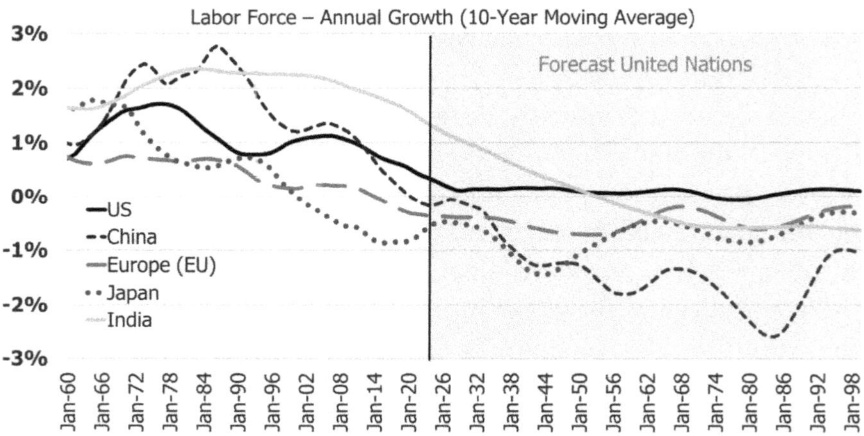

Source: The Great Rebalancing, United Nations, Our World in Data

China isn't alone, as other major economies like Europe and Japan are watching their labor force shrink as well. Europe's workforce is expected to shrink by more than 15 percent over the next 25 years, about 73 million fewer workers by 2050.

2050 is also projected to mark the first decline in India's working-age population. From that point onward, only one major economy, the United States, will still have a stable or marginally growing labor force. But that's hardly cause for celebration. Even with a stable workforce, the world's most crucial source of economic growth disappears: The pool of people driving economic growth has stopped expanding.

The reality is that labor, once the dominant engine of economic expansion, is now dragging GDP down. Labor is no longer a source of growth but a cause of economic contraction.

The Demographic Double Whammy

I would define demography as a "frustrating quest for pyramids." Countries with a healthy demographic profile, meaning many children and young people (the broad base of the pyramid), a continual inflow of people who can work (the middle of the pyramid), and a relatively small share of elderly who must be supported by the rest of the population (the narrow peak of the pyramid), have become rare.

The demographic profiles of countries such as China, Germany, Italy, and Japan bear little resemblance to pyramids. They look more like onions or mushrooms, or, in a striking yet slightly macabre comparison I once encountered, "urns." The world's demographic profile now resembles a circus tent far more than a pyramid. The upper tier of the population, the elderly, keeps expanding, while the base of children and youth continues to thin out.

Paradoxically, the further a country's demographics drift from the shape of a pyramid, the more its government and central bank seem to engage in a "pyramid scheme" to avoid facing the inevitable: a chronic shortage of growth.

I will return to that soon, but first, back to the onions, mushrooms, and circus tents. The changing composition of the population lies not only in falling birth rates but also in steadily rising life expectancy: A shrinking pool of workers must shoulder the burden of an ever-growing number of retirees.

This effect is captured by the old-age dependency ratio: the share of people aged 65 and older relative to the working-age population aged 15 to 64. The higher the ratio climbs, the grayer the population grows, and the heavier the burden on those still working becomes.

Old-age dependency ratios have surged dramatically over the past two decades. Back in 2005, more than five workers supported each retiree in the United States, reflecting a dependency ratio of 18 percent. Today, that number has fallen below four, meaning the dependency ratio has jumped to 26 percent. In Japan the ratio of elderly to workers now stands at one to two (dependency ratio of 50 percent): Two workers now carry the weight of one retiree. In Germany, home to one of Europe's oldest populations, fewer than three people are working for every person who no longer does.

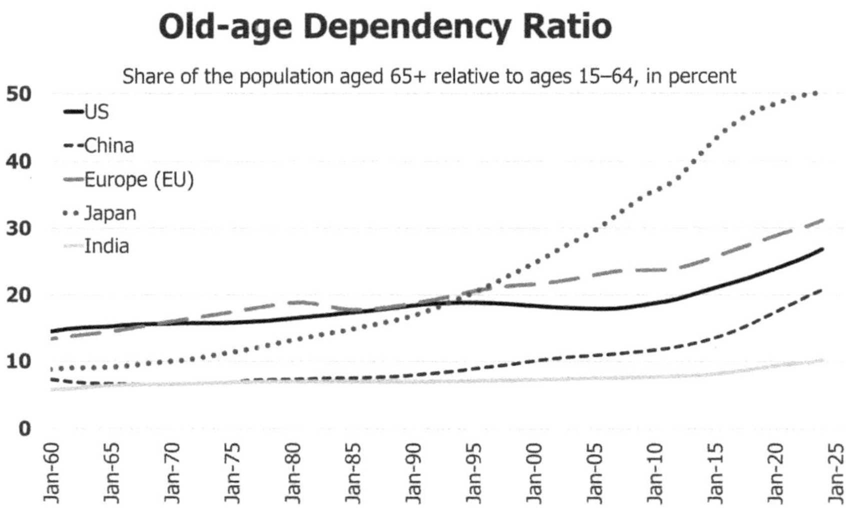

Source: The Great Rebalancing, United Nations, Our World in Data

And it gets much worse. Longer life expectancies and persistently low birth rates are profoundly reshaping populations around the world. A 2024 OECD study estimates that by 2050, Japan's old-age dependency ratio will climb to a staggering 79 percent. Put simply, Japan will soon have little over one worker for every retiree. In Italy and South Korea, ratios will reach Japan's current levels within 25 years, with two workers having to support one retiree. In China, the ratio has already doubled to 20 percent in just ten years, reflecting a drop from ten to five workers per retiree, and is on track to surpass 50 percent, leaving only two workers per elderly person.

Unless you're an economist, an old-age dependency ratio probably feels somewhat abstract. But when you translate aging, and the shrinking workforce that comes with it, into units of GDP, the true scale of its impact finally comes into focus.

The same OECD study estimates that GDP per capita will contract by roughly 8 percent over the next three decades as aging squeezes the labor force. Add to this the projected population decline across the OECD's 38 (mostly Western) member states, and the hit on total GDP will be even deeper than 8 percent. The OECD expects only two of its members, Mexico and Israel, to see a positive contribution to GDP from labor force dynamics.

A study by the National Bureau of Economic Research (NBER), the body that officially calls US recessions, found that a 10 percent rise in the share of people over 60 in the population cuts GDP per capita by about 5.5 percent. For context: The NBER expects the share of over-60s in the United States to rise by 11 percent between 2020 and 2030, meaning the total impact on GDP this decade will be even bigger.

Virtually every major economy is now grappling with this "demographic double whammy." From one side, too few children are born, causing the growth of the labor force to stagnate or decline. From the other, the number of elderly is rising rapidly, increasing pressure on the economy. Together, these forces trap economies in a structural shortage of growth that's nearly impossible to break.

Everybody In

"Everyone must be able, and willing, to take part." It's a well-worn cliché often trotted out by politicians, especially during election campaigns, to win over voters. It also features high on the list of "recommendations" from institutions such as the OECD in their efforts to offset the growth drag from aging populations. The logic is straightforward: If more people who can work actually do, the labor force expands even without population growth.

When estimating GDP, it's helpful to know how many people of working age actually take part in the labor market. The key measure here is the labor force participation rate, which captures the "active labor force," typically defined as the share of the population that either has a job or is actively looking for one. The latter group wants to participate but is temporarily unable to do so. Note that it refers to "the share of the population," not just those of working age (15–64) who are employed or seeking work. Plenty of people over 64 are still perfectly capable, and often willing, to work. This broader group is therefore often referred to as the total eligible labor force.

If you hoped the labor force participation rate could be a magic growth elixir, I'm afraid you'll be disappointed. In most economies, participation rates are trending downward. And once again, the culprit is aging. While many older people are capable of working, they do so far less often than those aged 15 to 64. To state the obvious, the older someone gets, the less likely they are to stay in the workforce. And let's be honest, who really wants grandma or grandpa still clocking in full time?

Of course, it's not only a question of ability. Baby boomers, the postwar generation of over-60s who thrived in decades of stability and prosperity and had many children, have become extremely wealthy, on average, of course. They enjoy generous pensions, valuable homes, and sizable savings, the perfect recipe for early retirement.

A study aptly titled "Where Is Everybody?" published by the Federal Reserve Bank of Philadelphia in 2017, draws exactly that conclusion. It is primarily the early retirement of Baby boomers since the global financial crisis that has driven participation rates lower and pushed dependency ratios higher. We will meet the boomers and their wealth again later in this book, when they begin transferring their assets to their children and grandchildren, an overlooked trend with major implications for future investment portfolios.

In the eurozone, aging exerts the same downward pressure on labor participation as it does in the United States. Eurostat estimates that without aging, the eurozone's participation rate would have been 1.6 percentage points higher between 1997 and 2023.

Do Women Provide the Answer?

Alongside the elderly, policymakers often point to another crucial group of potential workers to boost growth prospects: women. The idea that greater female participation could lift the overall labor force rate is, quite literally, old news. Although women's participation remains lower than men's, the gap is no longer explained by differences in education, rights, or pay.

Let's look at some of the data to back this up. In the 1960s and 1970s, women's education and equal rights rose to the top of political agendas, and the payoff has been enormous. Take the United States: Between 1970 and 1999, the entire rise in overall labor force participation was explained by women entering the workforce (see arrow in the chart below). Meanwhile, the share of men in work actually fell over that same period.

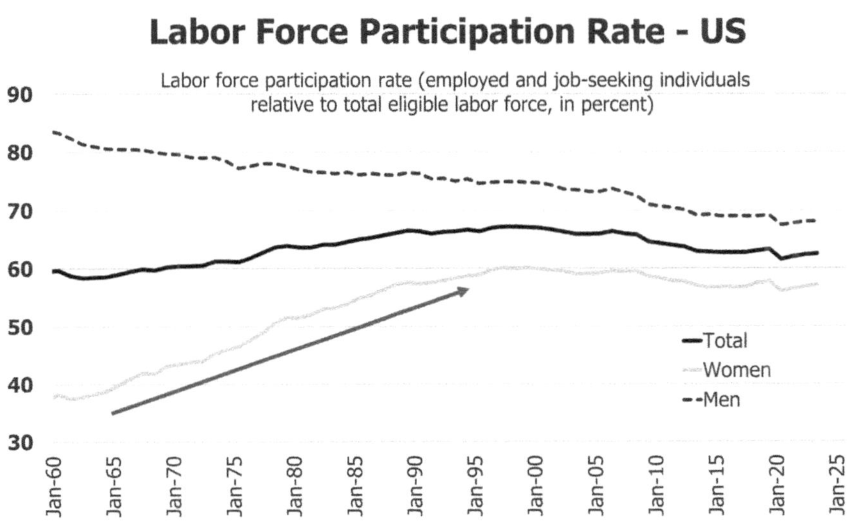

Source: The Great Rebalancing, World Bank

After 2000, women's participation plateaued, and the participation rate among both men and women began to simultaneously decline. Ever since the catch-up of women entering the labor market was completed, the explanation for the declining participation rate is the same as before: aging. Women, like men, are living longer, and, like men, they tend to work less as they age.

The overall labor participation rate is therefore primarily shaped by two factors: female participation and age. As the chart illustrates, from 1970 to 1999, the dominant driver was female participation, and since 1999 it has been aging.

A regression model helps predict how these two factors shape overall labor participation. A regression is a statistical model that maps the relationship between variables and how strongly they move together. In essence, it tries to explain one variable, the dependent one, using one or more others, the so-called explanatory variables. A regression model shows how well, or how poorly, those explanatory variables mimic the movements of the dependent variable. In this case, the regression equation measures how well age and female participation explain changes in the overall labor participation rate.

The regression results are striking: Age and female participation explain nearly every change in the overall US labor force participation rate. Together, they account for an astonishing 99 percent of the variation (the movements) in the overall participation rate. Age carries a negative coefficient in the model, meaning that a higher average population age reduces participation. Women's participation, by contrast, shows a positive sign, equally intuitive: The more women join the workforce, the higher overall labor participation climbs.

The beauty of a strong regression model is that it doesn't just explain, it can also predict. With reliable projections for age and female participation, the future trajectory of the overall labor force participation rate can be estimated with remarkable accuracy.

The United Nations provides such projections, estimating that the average age in the United States will increase by as much as two years over the next decade. Plugging that figure into the regression model results in a decline in the participation rate of nearly one percentage point, even before accounting for the likely additional drop in the female participation rate also due to aging.

The regression model isn't the only evidence pointing to lower overall labor participation; the data from China tell a similar story. Participation rates for both men and women in China, shown below, have been sliding fast for years. Although labor markets differ across countries, the fact that China's population is older, and aging much faster than America's, offers a clear preview of what lies ahead. In the next decade, China's population age is projected to rise by a remarkable 5.6 years, making a further, steep decline in the participation rate virtually inevitable, and signaling similar downward pressure in the United States.

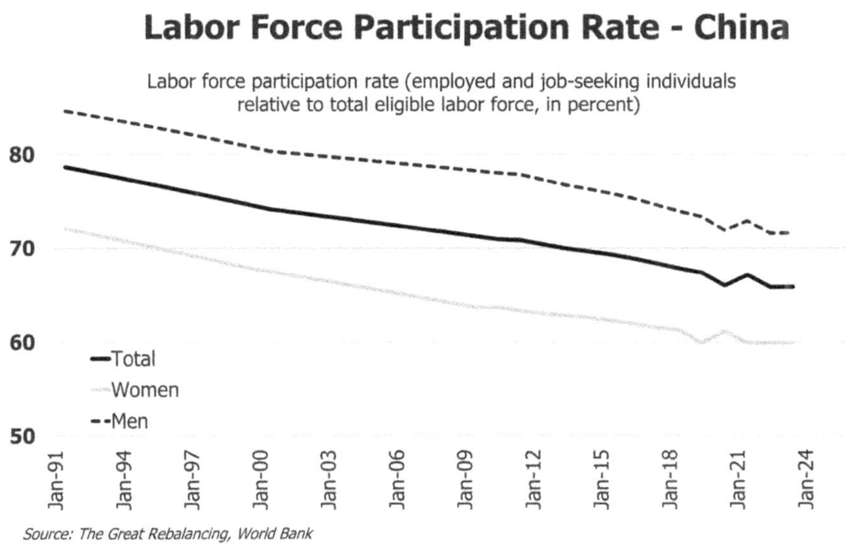

Is there really nothing that can push the participation rates higher? Yes, there is. Governments can lift participation by mandating later retirement, typically by raising the statutory retirement age. This trend is particularly visible in Europe. Denmark, Greece, Iceland, Italy, and the Netherlands all have official retirement ages of 67, three years above what is normally seen as the upper boundary of the working-age population, the now familiar range from 15 to 64.

Forcing people to work longer does raise participation, but with sharply diminishing returns. In Europe, participation is creeping higher, but remains well below levels seen in the United States or China. That's mostly because Europeans are far more likely to work part-time. When people are not working full-time, it's no surprise that the participation rate comes out lower. In addition, in Europe, participation among older workers, even before retirement, remains strikingly low. A maze of schemes, from early-retirement programs to unemployment and welfare benefits, makes it easy, even tempting, to stop working early. As a result, the effective retirement age is often far below the statutory one.

In Asia, the opposite is true. People frequently work years beyond the official retirement age. If European governments genuinely want people to work longer, they will have to make early retirement a lot less appealing. That's not the kind of message that wins elections.

Despite wide differences between labor markets, the underlying pattern remains the same. All major economies are set to face declining participation rates, simply because they all share the same defining driver: aging populations.

Too Much Balance?

That leaves one remaining factor for labor, the primary driver of growth: the number of hours worked. The chart on the next page shows average annual hours worked per employee. In Europe, Japan, and the United States, average working hours have been declining steadily. China is the notable outlier. Chinese workers not only work more hours than in other countries, but the number of hours they put in is actually on the rise.

But China is the exception that proves the rule. Across the globe, a mix of trends is converging to make people work less. Key examples include shorter workweeks and young people entering the labor market later. On top of that, there is a strong trend toward more people working part-time.

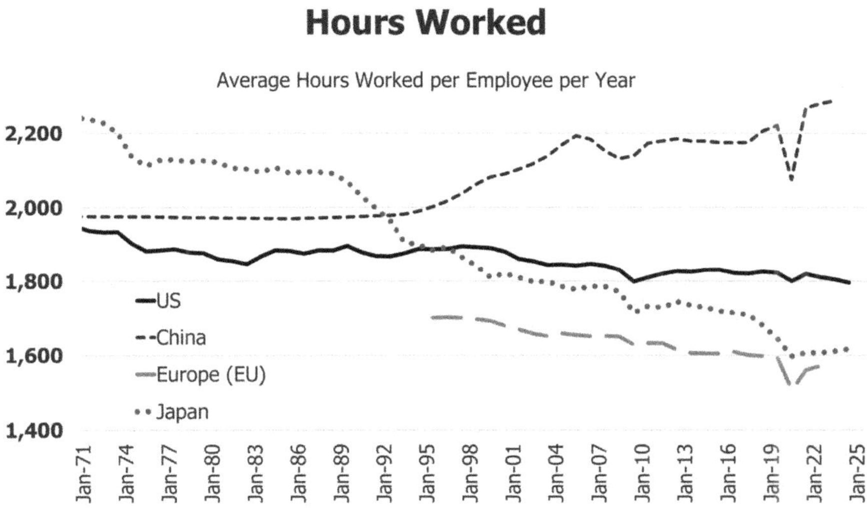

Source: The Great Rebalancing, OECD

The latter trend is especially prevalent in Europe. My own country, the Netherlands, is the undisputed champion, or rather the queen, of part-time work; more than half of Dutch women work part-time. Eurostat estimates that nearly one in five workers in the European Union are part-time workers. By comparison, only one in ten Americans works part-time, and in China, it is almost unheard of.

Given Europe's lavish benefits and social safety nets, it is hardly surprising that Europeans work the fewest hours of any major region. Compared with 1970, the average German has cut working hours by roughly a third. And since 2000, Germans have trimmed 9 percent off their working hours. Similar declines have occurred in Italy, the United Kingdom, and the Netherlands. In France, the *Loi Aubry* of 2000, the reform named after then-labor minister Martine Aubry, cut the official workweek to just 35 hours, a law that remains firmly in force today.

The part-time trend shows no sign of reversing anytime soon. Walk into any HR department and ask how they attract new workers these days and the answer is almost always the same: more time off. By 2025, over 200 companies in the United Kingdom had adopted a four-day workweek, mostly without any pay cuts. Earlier, smaller-scale experiments in Japan, New Zealand, and the United States produced similar outcomes: greater well-being, better work-life balance, and lower absenteeism.

Behind the push for shorter workweeks lies the bold assumption that fewer hours can be made up for with greater productivity. Not everyone is buying that logic, though. In July 2024, Greece went the other way, introducing a six-day workweek in certain high-pressure sectors struggling with acute labor shortages. The reason? A shrinking workforce.

This raises a vital question, central to the next chapter. Can productivity, the other primary engine of economic growth, compensate for the loss of labor?

Immigration

Before answering that question, a brief note on another much-debated factor shaping labor supply: immigration. Countries struggling with a shrinking labor force can choose to bring in workers from abroad. Framing labor migration in this way helps take some of the political heat out of what is typically a deeply polarized debate. From an economic standpoint, the rationale is straightforward: Labor shortages can be partly filled through migration.

This approach also allows policymakers to align migration policy with areas of greatest economic need. In an age of rapid polarization, where migration debates easily veer toward extremes, the economic lens offers much-needed balance. It also helps distinguish between mass migration, which suppresses growth, and targeted migration, which can stimulate it.

That said, countless studies show that even targeted migration can offset only a small fraction of the impact of aging. For large, developed economies, the resulting boost to GDP growth is typically no more than a few tenths of a percentage point, hardly a game-changer. In countries with strict immigration regimes such as China and Japan, the growth effect is close to zero. Even so, targeted migration remains a useful policy tool to cushion the decline of the world's original source of economic growth: labor.

CHAPTER 3
Elusive Growth

Introduction

The idea that fewer working hours boost productivity may sound logical, appealing even, but it is difficult to prove in practice. For some creative professions, one can indeed make a fair case that working less yields higher output. For manual labor that cannot yet be automated by machines, robots, or artificial intelligence, the story is very different.

No workers, no output. It's really that simple.

On top of that, older workers tend to be less productive. I don't want to sound impolite, but workers over sixty are, on average, a bit slower than their younger colleagues. Demographics drag productivity down with a force that is consistently underestimated.

The real challenge with productivity, however, is that it is notoriously hard to measure, and it can take decades before the payoff from productivity investments becomes visible.

Measurement Issues

While labor can be neatly broken down into measurable components such as the labor force, participation rate, and hours worked, the other driver of economic growth, productivity, is far more elusive.

Perhaps that explains why, within the Solow and growth decomposition frameworks, productivity carries the rather technical label of total factor productivity (TFP).

TFP tries to capture how efficiently labor and capital are combined to generate (more) output.

To complicate matters further, Solow treated TFP as a known variable to plug into his model to calculate growth, something that is nearly impossible in reality. The decomposition model, by contrast, treats TFP as a residual term. In other words, whatever portion of economic growth cannot be explained by labor is conveniently labeled productivity growth.

If you are starting to lose the thread, don't worry. Measuring productivity growth is messy, arbitrary, imprecise, and often raises more questions than it answers. Trying to peel productivity apart into neat, measurable factors like labor offers little value. Technological progress is, without doubt, the most powerful driver of productivity growth. Yet factors such as age, experience, innovation, infrastructure, knowledge, networks, production processes, research, and crucially, investment all play vital roles in driving productivity.

Labor Productivity

Just as policymakers have embraced GDP growth as the benchmark of success, productivity discussions often center on labor productivity. It's pretty straightforward to boast about rising output per worker, or per hour worked. It's virtually impossible to do the same with the contribution of new software or artificial intelligence to total output.

Moreover, focusing on labor productivity fits neatly with the other key growth driver: labor itself. The question is not just how much labor is available, an ever-shrinking pool as we learned from the previous chapter, but also how much that labor produces.

The chart above tracks US labor productivity growth all the way back to 1950. Each quarter, the Bureau of Labor Statistics (BLS) calculates labor productivity by dividing US GDP by the total number of hours worked. I then calculate the quarterly rate of change (growth) in labor productivity. To prevent outliers from distorting the underlying trend, I apply a three-year moving average, so each quarter, the rolling average shifts forward by three months.

The gray dotted line, the trend line, makes one thing abundantly clear: Based on BLS data, labor productivity growth has been slowing for decades. Put differently, labor productivity keeps rising, just more slowly with each passing year. Workers still generate more GDP per hour worked, but on average the incremental gain keeps shrinking.

Low-Hanging Fruit

The elusive nature of productivity growth makes it not only difficult to measure, but also a perpetual source of debate, especially since measured productivity growth is anything but stable, as the chart illustrates. When productivity jumps, technology evangelists rush to proclaim the dawn of a new economic golden age. Conversely, when productivity growth slows, eternal pessimists emerge from all corners, insisting that the great waves of economic expansion are long gone and that new technologies are coming for our jobs.

Today, hordes of economists debate whether the downward trend in productivity growth is a temporary phenomenon or a structural shift. Among the most influential voices in this debate stands Robert Gordon, the American economist and longtime professor at Northwestern University. In his landmark 2016 book *The Rise and Fall of American Growth: The US Standard of Living Since the Civil War*, he traces the history of productivity growth. Gordon concludes that the hundred years between 1870 and 1970 marked a "special century," characterized by extraordinary economic expansion and dramatic gains in living standards.

In his book, Gordon raises a fundamental question: Was that special century of electrification, cars, plumbing, telephones, and antibiotics the historical exception, a one-off explosion of progress unlikely to be repeated? He argues that post-1970 innovations, largely centered on communication, entertainment, and information processing, may be useful but lack the transformative impact on daily life and productivity of the great inventions of the Industrial Revolution a century earlier.

Tyler Cowen, professor at George Mason University and creator of the hugely popular and influential blog *Marginal Revolution*, offers a slightly different but complementary explanation for the structural slowdown in productivity growth. In *The Great Stagnation* (2011), Cowen argues that this decline stems from the US economy having already harvested its easiest growth opportunities, the proverbial low-hanging fruit. Once powerful growth drivers like the supply of free, undeveloped land, broad access to quality education, and widely applicable industrial breakthroughs have been largely exhausted. And that exhaustion has put a lasting brake on productivity growth.

Despite what the title of his book might imply, Cowen is not really that gloomy about new technological breakthroughs such as artificial intelligence and digitization. They are more complex and will take longer to reach their full potential. By "stagnation" Cowen doesn't mean the end of progress, but that we are merely in a waiting phase until the next wave of major innovations sparks a fresh surge in productivity. What Cowen and Gordon share is the conviction that today's innovations offer no guarantee of such a new productivity boom; the glory days of unfettered, technology-driven growth are, for now, behind us.

The conclusions of Gordon and Cowen inevitably ruffle the feathers of the perpetual tech optimists and hurt their limitless faith in exponential progress. To them, new sources of exponential, tech-driven growth are just waiting to be seized. "Disruption" has become the overused buzzword to describe the supposed far-reaching effects of these technological shifts.

The Productivity Paradox

In a 2016 blog post, Bill Gates initially sang the praises of Gordon's sweeping historical analysis. But when Gates reached Gordon's conclusion that US growth would never again rival the boom years of 1870 to 1970, because the fruits of the digital revolution cannot match the great inventions of the past, he reacted coolly but firmly: "I couldn't disagree more."

Gates countered that Gordon underestimates the digital revolution by limiting its impact to a handful of sectors, while its influence is far broader. Digitalization, Gates stresses, is transforming not just industries but also society as a whole, and, above all, how economies function and grow. Looking at how deeply technology is now woven into almost every aspect of our economies and societies, we must grant Gates at least some credit. It takes time before new technologies are so deeply embedded that they deliver large-scale benefits.

The loudest voice of optimism on productivity comes, of course, from Silicon Valley. Erik Brynjolfsson, professor at Stanford University, is known for his distinctly positive view of the impact of technological progress on productivity. What sets Brynjolfsson apart from the usual "tech gurus" is that his optimism isn't hype. Brynjolfsson rigorously supports his views with solid research.

The cornerstone of his argument is time. In "Artificial Intelligence and the Modern Productivity Paradox" (2017), Brynjolfsson (together with coauthors Rock and Syverson) argued that technology boosts productivity growth only once companies rewire their processes and organizations to take full advantage of it. Earlier breakthroughs such as electricity (a hallmark of Gordon's "special century") and the computer took years, if not decades, to realize their full potential.

In 2021, Brynjolfsson (again with Rock and Syverson) expanded his theory and gave it a brilliant name: "The Productivity J-Curve." According to Brynjolfsson, new technologies can initially cause productivity to decline because companies must invest heavily in new processes, systems, and skills. To get the most out of these technologies, companies need to transform, which takes time. Once these transformations are complete and firms can finally harness the new technology, productivity takes off, rising exponentially, and forming that signature J-shaped curve. It is not just about the supply of new technology but just as much about the evolution of demand from economies and societies before large-scale adoption can occur.

A 2024 study titled "AI Adoption in America: Who, What, and Where," co-authored by Brynjolfsson, examines the implementation and use of five AI-related technologies across an impressive 850,000 US companies. The authors conclude that fewer than 6 percent of firms had implemented at least one of these AI technologies.

According to Brynjolfsson, this is a textbook demonstration of the technology J-curve. The current moderate pace of productivity growth, clearly visible in the chart above, reflects that we are still at the beginning of large-scale AI adoption. Businesses, policymakers, and investors must continue to invest patiently and allow demand to mature in order to unlock the full potential.

Somewhere in the Middle

The key question, of course, is: Who is right? I believe the truth lies somewhere in between. When it comes to mobility, education, and the land we've already put to work, much of the low-hanging fruit has indeed been picked. At the same time, there remain vast challenges in energy, healthcare, climate, food supply, and aging populations, all areas where technology still has plenty of room to make a difference.

That last one, aging populations, however, has a demonstrably negative impact on productivity that is often underestimated. In a landmark 2017 article published in the *American Economic Review*, economists Daron Acemoglu, later a Nobel laureate, and Pascual Restrepo examined the relationship between aging and productivity, in an increasingly automated world. Their conclusion was that aging societies systematically lag behind in adopting new technologies. Older workers tend to be less flexible in acquiring new digital skills and are less receptive to major changes in how work is done. That resistance slows both innovation and productivity growth. These findings do not rule out the possibility of a future J-curve effect, though adoption will likely proceed more slowly, steadier, and far less dramatically.

Studies from the IMF, the OECD, and more recently, a policy report by former ECB President Mario Draghi (best known for his "whatever it takes" pledge during the European debt crisis in 2011-2012) persistently argue that massive, sustained investment in digitalization, education, and innovation is essential to limit the deeply negative drag of aging on productivity growth. That doesn't exactly sound like the next productivity J-curve is on the horizon. As I will demonstrate later, it is far from certain that these vital investments will ever happen, given their discretionary nature. They are anything but guaranteed: Every year, governments must formally approve budgets for education and innovation, and that space is shrinking fast.

Seen this way, modest but structurally declining productivity growth looks like the most realistic path ahead, not the exponential boom many still hope for. Not least because productivity growth in other countries mirrors the downward trend observed in the United States. In Europe and Japan, the pace of productivity growth is generally lower, and has fallen more steeply than in the US. In Germany, productivity growth has actually drifted below zero in recent years. In other words, in Germany, both labor and productivity are now dragging GDP into contraction.

If you are wondering why Germany is slipping further from the global stage, that's your answer. In China, productivity growth rose steadily until the global financial crisis but has since fallen sharply. Over the past three years, productivity growth has barely exceeded 2 percent. It's also worth noting that the availability of reliable productivity data pales in comparison to the wealth of data available on labor as a source of growth. This is not only true for China and highlights how elusive and hard to measure this source of growth really is.

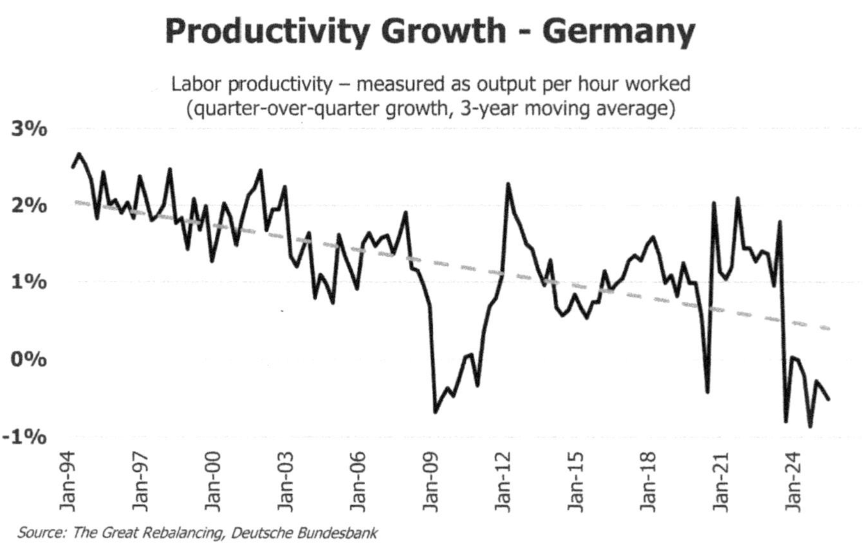

A Structural Shortage

Connecting this chapter to the previous one, the likelihood is close to 100 percent that global growth will decline or even stagnate, especially in regions where aging hits hardest. China, Europe, and Japan stand out as prime examples. The prospects for labor as a source of growth look bleak. The same wave of aging that erases labor as a source of economic growth makes a massive productivity-fueled economic boom unlikely, unless artificial intelligence delivers something truly extraordinary in the years ahead.

CHAPTER 4

Growth for Sale

Introduction

There's no mistaking the main takeaway of the previous chapters: The world is struggling with a deep, structural shortage of growth. Our hunger for economic growth runs deep, but the harsh reality is that most economies lack the intrinsic capacity to generate it.

The demographic forces are relentless. Across major economies, the labor force is shrinking, participation rates are falling, and the number of hours worked per employee is declining. The evidence that above-average productivity growth could offset these trends is far from convincing. The debate between economists like Robert Gordon, Tyler Cowen, and Erik Brynjolfsson shows there is no shared consensus about the future of productivity. What is certain, however, is that productivity growth, like the supply of labor, is buckling under the weight of aging populations.

How do we deal with the widening gap between the demand for and supply of growth? True to form, humanity found a way around it. If growth no longer arrives on its own, we simply manufacture it. After all, the Enlightenment taught us to seize control of our own destiny. And so, debt became the world's "magical" growth elixir, a tool to feed our insatiable hunger for expansion and an instrument through which growth can literally be purchased. This approach has now gone so far that the relationship between debt and growth has become utterly dominant.

Potential Growth

How much economic growth can we realistically expect? Sadly, not much. When you line up the figures for the labor force, participation rates, and hours worked, the inevitable conclusion is that labor is no longer driving growth, but instead, has started to hold it back.

For Europe and Japan, this could easily mean a one percentage point drag on GDP each year. While the available supply of labor remains larger in the United States, it will almost certainly weigh negatively on GDP as well. The Chinese work more hours, but their demographic outlook is by far the most unfavorable. Among the world's major economies, only India can still count on labor to deliver real growth.

What about productivity growth? Given its volatility and the opposing views about its future, I take the declining trend highlighted in the charts in the previous chapter as my baseline. For the United States, that points to an average productivity growth rate of just over 1.5 percent in the coming decades. For Europe and Japan, 1.0 percent labor productivity growth is already a generous assumption (Germany currently sits below zero), while for China, I use the recent average of about 2.5 percent.

Adding labor and productivity together, I arrive at potential GDP growth, the growth achievable on paper, of about 1 percent for the United States. For Europe and Japan, the same calculation yields zero growth, meaning their capacity to grow has already vanished. China lands at roughly 1.5 percent GDP growth per year, hardly a number to boast about. No politician wins elections by promising growth like that.

Meanwhile, estimates from policymakers, central banks, governments, and institutions such as the IMF and World Bank are consistently higher. People prefer positive outlooks to gloomy ones, so forecasts conveniently adjust to fit that preference. The next chart shows potential GDP growth estimates compiled by economists at data provider Bloomberg. In theory, those forecasts should be less tainted by optimism than those of policymakers, who tend to see GDP growth as proof of their own success.

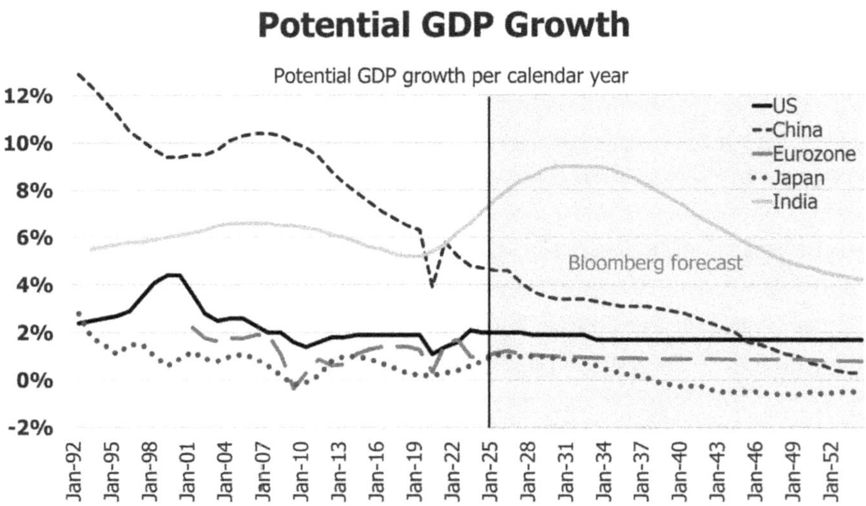

Source: The Great Rebalancing, Bloomberg

The chart shows forecasts of potential annual GDP growth for the world's five major economic blocs up to thirty years ahead. My focus, however, is mainly on the near-term horizon, since long-term projections become less relevant and increasingly uncertain. Too many variables can shift over such extended periods, making long-term growth forecasts little more than educated guesses. Often, you see long-term expectations gravitate toward an equilibrium value (as in the horizontal lines for Europe and the United States), which essentially signals that forecasters have no clue what will happen that far ahead. To still land on a number, forecasters take the easy route: They freeze the growth rate, along with labor and productivity.

For the period up to 2030, the average potential growth rate is pegged at 2 percent for the United States, 1 percent for Europe and Japan, 4 percent for China, and over 8 percent for India. These estimates are all substantially higher than my own calculations based solely on labor and productivity. This may partly reflect wishful thinking, though it is far more likely to indicate the presence of a magical growth ingredient.

Debt as the Source of Growth

How exactly does debt drive growth? Although the answer may seem obvious, many people struggle somewhat to visualize how it works in practice. Here is a concise overview of how debt fuels additional economic growth.

In essence, debt boosts consumption, investment, and government spending, provided it is used productively. That's why economists usually divide debtors into three groups: households, businesses, and governments.

When households borrow money, whether through auto loans, credit cards, student loans, or mortgages, they can spend more. In most major economies, consumer spending makes up the largest share of economic activity. More consumption equals more economic growth. Handing out "free" money has proven one of the most effective ways to accelerate growth through higher spending. The COVID crisis was an outstanding example, when governments flooded households and businesses with cash, leading to higher investment and consumption.

Businesses borrow to acquire machinery or other capital goods, to develop new products, or to roll out new technologies. This increases efficiency and production capacity, fuels job creation, and pushes output higher.

Governments can borrow to stimulate the economy directly, by building roads, constructing homes, or developing new energy infrastructure. They can also invest in education, innovation, and social programs to foster long-term productivity gains. Governments can even choose to borrow money to attract labor from abroad to expand the workforce, the positive side of immigration that I highlighted earlier.

The logic behind debt as a source of growth is straightforward; as long as borrowed money is used productively and translates into stronger growth, it's not inherently a problem. But if that condition breaks or debt simply grows too large, the system starts to crack, and only drastic action can set it right.

Debt in Historical Perspective

In a letter to Robert Morris dated April 30, 1781, Alexander Hamilton wrote, "A national debt, if it is not excessive, will be to us a national blessing."

Hamilton, one of the Founding Fathers of the United States and the architect of the early American financial system, was convinced that a well-managed national debt could support economic growth and anchor long-term stability. Manageability was key. Hamilton wanted to consolidate the debts accumulated during the War of Independence, establish a national bank, and finance interest payments through taxation.

To put Hamilton's idea of non-excessive debt in context, the Congressional Budget Office (CBO), the government agency that provides budgetary analysis for US policymakers, estimates that in 1790, one year after Hamilton became Secretary of the Treasury, the national debt stood at around 30 percent of GDP.

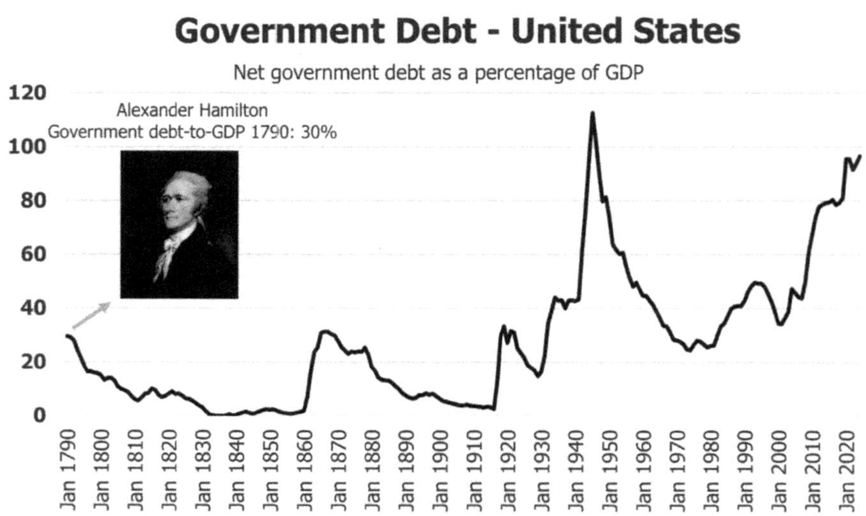

Source: The Great Rebalancing, Congressional Budget Office (CBO)

We'll cross paths with Hamilton again later in this book. He was also the visionary who proposed that the new US currency, the dollar, should literally look and feel like the Spanish silver dollar, which was widely available throughout the world at that time. Back in the eighteenth century, Hamilton already understood what some central bankers and politicians still fail to grasp today; if you want people to trust your currency, it must, at least in some way, be anchored in real value. Hamilton's insights were both forward-looking and revolutionary. Unfortunately, Hamilton failed to apply those insights in his own life. In a twist of irony, Hamilton ended up deeply in debt through numerous speculative land investments.

The Explosion of Debt

Back to the present day. The chart on the next page shows the total debt-to-GDP ratios of the five major economic blocs: the combined debts of businesses, households, and governments. Together with international trade, businesses, households, and governments make up total GDP. Today's debt ratios are galaxies apart from Hamilton's 30 percent benchmark. Even when focusing solely on public debt, the transformation over 235 years is staggering. According to the CBO and the Bank for International Settlements (BIS), often referred to as the central bank of central banks, US government debt currently stands at around 100 percent of GDP. That's over three times what it was in Hamilton's days.

Since the bursting of the dot-com bubble in 2000, total US debt as a share of GDP has risen by more than 70 percentage points to over 250 percent. In Europe, the debt ratio has climbed 50 percentage points since 2000, and in Japan an astonishing 80 points. Japan also holds the dubious honor of being the world's first economy with total debt four times the size of its GDP. Finally, in China, where reliable data are harder to come by, total debt has doubled in less than two decades and now approaches 300 percent of Chinese GDP, even higher than in both Europe and the United States.

Total Debt

Total debt of companies, governments, and households as a percentage of GDP

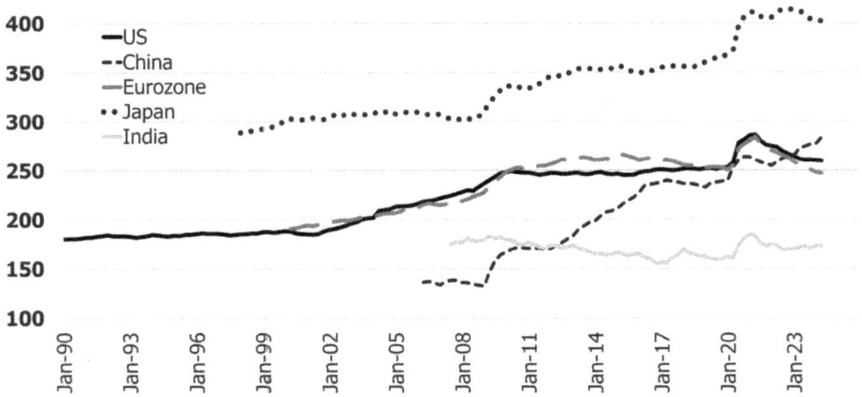

Source: The Great Rebalancing, Bank for International Settlements (BIS)

The optimistic reader may notice that debt ratios have eased slightly in recent years, except in China. True as that may be, it's an observation that must be interpreted with caution. During crises such as the pandemic, debt levels surge far more rapidly than average. When recovery sets in, a few years of strong economic growth usually follow, enough to nudge debt ratios lower. Yet they never return to precrisis levels, as the chart reveals.

In addition, the recent decline is also explained by a massive surge in inflation. This artificially boosts nominal GDP (GDP not adjusted for inflation), which is used to calculate debt-to-GDP ratios, but nobody truly benefits. Rising prices make the (nominal) economy look bigger. The real effect of rising prices is that savings and bond investments lose purchasing power, the real economy (GDP adjusted for inflation) stagnates, while nominal debt ratios drop as if by divine intervention.

Inflation sets off a massive and troubling transfer of wealth, rewarding highly indebted businesses, households, and governments at the expense of those holding mostly assets, instead of liabilities. Just as inflation erodes the real value of wealth, monetary debasement through inflation reduces the real burden of debt. Which makes it all the more striking that even after the recent surge in inflation, the verdict is clear: Our economies are increasingly powered by debt.

Debt Intensity

The debt-to-GDP ratio, where total debt is expressed as a percentage of GDP, is by far the most widely used measure of indebtedness. As with GDP itself, the reason is its simplicity. Policymakers and economists constantly look for intuitive, easily explainable variables to evaluate their policies and to allow for historical and international comparison.

Yet expressing debt as a share of GDP has a major limitation. It doesn't reveal how efficiently, or inefficiently, that debt is being used. How much economic growth can debt really buy? That's a vital question if debt is to fill the widening gap between our hunger for growth and its shrinking supply.

An insightful approach is the lens of debt intensity. This concept reverses the relationship between debt and growth. Rather than asking how large the debt is relative to the economy, the question becomes how much growth each unit of debt actually delivers.

The chart on the next page tracks the debt intensity of the US economy. I calculate debt intensity by dividing the quarterly change in US GDP by the quarterly change in total debt. To limit the impact of outliers, I take the average change in both GDP and debt over a five-year period, or twenty quarters. The gray dotted line traces the long-term trend in debt intensity.

What stands out is that, even though these are five-year averages, the US debt-intensity series remains remarkably volatile. This is due to fluctuations in corporate and household debt. A closer look at the data reveals that corporate and household debt swing far more wildly than government debt. The business cycle, shifting credit conditions, interest rates, and overall sentiment all drive sharp variations in household and corporate borrowing.

Beneath this volatility, however, appears a solid downward trend. The gray dotted line drifts unmistakably lower. In other words, every new dollar of debt buys Americans less growth than the one before. As a result, debt intensity increases over time. Between 1950 and 1980, the ratio of additional GDP to extra debt was around one, meaning that every dollar of debt injected into the economy yielded roughly one dollar of GDP. Over the past decade, the figure has fallen to just 0.4. Each new dollar of debt now produces only forty cents of GDP: The debt intensity of the US economy has spiked dramatically. Ever more debt is required to generate the same amount of economic growth.

Government Debt: The Engine of Growth

Policymakers and politicians tend to measure their success by GDP growth. Businesses and households care less about national growth and more about their own economic situation. Governments, however, are acutely aware of the drag on growth caused by aging populations and shrinking labor forces. It is therefore by no means a coincidence that government borrowing increasingly accounts for the swelling of a country's total debt burden.

With this in mind it's worth stripping out the noisy swings in corporate and household borrowing and measuring debt intensity based solely on government debt. This approach yields more stable outcomes and provides valuable insights into how effectively governments turn borrowing into growth. The results of that analysis are shown in the chart below.

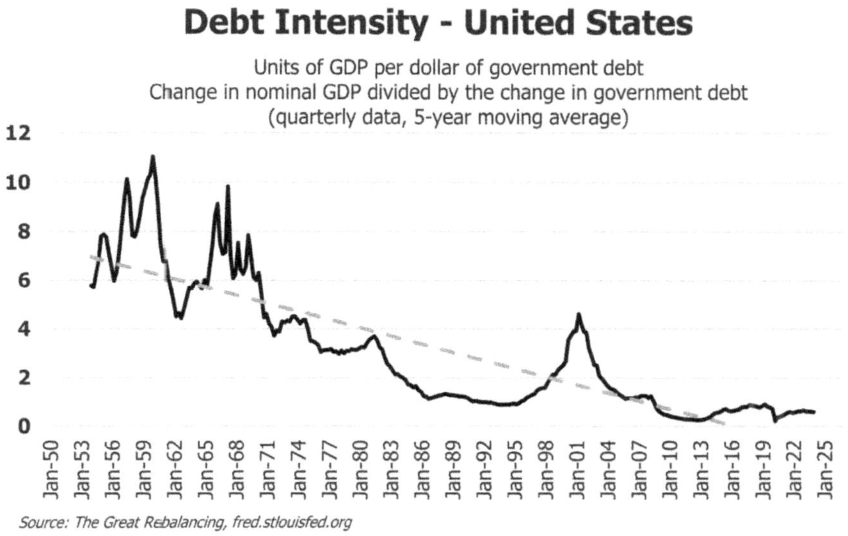

And these results are sobering. The debt intensity of the US government appears much calmer, yet also more ominous. In the 1960s, each new dollar of public debt was associated with an increase of six dollars or more in US GDP. Over the past sixty years, that figure has collapsed to just sixty cents. By this metric, the debt intensity of the US economy has increased tenfold. Worse still, each additional dollar of government debt now generates less than one dollar of output, meaning that massive injections of public borrowing are required to produce even a flicker of growth.

China's Growth Mirage

And that conclusion doesn't stop with America, far from it. Many investors and economists continue to believe that China's economy is fundamentally different from that of the US or Europe. Yet when it comes to its economic growth model, China runs on the same engine as every aging economy: debt-fueled expansion.

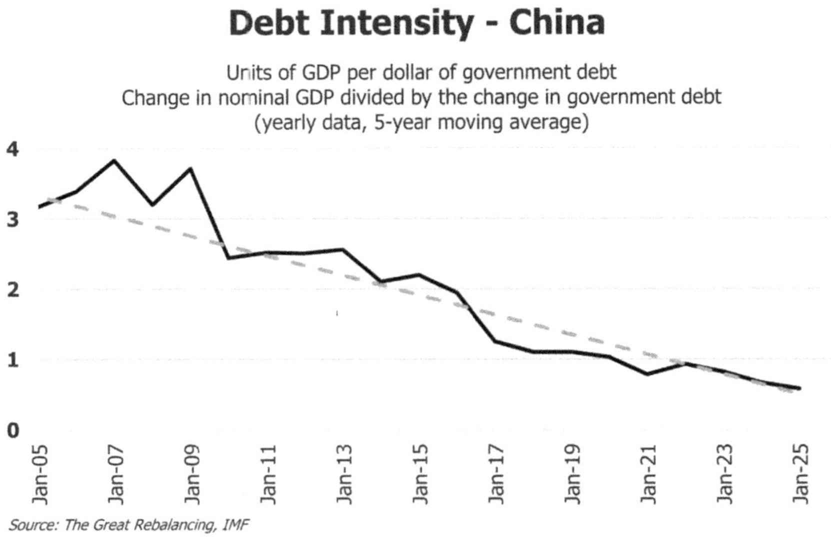

In 2024, China obtained only half a yuan of GDP growth for every yuan of new government debt. The country's debt intensity is at least as high as that of the United States. Many economists would be stunned to see how much leverage China needs to keep growing. Compounding the problem is Beijing's unwavering commitment to its sacred target of 5 percent annual GDP growth.

Recall that the combined contribution of labor and productivity to China's potential GDP growth amounted to just about 2.5 percent. Without debt as a crutch, China's potential growth is roughly 2.5 percent. Based on its 2024 debt intensity of 0.5, bridging that gap (from 2.5 percent to the targeted 5 percent) would require more than 5 percent of GDP in additional borrowing (2.5 percent extra GDP growth divided by a debt intensity of 0.5). That's just staggering, and it explains why China's debt burden is ballooning far faster than anywhere else. To hit that lofty growth target, China must unleash a flood of new debt every single year.

Finally, let's turn to Japan. Among all major economies, Japan faces the bleakest growth outlook. By 2040, the Land of the Rising Sun's potential GDP growth will have permanently sunk below zero. Japan's debt intensity, which is exceptionally high, tells a grim story.

No matter how much debt Japan pours into its economy, the effect on GDP has become negligible. This also explains why Japan's government debt sits well above 200 percent of GDP, far above that of other economies, also with deteriorating growth prospects. Japan is the leading example showing that the link between debt and growth is becoming ever more distorted. The less a country can grow, the more debt it requires merely to grow at all.

In short:

1) The lower a country's potential GDP growth, the higher its debt intensity.
2) As all nations age, economic growth will fade and debt ratios will keep climbing.

In the next part of this book, we will see how this combination brings deeply uncomfortable questions to the surface.

Refinancing Machine

Alongside traditional indicators such as debt-to-GDP ratios and debt intensity, there are other perspectives that expose our debt addiction with striking clarity.

One particularly revealing framework comes from Michael Howell of Crossborder Capital. In his view, it is not (just) the absolute level of debt, although that will continue to rise, but the constant need for refinancing that poses the greatest risk. Howell notes that in advanced economies, a staggering three-quarters of all financial transactions are devoted only to the refinancing of existing debt. Only a sliver of total debt issuance finds its way into new investment in the real economy. This immediately explains why debt intensity keeps climbing: Investments create growth, refinancing does not.

The real danger, Howell argues, lies in liquidity. Liquidity represents the total pool of available funding, shaped by factors such as the money supply, credit growth, lending standards, and bank balance sheets. When liquidity runs short to support the gigantic volume of refinancing, stress emerges: corporate profitability declines, bankruptcies rise, and sovereign creditworthiness comes under pressure. Borrowing costs climb through higher interest rates, feeding even greater concerns about refinancing risk.

Howell stresses that financial stability depends on an appropriate balance between debt and liquidity. The more debt, the more refinancing, and the greater the need for vast amounts of permanent liquidity. This need is particularly acute in the coming years, as an unprecedented volume of debt must be rolled over, likely at higher interest rates. Howell calls this phenomenon the "Maturity Wall."

The dominant role of refinancing in today's debt-driven world also reshapes the way central banks and governments operate. Policymakers can no longer get away with merely raising or lowering interest rates; they are forced to actively manage liquidity, driving ever more extreme interventions. This explains why the size of central bank balance sheets has exploded and why central banks have drifted far from their original mandate of price stability. Too little liquidity inevitably sparks financial market stress and strains the debt system, while too much liquidity fuels inflation. In practice, ever more liquidity is required just to keep the refinancing machine running.

The combination of our relentless desire for growth and the chronic shortage of it is pushing global economies ever deeper into debt's embrace. We have reached the point where debt is no longer merely a tool for creating growth; it has become the very foundation of the system itself. Policymakers keep feeding the illusion of endless growth, yet every bigger intervention drags us further from an economy once grounded in labor and productivity.

We stand at the edge of a new paradigm, one where economies, markets, and investments are being reshaped entirely, and old rules no longer apply.

Part II

The End of Discipline

CHAPTER 5
The Law of Debt

Introduction

It is now unmistakably clear: The economic growth we so deeply desire can only be manufactured with debt. And it takes ever more debt just to achieve modest growth. This raises a fundamental question: If debt is now the engine of growth, how do we keep it running? How can policymakers stop the debt-driven system from collapsing under its own weight?

The answer is that the old rules must be broken. The classic economic principle that debt is sustainable as long as economic growth outpaces interest rates no longer holds true. Governments, followed closely by central banks, must intervene continuously to prevent debt sustainability from collapsing the system. When debt is the last remaining source of growth, maintaining debt sustainability becomes the ultimate policy objective. Governments cannot allow this source to dry up as well.

This has profound consequences for how economies and financial systems function. Equally important, it compels investors to rethink their portfolios to make them better suited for a new financial paradigm.

The Law of Debt Sustainability

For decades, the relationship between growth (referred to as "g") and interest rates (called "r") has been at the heart of how economists judge whether a nation's debt is sustainable.

The change in the debt-to-GDP ratio can be expressed by the following formula:

$\Delta D = r\text{-}g \times D + PS$

- **ΔD** represents the change in the debt-to-GDP ratio over a given period. The Greek letter Delta (Δ) stands for change.
- **D** is the current debt-to-GDP ratio, measuring debt as a percentage of GDP.
- **PS** is the primary balance, meaning the budget deficit or surplus excluding interest payments.
- **r** denotes the interest rate, typically the 10-year government bond yield.
- **g** represents economic growth, that is, the rate of GDP growth.

Traditionally, this formula revolves around the relationship between the interest rate (r) and GDP growth (g). The logic is simple: As long as GDP growth exceeds the interest rate, debt becomes easier to carry and can be kept under control. After all, the sum of r-g is negative in this case. This negative number, multiplied by the current debt ratio (D), causes the debt-to-GDP ratio to shrink over time. Conversely, if a country grows more slowly than the interest rate, meaning the sum of r-g is positive, its debt as a share of GDP (D) rises. That's when debt sustainability starts to buckle.

To grasp the full impact of this relationship, we go back to 1944. Though others had hinted at the link between interest, growth, and public debt, it was the Russian-American economist Evsey Domar who gave it mathematical form. In his classic 1944 paper, "The 'Burden of the Debt' and the National Income," Domar argued that an economy can literally grow its way out of debt, provided growth is sufficiently high, higher than the interest rate at least. The year

1944 is crucial, as it ensured that the r-g formula was used for decades to downplay the potential risks of high (government) debt.

In 1944, many countries were burdened with towering debts as a result of World War II. Governments had borrowed heavily, first to finance the war and later to fund postwar reconstruction. Policymakers expected that peace, stability, and rebuilding would usher in a period of rapid economic growth. Domar's model fitted that narrative perfectly: As long as growth (g) exceeded the interest rate (r), debt would melt away as a share of GDP. It gave policymakers a powerful reason for optimism. Forget austerity or fiscal restraint; growth itself was the key to debt sustainability.

And at first, that expectation was met. Between 1950 and 1970, the US economy grew by an average of 5 percent per year, while postwar Western Europe achieved even higher growth rates.

Buoyed by Domar's elegant formula and the comforting rule of r < g, policymakers celebrated for more than three decades. As long as growth outpaced interest rates on government debt, and for decades it did, there was little to worry about.

Source: The Great Rebalancing, fred.stlouisfed.org

The Turning Point

In the early 1980s, however, the party came to an abrupt end. After a first wave of inflation in the 1970s, fueled by the abandonment of the gold standard in 1971 and the oil shocks of 1973 and 1979, central banks were slow to act. By the end of the decade, inflation, and, more dangerously, inflation expectations, had spiraled out of control. Fed Chair Paul Volcker had no choice but to slam on the brakes with massive rate hikes. The US 10-year yield soared to nearly 16 percent.

The early 1980s delivered a brutal wake-up call for policymakers, shattering decades of complacency. The long-held belief that growth alone could render debt manageable was shattered. Growth remained, but at interest rates of 16 percent, Domar's comforting formula suddenly turned against them. At those towering rates, debt sustainability was no longer a given.

After World War II, US government debt fell from more than 100 percent of GDP to barely 30 percent, a level Alexander Hamilton himself would likely have applauded. Yet with interest rates spiking above 10 percent, debt sustainability nonetheless began to strain under pressure. After all, the gap between interest rates and growth r-g had blown wide open, even as the US economy kept performing strongly.

Between June 1981 and June 1982, the 10-year yield averaged an eye-popping 14 percent, while nominal GDP growth hovered around 9 percent. The 5-percentage-point gap between r and g meant that, without intervention, debt would start climbing fast. Although not all debt had to be refinanced immediately at those higher rates, the imbalance between growth and interest rates was so large that America's debt sustainability was immediately called into question.

Elsewhere, interest rates also spiked, forcing central banks to make similar interventions. Confronted with this new reality, policymakers turned their attention to a component of Domar's model that had previously received little focus: the primary balance.

As shown in the formula above, a country's primary balance equals its budget surplus or deficit excluding interest payments on the debt. A primary surplus enters the equation as a negative term, reducing the debt ratio. That makes sense intuitively, since a surplus means the government spends less than it collects in taxes. Given the deeply unfavorable r-g dynamic, achieving a primary surplus became the top priority of fiscal policy in the early 1980s. Austerity was no longer optional; it was inevitable. Only a strong primary surplus could keep government debt in check. Taxes were raised and spending cut to prevent interest payments from rendering public debt unsustainable.

Since the 1980s, the once-celebrated Domar model has lost its shine. The era when r-g served as a comforting justification to smooth away debt concerns gave way to one defined by tight fiscal discipline and austerity. This shift laid the groundwork for the last sustained period of US budget surpluses, the late 1990s, roughly twenty-five years ago.

New Problems

Fast-forward to today, and it's no surprise that the r-g relationship is back to haunt policymakers. Only this time, it's not soaring interest that threatens debt sustainability, it's vanishing GDP growth. As shown in the previous chapter, potential GDP growth is already weak and is expected to decline further in the decades ahead due to aging populations and shrinking labor forces. Growth capacity has become so limited that even the smallest bump in interest rates can destabilize debt dynamics. As "g" in the equation moves toward zero, the system loses its only buffer against a rising "r."

The rate hikes by central banks after 2020, and the mounting debate over debt sustainability that came with it, underscore this vulnerability. Once again, Japan provides the most striking example. By the end of the next decade, the country will require negative interest rates simply to prevent its already towering debt from rising even further. As of this writing, Japan's 10-year yield stands at 1.6 percent, the highest in nearly two decades, yet hardly extreme by historical and global standards. Still, given Japan's meager growth potential, even this modest rate is enough to tighten the noose around its debt sustainability.

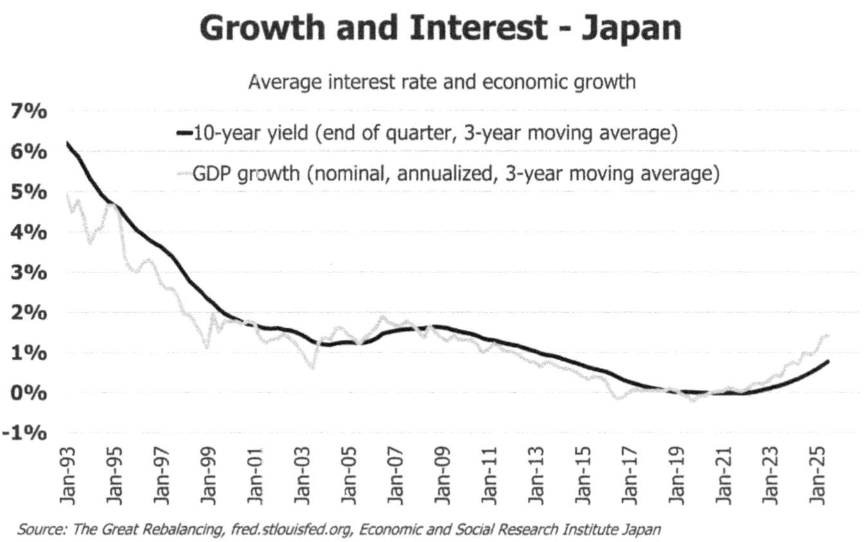

Because potential GDP growth keeps falling, primary balances must now be structurally positive to ensure debt sustainability. The opposite, however, is the case. Driven by their obsession with growth, governments worldwide are running record deficits, with little prospect of change. The last US budget surplus, now a quarter century ago, already confirmed this. And according to the OECD, Japan last achieved a primary surplus in 1992, more than three decades ago. The age of fiscal discipline is long gone.

Debt sustainability can no longer be fixed by conventional means, the r-g dynamic is *that* unfavorable, and fiscal budgets have stopped working as a stabilizing force. This reality is forcing policymakers toward increasingly extreme measures that cut deep into the fabric of our economic and financial system.

Government Dominance

Before exploring those measures, one final point. Although the r-g framework was developed for sovereign debt, with a few adjustments it can also be applied to corporate and household balance sheets. For companies, r represents the interest paid on outstanding debt or overall financing costs, while g stands for revenue or profit growth. When r exceeds g, debt grows faster than income, eventually leading to insolvency. Households face a similar dynamic: If wages and incomes fail to keep up with rising expenses such as mortgage payments, debt becomes unsustainable.

Nevertheless, there are two crucial differences that have a major impact on how the entire financial system operates. The first, and most fundamental, is that neither companies nor households control monetary or fiscal policy. Sovereign governments, by contrast, can refinance debt by issuing new bonds and having them purchased by central banks or other financial institutions. Or they can raise taxes and simultaneously impose capital controls to prevent wealth from fleeing. Companies and households have no such privilege. The ability of sovereign governments to control both debt and money supply is precisely what demands a fundamental reconsideration of how we structure investment portfolios.

The second difference ties directly to this point and was touched upon earlier: Government debt is growing ever more dominant. In sheer size, as the key driver of growth, and as the catalyst of change, governments now dominate the system like never before. To illustrate this: Until 1900, US federal government spending averaged less than 5 percent of GDP. After World War II, it climbed steadily from around 10 percent to over 40 percent. Since 2000, the share of US government debt in total debt has jumped from 28 to 43 percent of GDP, a rise of 15 percentage points. A similar trend holds across other major economies.

The expanding presence of governments and their debts is a central thread running through this book and the catalyst for The Great Rebalancing, demanding a massive overhaul of the way we invest. And it has a name: fiscal dominance. Its defining feature is huge: a complete loss of fiscal discipline.

CHAPTER 6
The Gap

Introduction

With policymakers, whether politicians or central bankers, it is more revealing to watch what they do than to listen to what they say.

Fiscal discipline is a perfect example of this. France, for example, continues to wrestle with the fallout of yet another political crisis. By late 2024, the government collapsed after a heated battle over a budget that was nowhere close to acceptable by any standard. For months, politicians bickered over half-hearted measures that might, at best, have nudged the deficit below 3 percent of GDP by 2029. In July 2025, Prime Minister François Bayrou again sounded the alarm, proposing to freeze pensions and even scrap two national holidays in a desperate bid to restore fiscal order.

That 3-percent deficit target originates from the 1992 Maastricht Treaty, the foundation of the Economic and Monetary Union. In that treaty, EU member states agreed that their budget deficits should not exceed 3 percent of GDP, and that government debt should remain below 60 percent of GDP. These were hard rules from a bygone era, designed to safeguard fiscal discipline and ensure debt sustainability. I wonder if politicians today ever think about those rules. Probably only for a moment in June 2025, when no fewer than nine of the twenty-seven EU countries were reprimanded by EU President Ursula von der Leyen for failing to meet the 3-percent deficit rule.

But even if deficit reduction were made a top priority, the odds of France achieving a structural deficit below 3 percent of GDP by 2029 are near zero. And that is only part of the problem. Because of demographic aging and a lack of economic growth, even a budget deficit of 3 percent is no longer sufficient to stabilize debt. Not for France, nor for any other major aging economy. The fiscal gap has simply grown too wide.

Mind the Gap

To see why most countries cannot get away with a budget deficit of 3 percent of GDP, we must go back again to the r-g formula from the previous chapter. Let's continue with the example of France. Suppose the French economy manages to grow by about 1 percent per year, despite the heavy drag from demographic aging. In that case, any interest rate above 1 percent will push the French debt-to-GDP ratio, already at 110 percent of GDP, higher, unless the country runs a primary surplus big enough to offset it. With so little growth to lean on, almost any deficit becomes unsustainable. French policymakers, however, evidently disagree, running an average annual deficit of 5 percent of GDP.

The need for budget surpluses is not merely a theoretical exercise based on the r-g framework. On the contrary, a growing body of economic research shows that sustained surpluses are required just to avoid economies from slipping backward. Much of that research centers on another crucial variable: the fiscal sustainability gap. This gap represents the budget surplus a government must achieve to maintain existing spending and commitments without causing debt to rise further. In other words, it's the surplus needed to guarantee the same future quality in education, pensions, social services, security, and healthcare, exactly the mandatory government expenses that are exploding in every aging economy.

The fiscal sustainability gap is a canyon that governments must somehow cross if they want to preserve living standards, a leap possible only with colossal, and frankly unrealistic, budget surpluses. Yet the fiscal gap rarely gets the attention it deserves, and is almost always grossly underestimated. And that's no surprise. Politicians rarely want to talk about the gap, assuming they even fully understand it. Another reason is that economists often present the concept in a counterintuitive, somewhat unwieldy way that obscures its urgency.

A report by the US Bureau of the Fiscal Service (BFS), part of the US Treasury Department, titled "An Unsustainable Fiscal Path," examined America's fiscal outlook all the way to 2099. The findings are nothing short of sobering. Without policy changes, US government debt is projected to surpass 200 percent of GDP before 2050, a doubling in less than twenty-five years. By 2099, US debt is projected to top an almost unimaginable 500 percent of GDP.

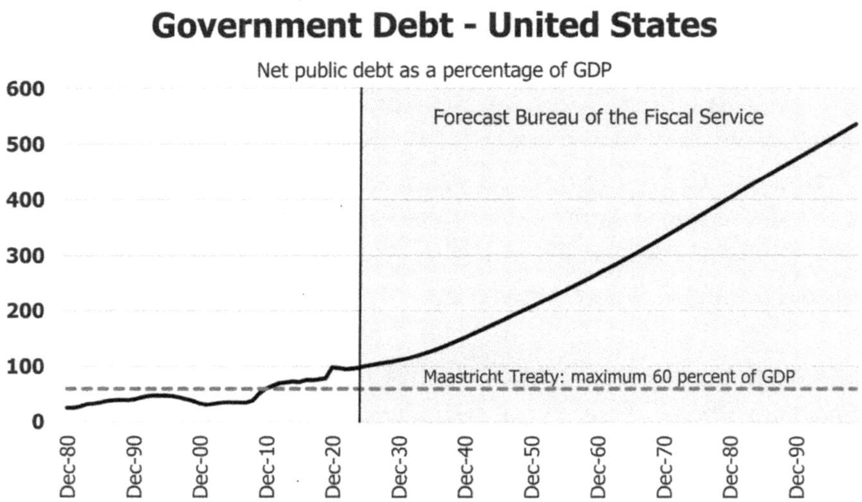

Source: The Great Rebalancing, Bureau of the Fiscal Service

The BFS then calculates the size of the budget surplus required to prevent the current debt level, now roughly 100 percent of GDP, from climbing higher. That surplus amounts to 0.6 percent per year. And here is where misinterpretation creeps in. Many people look at that 0.6 percent and think, "Alright, if Washington just spends a little less than it earns, and how hard can that really be, everything will be fine." What they forget is that the United States, like France and nearly every other major economy, runs a structural budget deficit. Recall that America's last budget surplus occurred a full twenty-five years ago.

The starting point for measuring the fiscal sustainability gap is therefore not zero. On the contrary, that 0.6 percent surplus stands against the deficit the United States is expected to run. In this case, against the projected budget deficit through 2099. In its analysis, the BFS assumes an average annual budget deficit of 3.6 percent of GDP. That sounds somewhat optimistic to me, yet it still translates into a fiscal sustainability gap of 4.3 percent of GDP (3.6 percent deficit plus the 0.6 percent surplus required to stabilize debt, rounded).

In plain terms, freezing today's debt ratio while honoring existing obligations would require the US government to cut spending by 4.3 percent of GDP, or raise the same amount in additional tax revenues. Under current policy, that's flatly impossible.

The International Gap

Other countries will provide different numbers, but the conclusion is identical. To safeguard the future quality of public services while keeping debt at today's already towering level, let alone reducing it, colossal budget surpluses are required. What governments have "achieved" for decades, however, is precisely the opposite.

To avoid drowning you in numbers, here is a glimpse of the fiscal burdens weighing heavily on governments everywhere. A 2024 study by the Japan Research Institute examined how Japan's combined central and local government debt could be reduced over thirty years from more than 200 percent of GDP today to 130 percent, a level last seen at the start of this century.

To highlight once again the importance of Domar's r-g-framework, the study assessed the fiscal discipline required under three now familiar scenarios:

- $r < g$, the interest rate is lower than GDP growth.
- $r = g$, the interest rate equals GDP growth.
- $r > g$, the interest rate exceeds GDP growth.

In the "middle" scenario, where growth and interest rates are equal, Japan would need to run a primary budget surplus of 2.8 percent of GDP every year for thirty years straight, starting immediately. Japan would need a remarkable stroke of luck to complete such a fiscal marathon. Since the start of this century, the country's average annual deficit has been 5.6 percent of GDP. The gap to close is therefore an enormous 8.4 percent (2.8 percent required surplus + 5.6 percent budget deficit). Over the past twenty-five years, Japan's primary balance was never once in surplus, making it clear that the country's fiscal sustainability gap is essentially unbridgeable.

That conclusion applies already to the scenario where the interest rate does not rise above GDP growth. Let's assume Japan's potential growth hovers around zero. In that case, even a modestly positive interest rate, the r > g scenario, would demand a staggering primary surplus of 4.5 percent of GDP every year for three decades. It is no coincidence that the Japan Research Institute's report carried the telling subtitle: "With the return to 'a world with interest rates,' the formulation and execution of a long-term plan cannot wait." Every tick higher in interest rates worsens Japan's debt problem. If the pieces of the puzzle are starting to fit together, great, that is no coincidence.

The European Central Bank (ECB) is not exactly famous for bold or intimidating titles, but it does produce charts that will make you pause. The ECB estimates that to bring eurozone debt back down to the once holy grail of 60 percent of GDP by 2070, governments would need to improve their primary balances by 2 percent of GDP immediately and permanently. If you also factor in the major challenges of aging populations, defense spending, and (absurd) climate investments, governments need to find an additional 3 percent of GDP in fiscal space. Taken together, this implies that eurozone governments would need to reform (read: improve) their primary budgets by about 5 percent of GDP, every single year, all the way to 2070.

That 5 percent figure is roughly the same magnitude as the fiscal sustainability gap confronting the United States. But note that the BFS analysis assumed merely keeping the current debt ratio stable. If the US were also to target a debt-to-GDP ratio of 60 percent, far greater fiscal discipline would be required.

Chart 5

Overview of fiscal efforts required in response to specific challenges

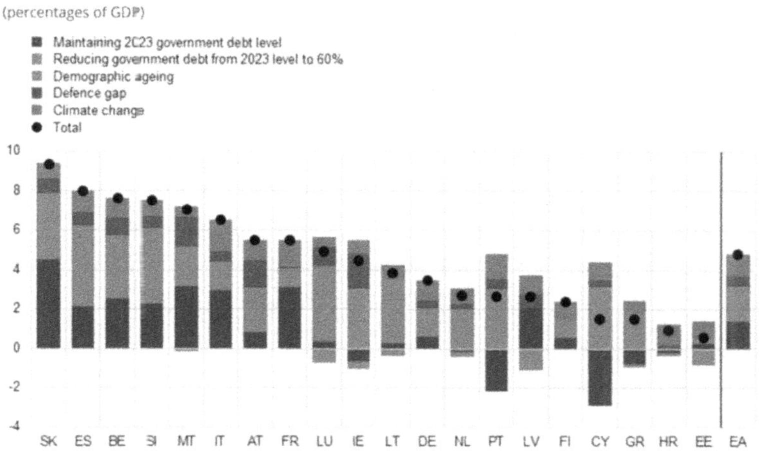

Sources: 2024 Ageing Report, European Commission's Debt Sustainability Monitor 2023, NGFS Phase IV simulations, IMF's October 2023 Fiscal Monitor, NATO, Eurostat and ECB calculations.
Notes: The chart depicts the required immediate and permanent one-off improvement in the ratio of structural primary balance to GDP to bring the debt ratio to 60% of GDP by 2070, incor[illegible]nancing for any additional expenditure until 2070 arising from an ageing population, defence and climate. See Box 1 for a description of the methodology.

In China and India, the picture is complicated not only by the familiar lack of reliable data, but also by the outsized role of local governments. A significant share of total debt sits at the local level. According to the IMF, Chinese local governments hold debt equal to 93 percent of GDP. For the central government, the IMF puts the figure at just 24 percent. This reflects a skewed fiscal system in which local governments shoulder most of the spending. Countries with such an uneven setup tend to have worse debt dynamics and a much larger fiscal gap than central government data suggest. In fact, China's vast mountain of local government debt, combined with its revenue streams that fluctuate heavily with the business cycle, has long been a source of financial instability.

Translating the Gap: Revenues and Spending

Let's return once more to the United States. A 2024 report by the Government Accountability Office (GAO), the US Congress's fiscal watchdog, titled "The Nation's Fiscal Health," reached conclusions strikingly similar to those of the BFS.

Because GAO is tasked with ensuring that tax dollars are spent effectively, it translates the fiscal sustainability gap into concrete spending cuts or revenue increases that Washington has to achieve to close it. In the interest of transparency, the agency even built a public website (scan QR-code) where users can run various budget scenarios. A quick visit reveals the sheer scale of the debt challenge.

For example, imagine the United States had signed the Maastricht Treaty and adopted a debt target of 60 percent of GDP. To hit that target, given that debt currently stands at around 100 percent of GDP, the federal government would need to boost annual revenues by more than 30 percent, or slash spending by 25 percent, every year over the next thirty years.

A quarter cut in government spending. Just imagine what that would mean for healthcare, pensions, infrastructure, and other pillars of daily life. Hospitals would close, retirement benefits would be cut, and bridges, roads, and railways would fall into disrepair. Cuts of that magnitude would inflict severe damage on America's quality of life.

Even if the goal were only to stop debt from rising further, massive fiscal adjustment would still be unavoidable. In that scenario, government revenues would need to rise by 23 percent, or spending would have to be cut by about 19 percent, permanently.

Given these staggering numbers, GAO's title, "The Nation's Fiscal Health," feels almost ironic. "The Nation's Fiscal Illness" would have been far more accurate. After all, it would take an effort of epic proportions to conclude that such figures reflect anything resembling a healthy financial condition.

Want to explore the US fiscal scenarios yourself? Visit the GAO website. To save you some time, after testing every scenario on the GAO site, I didn't find a single one that allowed for lower revenues or higher spending, not one.

CHAPTER 7
Fiscal Limits

Introduction

Why do politicians stay silent about the fiscal gap? Because it has become a chasm too wide to bridge. The sacrifices required will inevitably come at the cost of our standard of living; something will have to give. And since aging is the real culprit, it stands to reason that our retirement years, our pensions, will turn out less comfortable than we imagined.

Still, governments will try to close the gap, hoping to keep their debt-fueled growth model from collapsing under its own weight. After all, those who buy growth prefer not to answer uncomfortable questions about the bill. Traditionally, there are two obvious ways to reduce debt: spend less or bring in more income. The latter sounds simple. Why else would governments levy taxes in the first place? Yet in reality, the limits of taxation have basically been reached.

Aging populations, capital flight, and polarization are squeezing tax revenues. Who in their right mind wants to hand most of their paycheck to the government? Capital inevitably flows to where the skim is smallest. Wealthy households have plenty of ways to outmaneuver governments, while low-income earners are trapped. In short, the government's tax base looks increasingly fragile.

A Special Kind of Income

Whether companies can repay or refinance their debts depends directly on their ability to sell products and services people actually want to buy. The better those products and services match consumer needs, the stronger the cash flows, and the less likely that debt becomes a problem.

Yet even firms with exceptional products and services go under from time to time. Sometimes it's just bad luck. Companies have little control over the broader economy. During a recession, when GDP shrinks for two quarters or more, consumers spend less, no matter how great a product may be. New companies, firms that fail to sell enough, or those with thin financial buffers simply cannot meet their obligations and go under.

For sovereign governments, which can set and enforce their own policies, the situation is very different. Governments derive most of their income through taxes. Economic growth still matters; more growth means more tax revenues, but governments are far less vulnerable than a business that goes bankrupt or an individual who loses their job. They have one unique habit: a near-universal instinct to tax nearly everything that moves.

Who pays tax and what gets taxed together define the tax base. It represents the total sum of income, property, wealth, consumption, transactions, and other taxable economic activity. Taxes, therefore, are far more than a levy on wages and profits. While the tax base varies widely from one country to another, most governments tax a remarkably broad range of activities.

Here is a slightly cynical list of how that looks in practice:

- Tax when you work: income tax.
- Tax when you consume: VAT and excise duties.
- Tax when you invest: capital gains and dividend taxes.
- Tax when you own property: real estate and transfer taxes.
- Tax when you give something away: gift and inheritance taxes.
- Tax when you produce: carbon and environmental taxes.

All in all, that is a hefty amount of taxation. Whether you work, buy groceries, purchase a home, die, or invest in an interesting alternative fund, you inevitably pay tax. And as this list shows, wages, the main source of household income, are taxed not once, but multiple times. But is it really logical that the net salary of a diligent worker is taxed again the moment it is spent or invested?

The long list of already taxed incomes, assets, and transactions suggests that expanding the tax base is no easy task. Even if governments get creative and invent new sources of revenue, the base will likely shrink anyway for one simple reason: aging.

The OECD concludes in its extensive study "Funding the Future," on the impact of aging on government revenues, that these revenues will decline in thirty-four of the thirty-eight countries examined. Given the explosive rise in the old-age dependency ratio, measuring the balance between workers and retirees, it's hardly surprising that the fiscal model of governments is under severe pressure. It is primarily workers who provide the bulk of income and payroll taxes, along with most social security contributions. In nearly every major economy, these remain the core sources of public income.

Laffer's Curve

On paper, governments could offset falling revenues and weaker growth from aging populations simply by raising tax rates. In practice, this is far less straightforward.

In the fall of 1974, four men gathered at a Washington restaurant to vent their frustration about President Gerald Ford's planned tax hikes. Present at the table were Donald Rumsfeld, then Ford's chief of staff, Dick Cheney, his future successor, Jude Wanniski, journalist at *The Wall Street Journal,* and Arthur Laffer, professor of economics at the University of Chicago.

The two politicians were searching for alternatives to the temporary tax hike Ford was considering to fight inflation. During their conversation, Laffer argued that higher tax rates wouldn't necessarily raise tax revenues. Lower tax rates, by contrast, could spur economic growth and ultimately increase total tax receipts. To make his point, Laffer grabbed a napkin and sketched what would become famous as the Laffer curve.

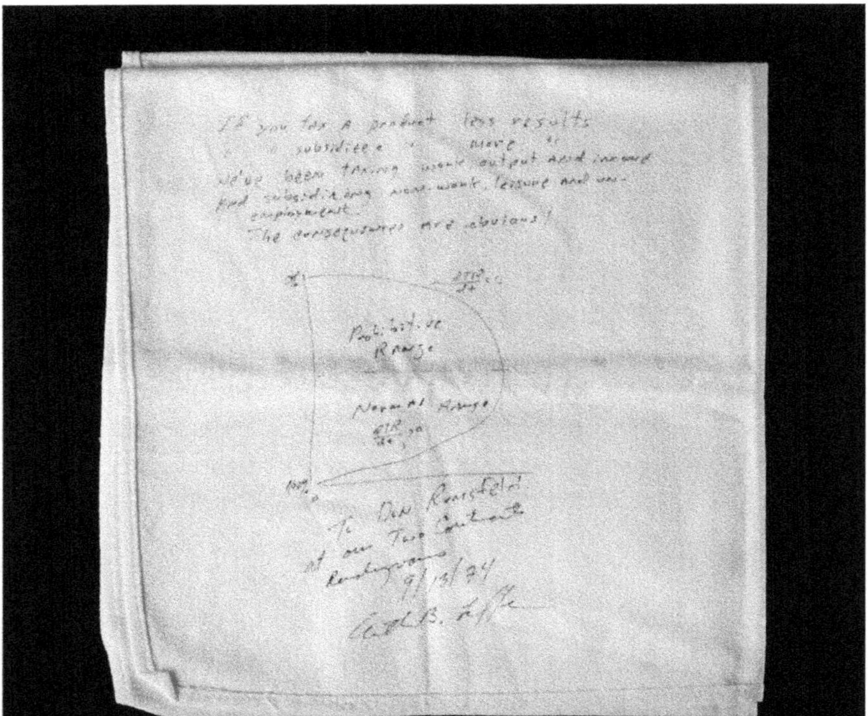

Source: National Museum of American History, Smithsonian Institution

The Laffer curve is a stylized illustration of how tax rates relate to government revenues. The original Laffer curve, now displayed in the National Museum of American History, is worth a look, though it is not exactly easy to read. As it turns out, ink on cloth is not the ideal medium for a clear economic diagram. Laffer also did not label the axes, and to make matters worse, he reversed them. He placed the explanatory variable on the vertical axis, and the dependent variable on the horizontal one, a cardinal sin in the eyes of most economists. Normally, the dependent variable, the one you are trying to explain or predict, belongs on the vertical axis, and the independent variable, the one you already know and use to predict the dependent one, is placed on the horizontal axis. So, in the case of the Laffer curve, you would expect the tax rate on the horizontal axis and tax revenue on the vertical one, because Laffer's entire point is that tax rates determine tax revenues.

That evening in 1974, Laffer took an unorthodox approach to make his case that higher tax rates do not always mean higher revenues. Below is a modern version of the Laffer curve, easier to read and, hopefully, more pleasing to the eyes of economists.

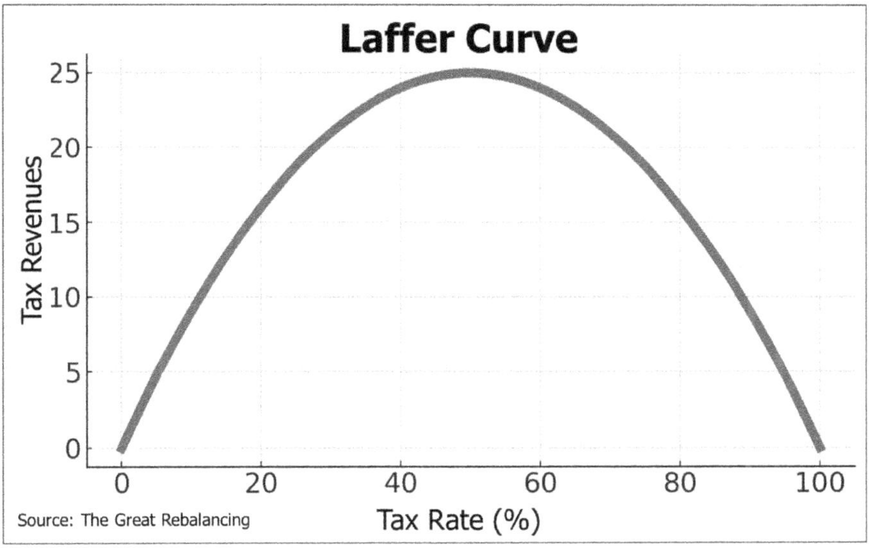

The message of the Laffer curve is simple, yet powerful. Raising tax rates to boost revenues works, but only up to a point. Go beyond that point, and higher tax rates start to backfire, driving revenues down.

Here is how to read the Laffer curve:

- Far left on the curve: When the tax rate is zero, revenues are, of course, zero.
- The rising part of the curve: Tax rates increase but remain within reasonable limits. Businesses and households continue to pay taxes while still consuming and investing.
- The peak of the curve: The optimal tax rate where revenues are highest. Businesses and households may complain about taxes, but

they still pay them and do not change their behavior too much.

- The downward slope: The tax burden becomes so heavy that people and companies try to avoid it, by working or investing less, evading taxes, or even leaving the country, causing revenues to decline.
- Far right on the curve: At a 100 percent tax rate, all profits and wages go to the government, so no one works, and revenues fall back to zero.

Like Solow, who published his theory in a prestigious journal, Laffer happened to be at the right place at exactly the right time. The fourth man at that Washington table, journalist Jude Wanniski, connected Laffer with two powerful politicians, Cheney and Rumsfeld, who would remain influential in Washington for decades. Moreover, Wanniski popularized Laffer's theory through his articles for *The Wall Street Journal* and his political network, bringing it to the attention of figures such as Ronald Reagan, who in the 1980s turned the napkin into policy with sweeping tax cuts.

No sound theory is complete without its critics, and the Laffer curve is no exception. Like most economic models, Laffer's theory is notoriously hard to prove. As the long list of taxes already confirmed, there is no single tax rate, and therefore no single optimal one, especially since most rates are intertwined. Instead, tax systems are a maze of rates, exemptions, and loopholes, making any "optimal" rate a moving target. Taxation has become a massive industry, with millions of firms, consultants, and advisors perpetually hunting for the best possible tax burden for their clients. And, of course, their mission is always to get as close to zero as possible. In addition, Laffer's curve is eagerly abused by politicians as a convenient excuse to announce or promise tax cuts.

Still, taxation has its limits. When it no longer pays to work, or when investment returns are too heavily eroded, people simply stop working or doing business. They evade taxes or move to places with friendlier rates. People work not to pay taxes but to support their families, pay their bills, build wealth, and secure their future. Governments that lose sight of this, as their revenues decline due to aging populations, soon find themselves on the wrong side of the Laffer curve.

Be honest: Would you still work if you had to hand over 100 percent of your paycheck to the government? What about 80 percent? Or 60?

Optimal Taxation

In many countries, tax systems have become so complex and costly that it is virtually impossible to determine the optimal rate in any standardized way. Most studies on optimal taxation therefore focus solely on the highest income groups. Because these incomes are typically taxed the heaviest and may thus appear to provide the best insight into the tipping point of the Laffer curve. On the surface, this approach may sound logical, yet it is flawed. While top earners have the highest salaries and face the steepest rates, paradoxically, those wages often represent only a fraction of their total income and wealth.

It is therefore plausible that top earners, despite facing higher tax rates, are ultimately less sensitive to tax hikes than households that depend entirely on their income to make ends meet. In economic jargon, the tax elasticity, the degree to which people change their behavior when tax rates rise, is likely higher for lower-income households than for top earners. Those earning modest wages are more likely to quit working, reduce hours, or underreport income when taxes go up. Several studies suggest that the turning point on the Laffer curve, based on the tax sensitivity of top incomes alone, lies somewhere between 50 and 60 percent. Once the tax burden reaches that range, revenues peak. Any further tax increase becomes self-defeating.

Thomas Piketty, best known for his book *Capital in the Twenty-First Century,* together with Saez and Stantcheva (2014), takes a different view. They argue that the optimal tax rate for top incomes is 73 percent or even higher. Yet their analysis is not neutral. Piketty ties the "optimal" tax rate to his broader goal of reducing income inequality, the central theme of his book. For him, higher taxes are a political instrument to narrow the gap between rich and poor. It is hardly surprising, then, that his optimal tax rate ends up much higher.

In contrast to Piketty's study, a range of research papers supports Laffer's original argument and shows that lower tax rates tend to boost economic growth. Tax cuts, in some cases, can even pay for themselves. Stronger GDP growth raises wages and consumption, which lifts higher corporate profits and employment, offsetting the revenue loss from the tax cuts. Some research finds that tax reductions can fund themselves by as much as 80 percent, even before accounting for long-term effects.

A Loss of Human Capital

Many studies on taxation, limited by complexity, focus exclusively on short-term data, comparing tax rates and revenues from one fiscal year to the next. What these studies fail to capture is how higher taxes erode the incentive to pursue education, develop skills, and gain work experience. If the payoff barely registers after taxes, what would be the point?

Knowledge and skills together make up human capital. When that capital becomes scarce, economies fall straight into the trap of slow economic growth. The competence, experience, and dedication of workers are among the strongest drivers of productivity. When employees stop investing in themselves or improving their skills because most of the reward ends up with the tax office, productivity inevitably declines.

The same dynamic occurs when high taxes sap the motivation to study or gain experience, feeding the belief that "it won't pay off anyway." Lower productivity means less growth, which in turn increases the reliance on debt to manufacture growth artificially.

The long-term impact of taxation on human behavior and capital is crucial. Of course, money is not the only reason people work, but the less of their salary they get to keep, the sooner they think: "why bother?" Governments themselves are often to blame for this reaction. In many countries, especially across Europe, the social safety net is so generous that for lower-income households, working hardly makes financial sense. They literally do not need to work for the money. Rarely do policymakers acknowledge the long-term damage the loss of human capital (because of higher taxes) inflicts on productivity and growth.

When you factor in the negative impact of taxes on human capital, the optimal tax rate automatically comes out lower. If taxes undermine the growth of human capital, tax revenues will eventually decline. Put differently, studies that limit themselves to annual tax rates and revenue comparisons overestimate how much pressure taxpayers can truly bear. A 2011 study by Mathias Trabandt (ECB) and Harald Uhlig (University of Chicago) concludes that when human capital is included, the optimal rate drops from around 60 percent to just 45 percent.

The Cumulative Tax Burden

This brings me back to the long list of taxes we face. The endless list of rates, tangled rules, and chaotic structures ensures that no study truly captures the cumulative tax burden. It is an impossible task, which likely suits many politicians just fine. Still, even a brief inventory of the many taxed items offers a decent picture of how much tax citizens actually pay. The takeaway is straightforward: The cumulative tax load is already so heavy that higher rates become counterproductive.

In the United States, the top federal income tax rate stands at 37 percent. Americans also pay state income taxes in most cases, although a handful of states impose no additional tax. In California, however, the state adds another 13 percent, and more still for top earners. As if that were not enough, some cities, including New York, levy an additional "local" income tax on top of federal and state taxes.

But that's not even the end of it. Beyond income tax, Americans also face levies on healthcare, capital gains, property, inheritances, and gifts. A US household with a high income, property, and investments can easily face a combined rate exceeding 50 percent, with peaks approaching 60 percent.

In other major economies, the top income tax rate is considerably higher than in the United States. Several countries levy top rates around 45 percent, excluding social security and pension contributions. Add in wealth, property, and transfer taxes, and the total effective rate for top earners easily climbs above 50 percent. In some countries, including Belgium, Canada, and Japan, the top rate nears 60 percent, and in certain cases even surpasses it. Faced with such tax rates, Laffer would likely have reached for a billboard instead of a napkin to make his point.

Norway's Exodus

That the Laffer curve is more than just a nice afternoon sketch becomes clear from the story of Norway. According to *Dagens Næringsliv,* Norway's equivalent of the *Financial Times,* more than thirty billionaires and multimillionaires left the country in 2022 after the wealth tax was increased. The number of ultra-wealthy who departed that year exceeded the total of the previous thirteen years combined, a striking case of capital flight.

At first glance, the tax increase seemed modest, from 0.85 to 1.10 percent, for Norway's wealthiest citizens. Yet because it applied to total wealth, that 0.25 percentage point rise was enough to drive a wave of the superrich literally out of the country. *CitizenX*, a technology platform that helps investors optimize their passports, estimated that the tax hike triggered an outflow of roughly fifty-four billion US dollars from Norway. The Norwegian treasury lost nearly $600 million in revenue, a fiscal hole that could not remotely be filled by the wealthy Norwegians who chose to stay. Net, the Norwegian treasury lost a staggering 448 million dollars. That's the Laffer theory in its purest form. The Norwegian policymakers who devised this plan clearly had no idea about the tax sensitivity of their wealthiest citizens, who collectively slammed the door on their way out.

That is, to put it mildly, remarkable. Barely a year earlier, in 2021, taxable wealth in the Norwegian municipality of Bø surged by 60 percent after the wealth tax was reduced. The result of this small "trial balloon" in Bø raises an obvious question: Why did the government decide to raise the wealth tax in 2022? Did they really not see the capital flight coming?

Perhaps not. But the fact is that by the end of 2021, Norway had a change of government. After the center-right coalition lost power, a center-left administration took office that October. As I will explain later, that fact tells you a lot. In an increasingly polarized world, the swings from right to left and back again have a growing impact on policy. The ideological contrasts have become sharper and "destructive politics" more common. What one side of the political spectrum builds and implements, the other rushes to dismantle, leaving behind suboptimal policy. The $448 million hole in Norway's budget stands as a painful example.

Taxation as a Competitive Tool

Most of the wealthy Norwegians who fled their home country because of rising taxes chose Switzerland as their new home. That is no coincidence. Switzerland boasts a large, innovative, and resilient financial sector built on a deep tradition of wealth protection and privacy. More importantly, in some parts of Switzerland, taxes are astonishingly low.

In cantons such as Schwyz and Zug, income tax rates hover around 20 percent, less than half the rate in most Western and Northern European countries. Moreover, some cantons offer what is known as "Pauschalbesteuerung," a lump-sum tax that allows foreign residents to pay a fixed annual tax amount based on their spending rather than their actual income or wealth. It goes without saying that the spending habits of Switzerland's ultra-wealthy somehow happen to align perfectly with those of the average Swiss household. What a coincidence.

Switzerland, in other words, competes for capital and talent through low taxes. There is usually a good reason why the superrich are that rich: They tend to be exceptionally good at what they do. The wealth Switzerland attracts through its generous tax regime isn't just counted in dollars, euros, or, as in the example above, Norwegian kroner; it also comes in the form of scarce human capital. It's human capital, getting increasingly scarce, that fuels the economic growth every nation desires.

As tasty as Swiss Emmental cheese may be, and as charming as its hidden mountain villages look, what truly draws the ultrarich is the country's minimal tax burden. The numbers speak for themselves. According to UBS's "Billionaire Ambitions Report" (2024), Switzerland, home to fewer than nine million people, hosts more billionaires than France (population of sixty-seven million) or the United Kingdom (population of seventy million). The country consistently ranks in the global top ten for both billionaires and *ultra-high-net-worth individuals* (UHNWIs) per capita. Measured by annual inflows of new wealth, the Alpine nation even ranks among the global top three.

The Race to the Bottom

Lower taxes to attract the wealthy are nothing compared to the global rivalry waged through corporate taxation. Why would policymakers settle for attracting individuals when they can draw in entire corporations? Over the past few decades, countries have systematically slashed corporate tax rates to lure businesses, create jobs, import human capital, and stimulate economic growth.

The chart below shows how countries compete for company headquarters by taxing corporate profits less and less. In the 1980s and early 1990s, corporate tax rates in major economies typically ranged between 40 and 50 percent. By 2024, those rates had dropped to just 20–30 percent. According to the independent think tank Tax Foundation, the GDP-weighted average global corporate tax rate declined from 47 percent in 1980 to just 26 percent in 2024, a stunning descent of 21 percentage points.

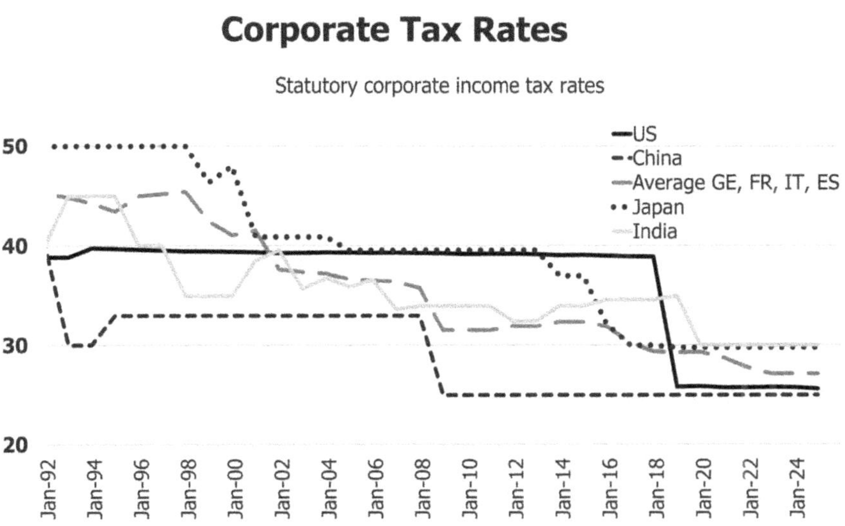

Source: The Great Rebalancing, https://taxfoundation.org/

In practice, corporations pay even less than the statutory corporate tax rates suggest. A 2022 GAO report found that the effective tax rate for large, profitable US corporations dropped from 16 percent to just 9 percent between 2014 and 2018. American companies already pay remarkably little tax, and those rates keep falling. It could not be more obvious. Governments, desperate for elusive sources of growth, keep enticing corporations with ever-lower tax rates.

Taxation and Polarization

The reality of these effective tax rates reveals that governments are remarkably willing to sacrifice tax revenues when it comes to corporations. By doing so, they hope to attract firms along with their investments, talent, and jobs. The increasingly skewed tax burden is simply accepted as the price of competition. Taxes on labor and consumption rise, while taxes on profits keep shrinking. As a result, countries compete for corporate headquarters often at the direct expense of their taxpaying citizens.

The consequences are predictable. The growing tax imbalance has become a driver of social polarization. The perception that ordinary people foot the bill while large corporations largely avoid their tax obligations fuels distrust in government and deepens social tensions. Judging by the striking gap in tax rates, that perception is not entirely unfounded.

These societal tensions are mirrored by rising political polarization. The result is "destructive policymaking," as I noted earlier. With the political center hollowed out, a change in government leaves nothing to build on. Political parties drift ever further apart, leaving two extremes: the far left and the far right. Supercharged election campaigns only worsen the divide, while billions are spent undoing the previous administration's policies, often with little success due to the relentless resistance of that previous administration. Together, social and political polarization ensure that, even if there were room to raise taxes, doing so would amount to political suicide.

Polarization, oddly, "benefits" countries with fewer political parties. In much of Europe, it therefore creates political gridlock, paralyzing progress and diluting policy objectives. Politics and polarization are a toxic combination.

This is more than an assumption. The IMF's 2024 study, "Fiscal R-Star: Fiscal-Monetary Tensions and Implications for Policy," examined whether fiscal and monetary policy can still be aligned. The authors found that the more divided the political landscape, the harder it becomes for governments to take responsible budgetary action. Polarization breeds delays, weak compromises, and short-term fixes that postpone structural reform. The result is a chronic erosion of fiscal discipline.

According to the IMF study, political polarization in developed economies is now at its highest level since the 1940s. In other words, the will and discipline to restore sound public finances have all but evaporated.

Fiscal Boundaries

Governments hold the unique privilege of taxation, which in theory should allow them to close widening deficits. In practice, they fail to do so. For households, the tax ceiling already appears to have been reached. Higher taxes risk triggering large-scale capital flight, as illustrated by the example of Norway. Governments refuse to tax corporations more heavily, fearing job losses and the exodus of talent and investment.

At the same time, rising political polarization has created a climate where genuine fiscal reform is nearly impossible and any proposal to raise taxes is brutally punished at the ballot box. It is therefore highly unrealistic to expect taxation to deliver a lasting, meaningful contribution to fiscal discipline.

CHAPTER 8

Exponential Spending

Introduction

Any good accountant will tell you there's another way to balance the books: spend less. Let me dispel that illusion right away: The odds that governments will balance their budgets through spending cuts are far slimmer than the odds they will do so by raising taxes.

This chapter lays out why we are trapped in a system that depends entirely on debt. Governments cannot meaningfully cut spending without unleashing painful economic, social, and political fallout. Without exponential growth in government spending, the welfare state, or anything resembling it, simply cannot survive.

Mandatory Spending: The Elephant in the Room

For decades, population growth and productivity gains formed the backbone of economic expansion. Today, economies, and their governments, have been overtaken by reality: unprecedented aging and shrinking workforces. These are major trends that inevitably drive an explosion in mandatory government spending. That small word *mandatory* makes all the difference here: It is simply impossible for governments to cut spending deeply enough to halt the relentless buildup of debt. But what exactly falls under mandatory government spending?

In general, it refers to all expenditures a government must make, regardless of who holds power or how the economy performs. These are obligations embedded in society, enshrined in permanent legislation, and not subject to annual budget approvals. Mandatory programs often pay out automatically: pensions, healthcare subsidies, and income support, to name a few.

The two largest categories of mandatory spending are social security and healthcare. Social security includes pensions, disability benefits, unemployment insurance, and other income-support programs such as welfare, child allowances, housing subsidies, and food assistance.

Healthcare spending spans a wide range of costs, from public health programs, elderly care (such as Medicare in the US), hospital and pharmaceutical subsidies, and healthcare allowances. In some countries and regions, such as the European Union, universal healthcare systems, including long-term and elderly care and public health insurance, also fall into this category.

It takes little imagination to see that mandatory spending on social security and healthcare soars in aging societies. Increasingly fewer workers simply cannot carry the cost of an ever-expanding elderly population. These costs are already astronomical and are set to rise steeply in the decades ahead.

According to the Congressional Budget Office (CBO), mandatory spending by the US federal government in fiscal year 2024 totaled

$4.1 trillion. The US government's total outlays that year were $6.8 trillion, meaning that mandatory programs accounted for just over 60 percent of total government spending. So, without sweeping legislative change, Washington can do little to alter almost two-thirds of its budget.

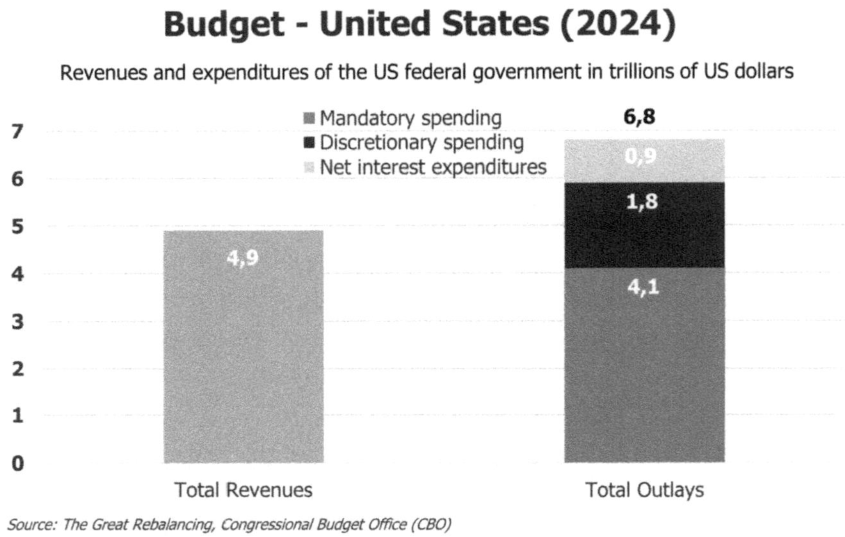

That $4.1 trillion equals roughly 14 percent of US GDP, nearly four times what the US spends on defense, justice, education, and transportation combined. Per capita, mandatory spending amounts to about $12,000. For a family of four, that's nearly $50,000 per year, equal to 60 percent of the median American household income.

The CBO's most revealing data, however, appear not in its fiscal-year summaries but in its "Long-Term Budget Outlook." This CBO report holds an annual analysis of the US budget for the next thirty years. One of its key projections shows mandatory spending, driven largely by healthcare, will climb from 14 percent to over 16 percent of GDP over the next three decades. The US government's mandatory outlays are rising, both in absolute size and as a share of the economy. That almost certainly means deeper deficits and an even higher mountain of debt. In addition, these deficits are structural, since mandatory programs are locked in and cannot easily be adjusted, which puts all other, nonmandatory spending under growing pressure.

The Costs of Aging

Much like taxation, healthcare systems are complex and difficult to compare across countries. There are major differences in how costs are split between governments and citizens, and the line between "healthcare" and "social security" is often blurred. Expenditures that count as healthcare in one country may be classified as social benefits in another.

Most EU countries run universal healthcare systems, allowing nearly everyone access to medical services. These systems are financed largely through tax revenues and mandatory social contributions. One advantage of such universal systems is that governments can negotiate directly with healthcare providers and pharmaceutical companies, keeping overall costs in check. But this centralization comes with a price: Governments end up footing most of the bill.

The European Commission's triennial "Ageing Report" confirms exactly that. It is one of the Commission's most important strategic reports, projecting public spending on pensions, healthcare, and education across the EU through 2070. Between 2014 and 2019, the EU as a whole (governments, companies, and households combined) spent roughly 8.5 percent of GDP on healthcare. That figure excludes long-term care, which the European Commission lists as a separate category. Hardly surprising, since the report specifically studies the impact of aging. After 2019, spending surged to well above 9 percent of GDP, driven in part by the pandemic. The costs of healthcare are staggering, around €1.4 trillion in 2021 alone. And because of the system's design, EU governments bear the bulk of these costs. In each year between 2014 and 2021, EU governments accounted for about 80 percent of all healthcare spending.

China, by contrast, presents the opposite picture. After Mao Zedong's death in 1976, the collectivized healthcare system collapsed. This system was epitomized by the so-called "barefoot doctors," semi-trained practitioners who delivered low-cost healthcare to China's rural communes. In the 1960s and 1970s, some 80 percent of China's population lived in the countryside, and Mao insisted that the healthcare system should serve not just the cities, but above all "the peasants, the workers, and the soldiers."

After the Maoist system disintegrated in the 1980s, China didn't start rebuilding a public system until the late 1990s. Today, it consists of a patchwork of national and urban programs marked by deep inequalities. While nearly all citizens are now insured, out-of-pocket costs remain high: Chinese households pay almost one-third of their medical costs themselves, about three times as much as in Western economies.

Crucially for fiscal policy and mandatory spending, China is rapidly expanding its public health infrastructure. Its Five-Year Plan, the country's main economic and social blueprint, channels billions into improving healthcare coverage, efficiency, and access. Meanwhile, China is aging at record speed. Between 2020 and 2040, its population over sixty-five will double, meaning the real surge in healthcare demand is still ahead.

China's health system resembles an S-curve, where a slow start is followed by rapid growth that eventually levels off as saturation sets in. The combination of a rapidly broadening healthcare base and explosive demographic aging means China stands on the brink of an exponential surge in healthcare costs. The foundation is in place: nearly universal coverage and massive investment in healthcare infrastructure. The steep climb will begin once the wave of elderly citizens starts drawing on the system. Once China hits the steep section of the S-curve, both public spending and healthcare costs will soar dramatically.

To put this into perspective, the World Health Organization (WHO) reports that in 2022, per-capita healthcare spending in China was $672. For comparison, Germany spent $6,182 per person, while the United States spent an astonishing $12,434 per capita. It will take years before China's healthcare costs even begin to approach those of Germany, let alone the United States. Yet the gap is so vast that, even with substantial out-of-pocket contributions, healthcare spending will become a major burden on China's public finances in the decades ahead.

The next chart illustrates the trend in healthcare spending across the world's major economic blocs. With the exception of India, healthcare spending as a share of GDP is rising everywhere. In other words, healthcare costs are outpacing economic growth, a dynamic clearly reflected in government budgets. The effect intensifies as governments take greater control of healthcare to manage aging populations.

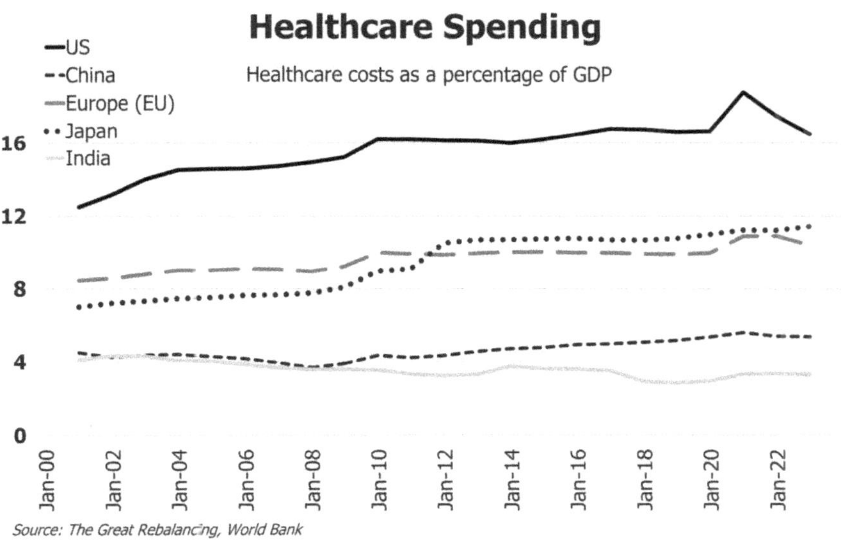

Governments have little choice, with the old-age dependency ratio skyrocketing. A shrinking labor force simply cannot sustain more retirees; they generate too little in taxes and social contribution income to fund the system. Governments must therefore choose: either plug the gap with more debt or scale back healthcare spending. Even though healthcare ranks among the largest mandatory expenses, the odds that governments will shrink their deficits through cuts here are close to zero. On the contrary, both European Commission and CBO projections point to healthcare costs rising relentlessly for decades to come.

The Infinite Costs of the Welfare State

The United States may lead the world in healthcare spending, but Europe is the undisputed heavyweight of the expensive welfare state. Most eurozone countries maintain a vast, government-funded patchwork of fixed contributions, subsidies, and transfers aimed at guaranteeing a minimum standard of living. Social security sits squarely at the core of this system.

The European Union's definition of "social spending" underscores just how broad the category is, far larger than healthcare: "Social protection benefits are transfers to households, in cash or in kind, intended to relieve them of the financial consequences of a series of fundamental risks and needs. These include disability, sickness, old age, the death of a breadwinner, family responsibilities, unemployment, housing, and social exclusion."

That's quite a mouthful, and a long list of expenses that, once again, fall overwhelmingly on government budgets. In 2023, EU governments spent €3.3 trillion on social security, equal to 19.2 percent of GDP. That is nearly two-and-a-half times total healthcare spending and fully 40 percent of all government outlays in the European Union. This is the welfare state, in full view.

Although the category "old age" is tucked away in the definition, it is by far the largest cost item. Of that 19 percent of GDP spent on social security in 2023, more than half, 10.4 percent, was devoted to old-age benefits. And within the "old age" category, there is a clear standout that absorbs the lion's share of costs: pensions.

The dominance of old-age spending within the social welfare budget is hardly surprising, but therefore no less worrying. Many assume that the fiscal impact of aging shows up primarily in healthcare costs. In reality, the link to social security expenditures is far stronger. With aging set to accelerate over the coming decades, it doesn't take a PhD in economics to understand where these mandatory expenses are headed. Yet few fully grasp how massive a burden social security will place on public finances.

The French Cost Wall

To make this more concrete, let's look again at France. With total social security spending above 30 percent of GDP, and an elaborate system of pensions, healthcare benefits, and government transfers, France stands out as one of the most expansive welfare states in Europe. From the chart below, it's clear that today's 30-plus percent of GDP is already in a category of its own (top line). Yet in the decades ahead, this share will climb to levels that will inevitably trigger urgent questions about the sustainability of France's welfare model. All signs point to the same conclusion: The French welfare state is well on track to become unaffordable.

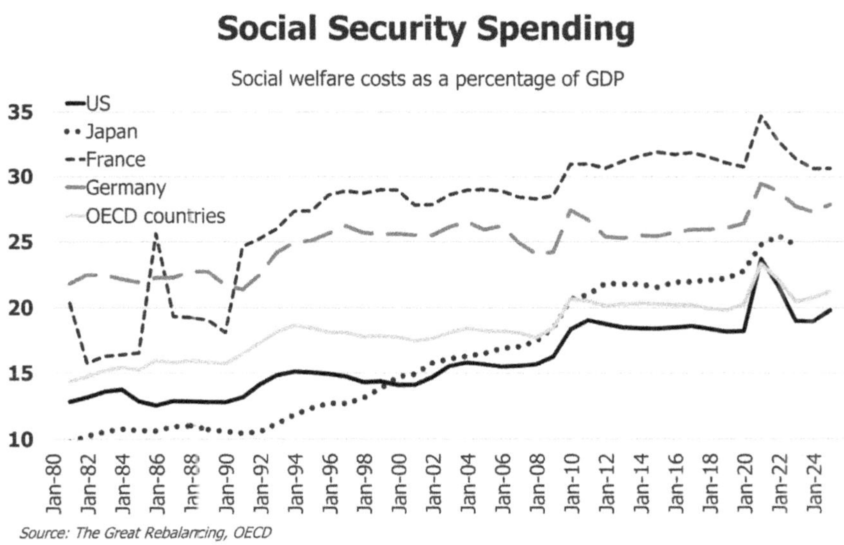

Let me support that statement with a few numbers. The starting point for this is the link between demographic aging and mandatory social security spending. As an indicator of aging, I use France's median age. The median age marks the point at which half the population is younger and half is older. In other words, it is the exact middle value when the ages of all French citizens are lined up from youngest to oldest. The median is less sensitive to outliers compared to the mean. For instance, if a country has ten people, nine of whom are twenty-five years old and one who is seventy-five, then the median age is twenty-five. That is the value, in this case the age, dividing the ordered list right down the middle. The average age would be thirty, pulled up by the one seventy-five-year-old, even though no one in the country is actually that age.

The median age allows us to map the relationship between aging and the rising burden of social security spending. In the chart below, France's median age is plotted on the horizontal axis, while French government spending on social security as a share of GDP is plotted on the vertical axis. The series begins in 1980. To smooth fluctuations, I use a three-year moving average that advances one year at a time, for example, the data for 1980–1982, 1981–1983, and so on.

The chart reveals a clear positive relationship: higher median age, shown on the right side of the horizontal axis, corresponds to higher government spending on social security (vertical axis); a younger population, on the left of the horizontal axis, corresponds to lower spending. In short, the older the population, the heavier the social security burden on the French state.

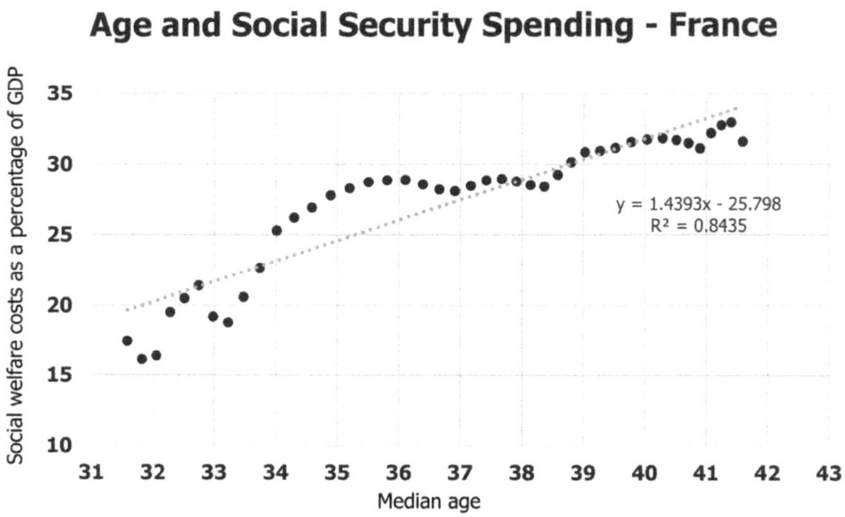

Source: The Great Rebalancing, OESO, Our World in Data

The chart also reports the formula of the best-fit line: "1.4393 × x – 25.798." The "x" represents the median age. If you know the median age, you can estimate social security spending as a share of GDP using this formula. The chart also reports the R^2 (R-squared), a key statistic measuring the strength of the relationship between the two variables, with values ranging from 0 to 1. (An R-squared of 0 means there is no relationship at all, while an R-squared of 1 indicates the fit between the variables is perfect.) In that case, knowing one variable allows you to predict the other with perfection. So, with an R-squared of 0.84, as shown in the chart, the relationship is particularly strong.

The stronger the relationship, the better the forecasts become. In other words, if you know France's median age ten years from now, you can predict its social security spending with remarkable precision. As noted in Chapter 2, the United Nations provides reliable projections for future median ages across countries. Each year, they conduct an extensive analysis of future median ages across countries based on factors such as birth and death rates, life expectancy, migration, and trends in health and population growth.

The United Nations projects that in ten years, France's median age will reach 43.4 years, an increase of 1.8 years compared with today. Plugging that number into the formula shown in the chart implies French social security spending will rise to a whopping 37 percent of GDP. That is a 5 percentage-point increase from the current level.

There's more. The cost wall France is heading toward may prove even steeper than that. Instead of age, the old-age dependency ratio can serve as the explanatory variable for social security spending. This ratio captures how the pool of workers funding social programs keeps shrinking, while the group relying on them, the elderly, is expanding rapidly. As the old-age dependency ratio rises, you can safely assume that social welfare spending will rise as well.

The relationship in France between the old-age dependency ratio and social welfare spending is again strong, though slightly weaker than the one based on median age (R-squared of 0.7). Using the EU's projection for France's old-age dependency ratio ten years from now, the model predicts social security spending reaching an unprecedented 43 percent of GDP. That would represent an 11 percentage-point increase from the current level. While this estimate is marginally less precise than the median age projection, the conclusion is virtually certain: French social security spending will be far higher in ten years from now.

I linger on these statistical relationships and spending projections, hardly the most thrilling reading, because they vividly illustrate the challenges aging societies face. Consider the projected increase in French social security spending from 32 percent to 37 percent of GDP as the median age rises. If all else remains equal, and the government covers the increase through borrowing, hence debt, the budget deficit would (theoretically) rise by the same 5 percentage points.

That might not sound dramatic, but it absolutely is. Recall the fiscal sustainability gap, the budget surplus governments must somehow achieve to meet all obligations without letting public debt rise further. As shown in Chapter 6, the European Commission estimates France's fiscal gap at 5.5 percent of GDP. If social security spending alone adds 5 percentage points (of GDP) to the deficit, then that estimate is far too conservative. Of course, social security spending does not evolve in a vacuum. But that hardly makes the picture more reassuring. A glance at healthcare costs suggests the exponential impact of aging will prove far greater than most economists or politicians dare to acknowledge.

This goes a long way toward explaining France's chronic political paralysis. France is a textbook case of a rapidly aging welfare state in which pressure on government finances translates directly into constant social tensions and political instability. The only way to release the pressure is to let debt rise further, which in turn deepens concerns over debt sustainability. If you're still holding out hope that France will post a Maastricht-compliant deficit of 3 percent of GDP by 2029, it is time to let that illusion go.

Finally, while France is a leading example of an unaffordable welfare state, many major economies display the same pattern. Mandatory social security expenditures consume an ever-larger share of both GDP and government budgets. Put differently, as societies age, households grow increasingly dependent on government transfers. Workers simply can't keep pace with those rising costs, leaving governments to fill the gap. The American think tank Economic Innovation Group captured this dynamic in its study "The Great Transfer-mation." The study found that in a majority of US local communities, more than 25 percent of total personal income now comes from government transfers. Fifty years ago, such transfers were rare.

Discretionary Spending

Bear with me; there are a few more numbers we need to unpack. They are crucial to grasp that our debt-driven system cannot change without bold social choices, the kind policymakers instinctively shy away from.

On paper, the area where policymakers still have room to maneuver is discretionary government spending. These are expenditures that require periodic approval by a parliament or Congress and are therefore not considered "mandatory."

Think of spending on education, security, transport, culture, science, and defense. Without doubt, these are major pillars of society, which makes it all the more striking that their share of total government spending is relatively small. As shown in the earlier CBO chart, discretionary spending in 2024 amounted to barely one-quarter of total US government outlays, $1.8 trillion out of $6.8 trillion. In the EU, culture, education, science, and security together make up just 15 percent of total government spending. In Japan, where mandatory social spending is rising faster than in any other major economy, the picture is no different. So, even if deep cuts in these nonmandatory spending categories are implemented, they would barely dent the unprecedented rise in mandatory spending.

The phrase "even if" is chosen carefully, and for good reason. I doubt many readers, seeing that list of discretionary spending, would think that these are easy targets for cuts. Much of this spending is so deeply embedded in the fundamentals of society that there is virtually no scope for structural cuts. Take education, for example. In aging economies with shrinking workforces, high-quality education is vital to prevent the last remaining source of growth, productivity, from sinking as well. Less education inevitably fuels deeper inequality and, in the end, greater social unrest.

When it comes to security, political choices are no longer truly voluntary. As polarization grows, so does the need to allocate more resources to public order, cybersecurity, and counterterrorism. Transport and infrastructure spending are often labeled "discretionary," yet economic reality tells a far more complex story. These are the familiar, yet factual, stories of decades of underinvestment in bridges, railways, and road networks that constrain economic growth. Cutting back on transport and infrastructure makes little sense, given their direct link to growth, particularly once the multiplier effect is considered.

The multiplier effect measures how much one euro or dollar of investment ultimately generates beyond its initial amount. For example, a local government builds a bridge connecting two parts of a city. A construction company wins the contract, buys materials and machinery, and hires more workers. Those new workers spend their wages on housing, groceries, dining out, or a nice vacation. The bridge shortens commuting times, reduces traffic congestion, and improves business accessibility. The local government may decide to charge tolls to generate more revenue. In short, a single investment triggers a chain of economic effects that together define the multiplier effect.

China and India understand the infrastructure multiplier better than anyone. In many emerging markets, discretionary infrastructure spending forms the backbone of economic growth. In these countries, it's not about replacing or connecting bridges but about building one for the very first time, alongside new railways and highways that deliver an enormous boost to economic expansion. In recent years, China has repeatedly turned to industrial and infrastructure investment whenever its economy slows. These investments are anything but discretionary and add increasing pressure on public finances and accelerate debt accumulation.

The Limits of Good Spending

High-multiplier spending may seem like a no-brainer in a world starved of economic growth. Yet in a world awash in debt, even this kind of spending offers no guarantees. The "good debt" Alexander Hamilton once extolled simply no longer exists.

In a 2021 report with the ambitious title "Effects of Physical Infrastructure Spending on the Economy and the Budget Under Two Illustrative Scenarios," the CBO concluded that infrastructure spending boosts growth and tax revenues, but only if it is not financed by more debt. In their first scenario, investments are funded by spending cuts elsewhere, resulting in higher productivity and even a modestly declining budget deficit. But in their second scenario, where investments are financed by borrowing, debt and interest costs outpace the revenues. The benefits of the multiplier effect are wiped out by rising interest costs and the crowding out of private investment.

Eventually, debt grows so large that even the smartest investment can't tip the balance back into the black. At that point, even building bridges stops making sense.

Beyond Discretionary

Two major categories of discretionary spending remain unmentioned, for the simple reason that, especially on my continent, Europe, they are no longer discretionary at all. They are climate and energy, and defense.

Climate Costs

Climate spending is a "hot topic" when it comes to government budgets. On paper, climate spending is still discretionary, but in reality it is bound up in local and international laws, regulations, and treaties. What is striking, again especially in Europe, is how little governments account for uncertainty, something that is standard practice in economics and science in general. Climate change is presented as a foregone conclusion, leaving no room for error, and leading to ever-rising spending. In Europe, climate policy has taken on the tone of a religion rather than an economic debate.

Rather than balanced decision-making that weighs climate against other important issues, climate is almost always prioritized, even when the justification is weak. Every deviation from long-term climate goals, no matter how unrealistic, triggers yet more spending to "get back on track."

Brussels is the ultimate example. For the 2021–2027 period, the EU set aside €578 billion, more than 30 percent of its entire budget, for climate-related spending. Through countless programs, Brussels funnels money into green tech, sustainable transport, and energy-efficient buildings. Climate goals are embedded across all EU policy domains, leaving little room for deviation. If targets appear at risk, budgets are simply raised again, even when the shortfall has nothing to do with effort. According to the European Commission, meeting climate targets will require at least €620 billion in extra green investment each year through 2030.

No surprise, governments will shoulder the overwhelming share of these additional costs. Conveniently, EU budget rules carve out exceptions for green investments, handsomely allowing for additional borrowing. And with that, the circle is complete. In Europe, climate spending is anything but discretionary, soaring rapidly and funded predominantly by governments. Budgets will need to stretch further, with a further rise in debt-to-GDP ratios as the predictable outcome.

In other parts of the world, climate policy is treated less ideologically, giving spending a more genuinely discretionary character. China invests heavily in clean energy, primarily for economic, not ideological, reasons. The European market for electric vehicles is now dominated by Chinese manufacturers. For China, energy is an engine of economic growth, and the more of it, the better. That is why China invests heavily in both green and brown energy, the exact opposite of Europe where nuclear plants and gas fields were shut down despite heavy dependence on Russian energy.

In the United States, climate policy swings with whoever happens to be in power. Under President Biden, the Inflation Reduction Act (IRA) unleashed nearly $370 billion in climate-related incentives, tax credits, subsidies, and investments spanning clean energy, electric vehicles, and power grids. This approach rested partly on economic incentives; households and businesses were rewarded financially for going green. In that sense, climate spending functions as a discretionary policy tool. With a political shift, such as Trump's return to power in 2025, these subsidies and incentives were reversed or curtailed. Unlike in Europe, US climate policy remains primarily an instrument of fiscal politics.

Defense: From Peace Dividend to De Facto Mandatory

Officially, defense spending is classified as discretionary spending, i.e., expenditures that require periodic political approval, yet a reclassification to mandatory spending would not be out of place. Since Russia's invasion of Ukraine, defense has been rapidly morphing into a de facto mandatory category. Especially in Europe, where defense was neglected for decades, politicians are now racing to lock in higher spending permanently in their budgets.

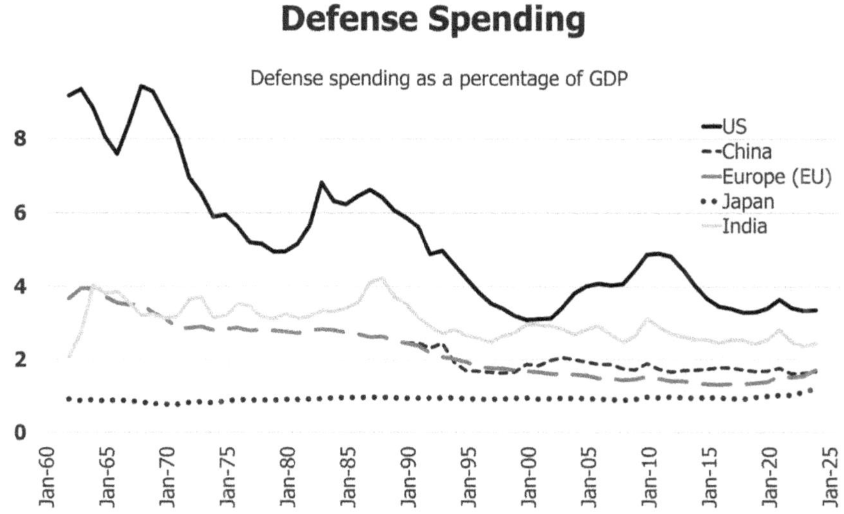

Source: The Great Rebalancing, World Bank

Permanently elevated defense spending would mark a clear break from the past. After the Cold War ended in the early 1990s, defense budgets plummeted. Policymakers wasted no time cashing in the so-called "peace dividend," redirecting those freed-up funds to mandatory categories such as healthcare and social security. In doing so, they conveniently postponed the hard questions about the long-term sustainability of those aging-dependent commitments.

Even Russia's 2014 annexation of Crimea, an unmistakable warning sign in hindsight, failed to restore defense as a priority. At the 2014 NATO summit in Wales, member states solemnly declared that a united, free, and peaceful Europe had been fundamentally undermined. In response, they committed to spend at least 2 percent of GDP on defense. It was an empty promise; very little of it ever materialized. Germany spent barely 1 percent of its GDP on defense in 2014, a figure that remained unchanged for the next five years. By 2023, Germany was still half a percentage point shy of the target it had pledged a decade earlier.

Sadly, it often takes a shock or crisis to break the status quo. Over time, politicians have grown increasingly reactive, hardly a flattering trait. For Europe, it took a war on its own continent and an angry man in Washington to finally spur action. US President Trump repeatedly insisted during his campaign that NATO's 2-percent defense target should be seen as a floor, not a ceiling. In 2023, the United States devoted more than 3 percent of its GDP to defense. And in early 2024, during a campaign rally, Trump warned that NATO members failing to meet the target would not be defended in the event of a Russian attack.

A year later, his vice president, JD Vance, launched a blistering attack on Europe at the annual Munich Security Conference. He argued that European countries invest far too little in their own security and remain dangerously dependent on the United States. He stressed that most European nations no longer possess armed forces capable of adequately defending their own territory. Vance's speech is well worth watching. The uneasy and indignant faces in the audience as Vance tore into Europe's failed policies speak volumes.

Trump's warning about refusing to defend NATO members underspending on defense was, of course, at odds with the alliance's core principle, Article 5 (an attack on one member is considered an attack on all). Even so, a growing number of European politicians, spurred by the grinding war in Ukraine and Washington's shifting foreign policy, now recognize that defense spending must rise sharply. It's exactly this realization that gave rise to the EU's "Readiness 2030" plan. Originally, Ursula von der Leyen, President of the European Commission, had dubbed the plan "ReArm Europe," apparently on her own initiative. Several member states, however, found that name a bit too provocative. The emphasis, they argued, should be on the EU's readiness and strategic autonomy, rather than on mobilizing weapons.

To achieve that, Readiness 2030 calls for €800 billion in defense spending over four years. That equals roughly 5 percent of the EU's entire GDP, a massive sum. Where will the money come from? You already know the answer: more debt. Of the €800 billion, €650 billion will come from additional borrowing by member states through loosened EU budget rules, while the remaining €150 billion will consist of EU-backed loans for air defense, artillery, drones, cyber capacity, and logistics. That touches on one of Europe's most sensitive political issues: Eurobonds, jointly issued debt that makes EU or eurozone countries collectively liable. Will Germany and the Netherlands, two of the few nations that have actually kept their debts in check, risk their creditworthiness for the sake of the eurozone?

The pattern is unmistakable. All additional spending, defense or otherwise, is financed through borrowing and requires looser budget rules, with a predictable result: more debt. This is exactly how debt-driven economies operate. While Europe is currently the epicenter of the defense-spending imperative, the rest of the world will not stay on the sidelines. Geopolitical tensions are mounting. The US-China relationship continues to deteriorate, with rising unease around Taiwan. Russia remains a persistent threat, and it is still hard to imagine what a definitive end to the conflict in the Middle East would look like.

This raises the question of whether we are entering a new era of the classic "guns-or-butter" model. Confronted with towering debt and bloated budgets, governments are forced to choose between defense, security, and weapons on one side, and education, healthcare, and infrastructure on the other. But because that choice feels politically impossible, many policymakers take the path of least resistance: more debt. Especially in an era of rising geopolitical strain and deepening polarization. Yet, not choosing is a choice too: even more debt.

Interest Costs

Where there is debt, there is interest. Borrowing money is not free. With tax rates maxed out, mandatory spending surging, fiscal discipline eroding, and debt piling ever higher, interest costs have become a critical pillar holding the system together.

Interest costs are often listed as a separate spending category. Yet make no mistake, they are unmistakably mandatory expenditures. Businesses and households that fail to pay interest go bankrupt. Governments that fail to meet their interest obligations will quickly find no one willing to lend to them. Separately listing interest costs simply underscores how heavily the cost of debt weighs on public budgets and the broader economy. And as will become clear, interest costs lie at the very heart of The Great Rebalancing of investment portfolios worldwide.

The Coming Cost Explosion

Let's return to the CBO's "Long-Term Budget Outlook." The forecasts in this report are used by numerous institutions and research groups for further analysis. Among them is the widely respected Committee for a Responsible Federal Budget. In a series of analyses, the committee has warned that US interest costs are "set to explode." For 2025, federal interest costs are projected to reach 3.2 percent of GDP, a record. That translates into more than one trillion dollars, larger than the total GDP of the Netherlands, Turkey, or Switzerland. In 2025, the US government will have spent more on interest payments than on defense.

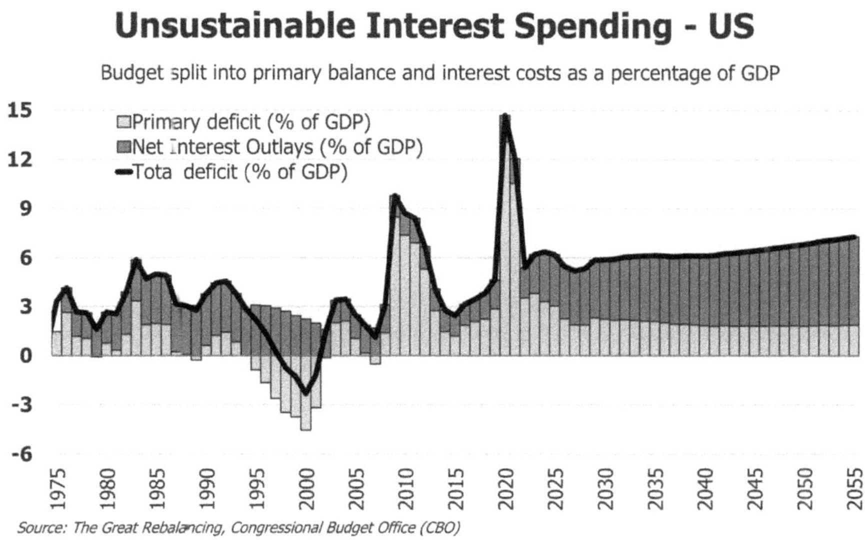

After 2025, interest costs are projected to climb steadily over the next thirty years, reaching 5.4 percent of GDP. That is an additional annual deficit of 2.2 percent of GDP, again, assuming all else equal. The Committee for a Responsible Federal Budget goes on to project that by 2045, the average interest rate on US debt will exceed the country's GDP growth. In other words, from that point onward, Domar's formula flips: r > g, meaning interest exceeds growth, and US debt becomes unsustainable. The committee puts it bluntly: "The average interest rate on debt will exceed the economic growth rate by 2045, sparking the beginning of a debt spiral." A debt spiral, then. That does not bode well, especially given that the CBO's growth assumptions look rather optimistic.

In Japan and most eurozone countries, interest costs as a share of GDP are significantly lower than in the US. But that does not mean that these countries are better positioned. France will pay interest costs equal to about 2 percent of GDP in 2025, and that figure will rise in the years ahead. Given that France's potential GDP growth barely reaches 1 percent, and is trending downward, those seemingly low interest costs look far less benign. Italy, which would almost certainly have been forced back to the lira without the ECB's extraordinary policies of the past fifteen years, faces interest costs approaching 4 percent of GDP. Against potential growth rates even lower than France's, and a public debt ratio of 135 percent of GDP, the question of whether Italy's debt is sustainable without permanent ECB support basically answers itself.

Japan's interest costs, however, are below 1 percent of GDP. In the years after the COVID crisis, they were nearly zero, the result of extraordinary Bank of Japan policy. Is it a coincidence that one of the world's oldest economies, with a shrinking population, negligible growth potential, and by far the largest debt pile, pays the least in interest?

Finally, one more look at the United States. The figure on the left page shows how net interest costs are becoming increasingly dominant within US government spending, pushing the budget deeper into deficit. By 2055, interest payments are expected to consume 20 percent of all federal outlays. The US government will have to spend one out of every five dollars simply to service its debt. At that point, interest costs alone will propel debt higher, triggering even greater interest costs in return. This is the debt spiral that takes hold once GDP growth is no longer sufficient to keep debt in check.

An Unpleasant Sum

Taken together, the last three chapters paint a sobering picture: Governments worldwide are fighting a losing battle. Aging populations, exhausted tax bases, exploding healthcare and social security costs, newly entrenched categories of mandatory spending, and surging interest costs have left governments with their backs against the wall.

The idea that sound fiscal discipline could still bring budgets into balance is hopelessly outdated. To prevent debt from rising, governments would need to enforce massive primary surpluses year after year. Only radical decisions that sharply cut living standards, unleashing waves of social and political upheaval, could achieve that on paper.

What remains is a spiral of widening deficits, more debt, and rising interest costs. Is there nothing that can break this spiral? “Break” may be too strong a word, but as the final chart in this section above shows, there is one crucial lever that can at least extend debt sustainability for as long as possible.

Part III

A New Paradigm

CHAPTER 9
Toward Fiscal Dominance

Introduction

Today's economy runs almost entirely on debt and is simultaneously being crushed by the weight of that very same debt. The reality is that this will not end anytime soon, now that our intrinsic sources of growth have been exhausted.

Taxes and spending cuts can no longer produce the budget surpluses needed to stop debt from spiraling out of control. Policymakers therefore need to come up with an alternative solution. One that makes debt more affordable and manageable. Such a solution exists, but it comes with one critical condition: Central banks must sacrifice both their official inflation targets and their independence.

That is why the answer governments crave so deeply has been aptly named "fiscal dominance." Meaning, monetary policy must bow to fiscal policy. Skyrocketing debts render central banks subordinate, though no central banker will dare to say it out loud.

More Affordable and Sustainable

So where does the debt-driven growth model go from here? How can the system remain standing when fiscal discipline is no longer on the table? Governments risk being trapped in a tightening spiral of widening deficits, swelling debt, and soaring interest costs.

Yet there is a way to interrupt, or at least slow, this spiral, a way that spares policymakers from draconian tax hikes or politically impossible spending cuts. To better understand the mechanics of debt, it helps to think of the risks in two simple categories:

- **Affordability**

Interest determines the affordability of debt. As long as you can keep servicing the interest, debt isn't an immediate problem. This is best captured by Domar's now-familiar r-g formula. As long as the interest rate stays below the growth rate, debt remains sustainable, unless a persistent primary deficit tips the balance.

- **Size**

Debt has a size, or better yet, a value. When the value of debt drifts too far from the underlying cash flows or assets, the risk of things going wrong rises sharply. For a country or government, the key benchmark is the value of debt relative to the size of the economy (GDP).

When you look at debt risks through this lens, the solution almost reveals itself. How do you improve debt affordability? Very simple: by lowering interest rates. And how do you shrink the real value of debt without generating surpluses or strong growth? By letting inflation do the work. For example, if inflation runs at 10 percent, the real value of debt falls by roughly 9 percent after one year (for example, €100 ÷ 1.10 = €90.9). After two years, the real value of debt is down over 17 percent (€90.9 ÷ 1.10 = €82.6). And so on.

The chart on the next page shows how inflation erodes the real value of debt. It's the cumulative effect that matters most: Even a modestly higher inflation rate, sustained long enough, can dramatically reduce the real burden of debt. You can think of inflation's impact as compounding interest in reverse.

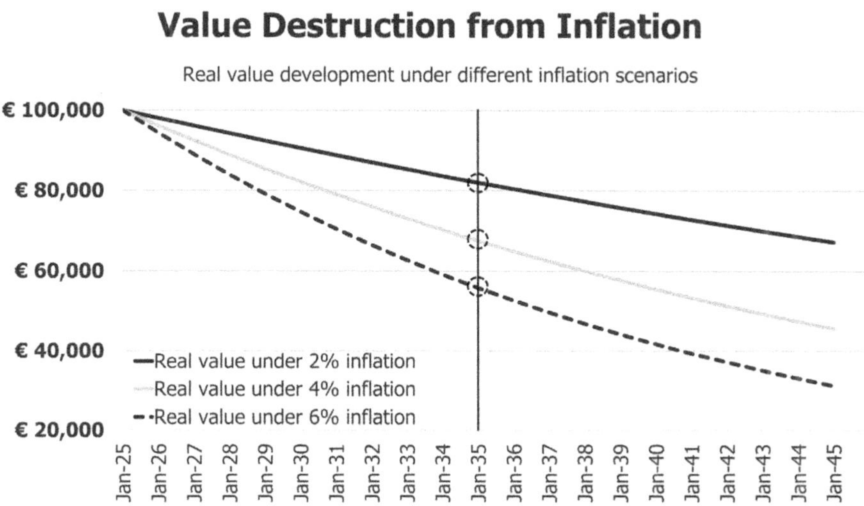

Source: The Great Rebalancing

Suppose that on January 1, 2025, a government carries debt worth €100,000. The chart shows what happens to its real value under three inflation scenarios: 2 percent, 4 percent, and 6 percent. If inflation holds steady at 2 percent, the real value of the debt drops to €82,000 after ten years. At 6 percent inflation, it plunges to €56,000. The nominal debt remains unchanged, but its real value is almost halved. At 6 percent inflation, the debt's real value is €26,000 lower than under a 2 percent scenario. Starting from €100,000, that means the real value of debt falls 26 percentage points more over ten years with 6 percent inflation than with 2 percent.

So, along with low interest rates, higher inflation greatly extends debt sustainability. Since it is far easier to push interest rates down and let inflation rise than to hike taxes or cut spending, this path shines to policymakers like a pot of gold on the horizon. Provided, of course, that they openly admit public finances come first. After all, those same low rates and higher inflation quietly eat away at private wealth too.

And therein lies the problem. Policymakers have an effective fix for debt sustainability right at their fingertips, so long as they can deploy it quietly. Publicly advocating low rates and high inflation would be political suicide. Tolerance for inflation is near zero, especially after the huge post-COVID spike. Any policymaker who openly welcomes such a strategy would sacrifice their political support in today's polarized societies. Openly advocating for low rates and high inflation is therefore not something policymakers typically do.

But what if there were an actor capable of lowering interest rates and allowing inflation to rise, without ever stating it as its goal? You guessed it: Central banks are the perfect instrument for governments intent on preventing debt from toppling the system. The beauty of it is that central banks remain generally regarded as independent institutions and are seen as the ultimate guardians of price stability. Welcome to the age of fiscal dominance.

What Is Fiscal Dominance?

Fiscal dominance is an economic and financial market regime in which monetary policy, the control of inflation, becomes subordinate to the fiscal policy of governments. Central banks then deploy their tools, such as interest rates, liquidity, and the money supply, not primarily to maintain price stability but to ensure debt sustainability.

Fiscal dominance is the necessary pillar of the debt-driven economic growth model we know today. Yet the idea itself is far from new. In 1981, economists Thomas Sargent (later a Nobel laureate) and Neil Wallace published their influential paper "Some Unpleasant Monetarist Arithmetic" in the fall issue of the *Federal Reserve Bank of Minneapolis Quarterly Review*.

Sargent and Wallace argued that monetary and fiscal policy cannot operate independently. When governments run persistent, large deficits and fund them through debt issuance, as most major economies do today, central banks are eventually forced to purchase that debt by creating money. This process is called debt monetization, and ultimately fuels inflation. In other words, fiscal policy ends up dictating monetary policy, forcing the very institutions meant to guard price stability to fall in line.

Sargent and Wallace described this as an *unpleasant arithmetic* because tight monetary policy today, where central banks refuse to monetize debt and create money, still leads to inflation later. Structural budget deficits make both debt and interest costs unsustainable without monetary financing. So even if central banks prioritize fighting inflation by avoiding bond purchases now, they will eventually be forced to reverse course, allowing fiscal policy to dominate monetary policy. As Sargent and Wallace wrote: "Tighter money today lacks even a temporary ability to fight inflation."

After the global financial crisis, the European debt crisis, and especially the pandemic, the concept of fiscal dominance took on new urgency. Debt exploded during the pandemic, followed by a prolonged period of extraordinarily high inflation. That inevitably raised tough questions about the effectiveness, and the true priorities, of central bank policy. Throughout each of these crises, central banks purchased massive amounts of government debt, never with the aim of meeting their official inflation target, but to preserve debt sustainability under the banner of crisis management. Fiscal dominance was suddenly impossible to ignore.

Prominent economist John H. Cochrane further develops this idea in his 2023 book *The Fiscal Theory of the Price Level.* Cochrane, affiliated with Stanford's Hoover Institution, builds on Sargent and Wallace's framework by arguing that not only money creation, but also the mere expectations of a government's fiscal health, determine the price level, and therefore inflation.

How does this mechanism work? Cochrane explains that government debt functions much like a share of stock. People treat debt, or government bonds, as a promise the government will one day honor with tax revenues. If people lose faith in that promise, because the debt is too large or future revenues (taxes) are insufficient, the value of that debt declines. According to Cochrane, this adjustment occurs through a rise in the general price level, i.e., inflation, which reduces the real value of the debt. The exact same principle as the earlier chart, showing that debt loses value faster at 6 percent inflation than at 2 percent.

Cochrane examines not only the effects of central bank money creation, as Sargent and Wallace did, but also people's expectations about the government's debt itself. From this perspective, he explains why no spike in inflation followed the 2008 global financial crisis, even though governments borrowed heavily at the time: People trusted governments to conquer the crisis and repay their debts. That trust, however, proved misplaced. Debt ratios failed to return to precrisis levels. Fifteen years on, that breach of trust became painfully clear.

Between 2021 and 2023, inflation did surge because by then, people, having learned from the 2008 crisis, doubted that governments would ever repay the colossal COVID debts. Cochrane's theory thus extends the "unpleasant arithmetic" of Sargent and Wallace and better captures today's reality. Inflation arises not only from money printing, but also from the eroding trust people have in their governments.

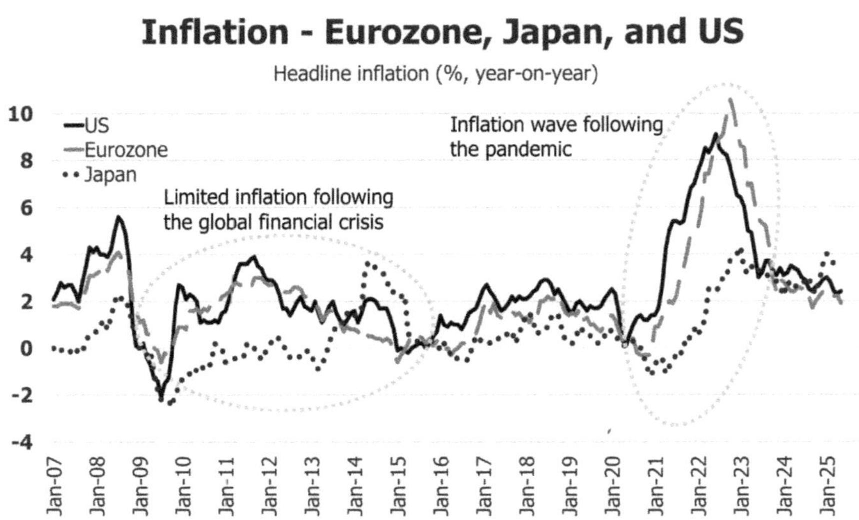

Source: The Great Rebalancing, Bureau of Labor Statistics, Eurostat, Ministry of Internal Affairs and Communications

Far-Reaching Consequences

Fiscal dominance carries profound and far-reaching consequences. It shows that the most iconic line by Milton Friedman, one of the most influential economists of the twentieth century, "Inflation is always and everywhere a monetary phenomenon," requires nuance. Inflation is not always and everywhere the direct product of independent central bank policy. When governments run chronic budget deficits, accumulate excessive debt, and face mounting interest costs, central banks inevitably lose both control and their independence.

They are forced into a looser monetary stance than their price-stability mandate would allow, because tighter policy would ultimately lift inflation anyway. Yet by cutting rates, purchasing bonds, and injecting liquidity, they end up stoking inflation all the same. This helps explain why, despite a barrage of rate hikes after the pandemic, central banks failed to bring inflation back under control. They moved too late, lost credibility, and watched public trust in governments sink to new lows. It is no coincidence that this "unpleasant arithmetic" makes inflation inevitable, as Sargent and Wallace demonstrated more than forty years ago.

Since central banks were designed as independent guardians of price stability, they will never admit that fiscal dominance has quietly overtaken that mandate. Obviously, that is music to the ears of policymakers whose true objective is not price stability, but keeping the debt-driven growth model alive, gladly enlisting central banks to make it happen.

A vivid example came in June 2024, when Isabel Schnabel, a member of the ECB's Executive Board, denied that the Bank's monetary policy was being overruled by fiscal policy. She argued that the ECB had preserved its independence, and had pursued price stability vigorously, including raising interest rates by 4.5 percentage points within just fourteen months. That statement, however, deserves at least some context. The first rate hike did not occur until July 2022, when inflation had already risen to 8.6 percent.

Consistent with the theory of fiscal dominance, which holds that inflation is unavoidable, Eurozone inflation remained well above the ECB's 2 percent target through the end of 2023. After the post-pandemic surge in inflation, central bankers became acutely aware of the "danger" posed by fiscal dominance. Schnabel rightly emphasized that future fiscal discipline is essential to protect the ECB's independence and to prevent fiscal dominance. Unfortunately, as shown in the previous chapter, genuine fiscal discipline is already a relic of the past.

Central bankers invariably reaffirm their independence and their dedicated focus on inflation, yet occasionally hint at the growing influence of fiscal policy. Andrew Bailey, governor of the Bank of England, acknowledged that the surge in public debt after the pandemic had affected both the economy and inflation. He called for closer coordination between monetary and fiscal policy but stopped short of admitting that runaway deficits had begun to tie central banks' hands.

Of course, the evidence of growing fiscal dominance also leads us to former ECB President Mario Draghi's legendary phrase, "Whatever it takes." Those words had nothing to do with fighting inflation and everything to do with holding the eurozone together by propping up heavily indebted member states. Most central bank bond-buying programs, in truth, are not primarily aimed at controlling inflation, but at preserving the financial system and ensuring debt sustainability.

Fiscal dominance thus offers an artificial remedy for a debt-addicted system: low interest rates and high inflation. But that comes at a steep price: the loss of central bank independence and the breakdown of the very principles on which sound economics rests. You only need to look around; the evidence is everywhere.

CHAPTER 10
The Proof

Introduction

Economists tend to prove theoretical concepts such as fiscal dominance through abstract models, formulas, and academic reasoning. But simply looking around often works just as well, if not better. Fiscal dominance is no exception.

There are ample signs that debt sustainability now exerts a powerful influence on central bank policy, financial markets, and, crucially, your investment returns. This chapter presents an overview of the most compelling evidence showing that fiscal dominance, where central banks bow to government policies, is taking control of global financial markets.

Structural Deficits

To know where to look for signs of fiscal dominance, it helps to outline its defining features:

- Structural budget deficits and rising debt-to-GDP ratios
- A broken link between debt and interest rates
- Higher and more volatile inflation
- Extraordinary central bank policies

At the heart of fiscal dominance are governments running structural budget deficits. The word *structural* is key here: It implies that debt sustainability can be maintained only if monetary policy adapts accordingly. It therefore makes sense to start by examining fiscal deficits and debt ratios.

As shown in Chapter 6, the debt ratios of nearly all major economies have risen steadily, far beyond the EU holy grail threshold of 60 percent of GDP. Debt isn't just supporting the economy anymore; it is now the system's lifeblood.

The chart on the next page shows US budget balances as a percentage of GDP since 1962. Deficits show up as negatives, surpluses as positives. If you recall from Chapter 5, it has now been roughly a quarter of a century since the US government last ran a surplus. Since the global financial crisis (2008–2009), deficits have ballooned, regardless of whether the US economy was in recession or not. The average annual deficit since then amounts to an astonishing 6.2 percent of GDP, more than double the 3 percent threshold that economists and the Maastricht Treaty regard as fiscally sound. In just two of the seventeen years since 2008 did the US manage to stay within that fiscal boundary, a rarity, to say the least.

I add once more that the 3 percent of GDP rule is very likely too lenient, given the structural decline in potential economic growth and debt ratios that are miles away from the 60-percent-of-GDP benchmark. A 2 percent budget deficit ceiling would be more realistic, and in the case of Europe and Japan, the threshold is even lower.

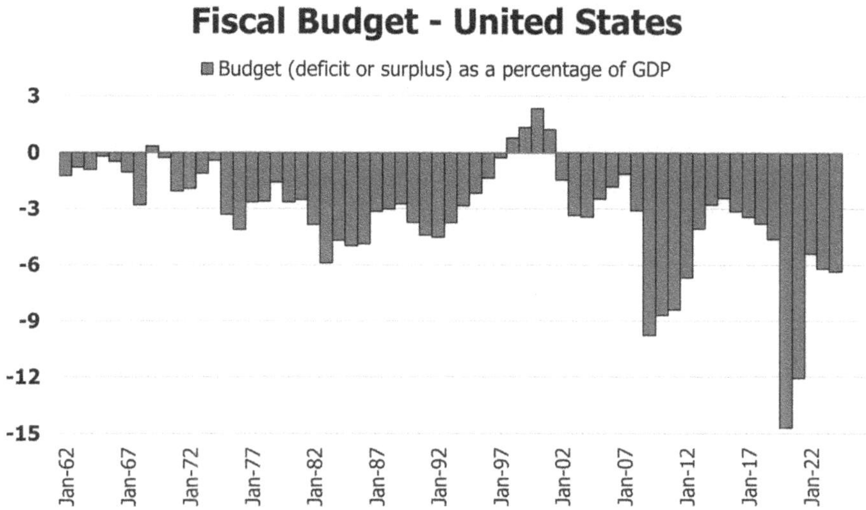

Source: The Great Rebalancing, Congressional Budget Office (CBO)

In addition, the fiscal outlook is anything but bright. According to the CBO, US budget deficits will remain above 6 percent of GDP annually for the next two decades, rising to over 7 percent by 2055. Like the OECD, the CBO expects public debt to climb ever higher in the decades ahead. The answer to the question of whether the US faces structural budget deficits is an unequivocal "yes."

In the eurozone, the average deficit since the global financial crisis has been 3.3 percent of GDP. At first glance, that might seem modest next to the US figures, but I do not share that opinion. First, the region's growth potential is so weak that deficits anywhere near 3 percent are nowhere near sustainable. The eurozone no longer has the capacity to grow its way out of debt, not even slightly.

Second, and more importantly, the aggregate eurozone budget deficit is entirely irrelevant. Every euro crisis has shown that, to hold the bloc together, policy must always be tailored to the weakest link within the zone. The sovereign debt crisis of 2010–2012 remains the clearest example: Greece and Italy forced the ECB to slash rates to zero, flood the market with cheap refinancing loans, and buy unlimited amounts of government bonds, despite the stronger economies in the north.

During the pandemic, the Stability and Growth Pact, originally designed to enforce fiscal discipline, was suspended when the European Commission invoked the *escape clause.* Fiscal rules were shelved, and a €750 billion recovery fund, NextGenerationEU, was launched to support weaker member states.

By design, the ECB's policy must focus on the countries with the largest deficits and highest debt ratios. The eurozone thus represents an extreme form of fiscal dominance: The structural budget deficits of a single member dictate the monetary policy of nineteen others.

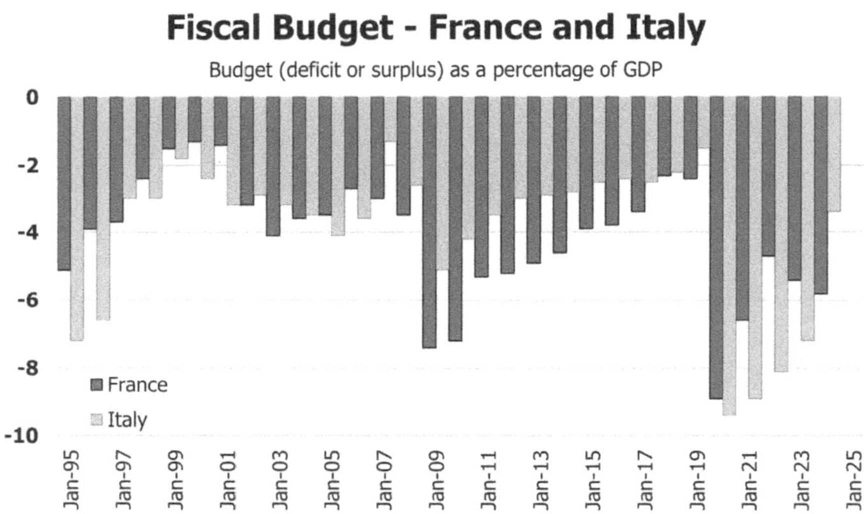

Source: The Great Rebalancing, Eurostat

When it comes to deficits, France now stands out as the weakest link. Since 2008, its shortfall has averaged 5 percent of GDP per year, utterly unsustainable for an economy that barely grows 1 percent a year and is burdened with debt of 110 percent of GDP. From 2008, French public debt has risen by 40 percentage points. I already discussed the odds that France will meet the 3 percent deficit limit. Don't count on it.

Italy performs slightly better, with an average deficit of "just" 4.2 percent of GDP per year. But then again, with a debt ratio of 135 percent, more than twice the 60 percent prescribed by the Maastricht Treaty, what else can you expect with debt sustainability already at risk?

Wherever you look, it's the same story everywhere. Japan's average deficit since 2008 comes to 5.4 percent of GDP. That deficit belongs to a country that barely grows, weighed down by the crushing costs of an aging society. If you were to draw a trend line through Japan's budget deficit chart, it would slope downward more steeply than that of any other major economic bloc. The deficits are huge and keep widening as time progresses. In the past thirty years, Japan has failed to keep its deficit below 3 percent more often than not.

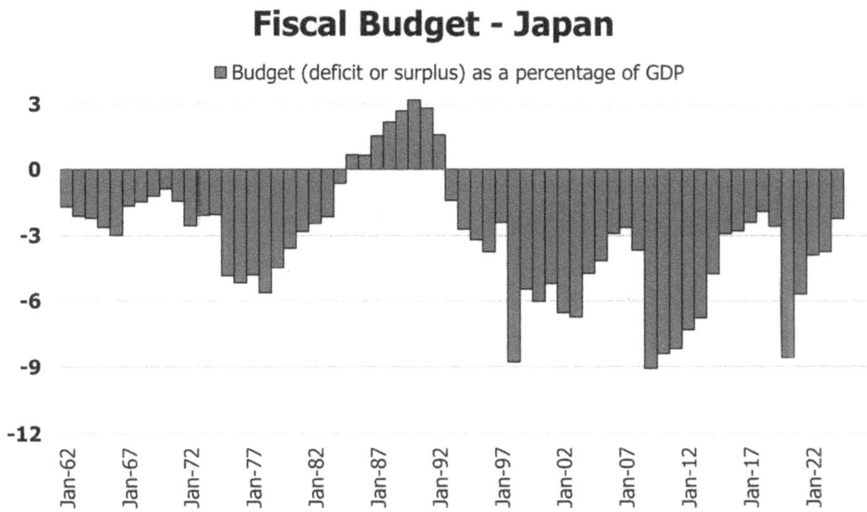

Source: The Great Rebalancing, OECD

Hidden Debt

Finally, China. Here, the fiscal picture has changed dramatically. Until roughly a decade ago, China ran deficits comfortably within the 3-percent-of-GDP threshold. Since 2015, however, fiscal discipline has collapsed and deficits have consistently exceeded 3 percent. That turning point stems from China's rapid aging, which has struck with full force over the past ten years. The shift to a shrinking labor force, as outlined in Chapter 2, has everything to do with it.

Beyond the impact of aging, Beijing's central government has increasingly absorbed the debts owned by local authorities. Policymakers have relied heavily on local government financing vehicles (LGFVs) to stimulate growth, for example by investing in housing construction and infrastructure. To fund these efforts, those financing vehicles have taken on enormous sums of debt. Debt that never shows up on the official balance sheets of Chinese local governments.

By 2024, China's local debt had ballooned to an estimated 66 trillion yuan, about 9 trillion US dollars. To put that number in perspective, these hidden debts, accumulated through opaque financing structures, are equivalent to one quarter of the total US national debt.

With numbers like that, it's hardly surprising that hidden debt now makes up the lion's share of China's total government obligations. In 2024, these hidden liabilities represented roughly 40 percent of total government debt, even after the central government was forced to take over part of the debt to prevent a collapse. According to research firm Rhodium Group, by the end of 2022, only one-fifth of China's LGFVs generated enough cash flow to cover their short-term debt and interest payments. These hidden debts are the chief reason credit rating agencies such as Moody's and Fitch have downgraded their outlook on China's debt sustainability. These data make one thing clear: Focusing solely on central government debt misses the real picture, the actual debt burden.

The combination of a shrinking population, unrealistic growth targets of 5 percent GDP per year, and a mountain of hidden debt makes it highly likely that China's deficits will deepen even further in the years ahead.

A Broken Link Between Debt and Interest Rates

To demonstrate that fiscal dominance is now firmly established as the new economic regime, budget deficits come under increased scrutiny. After all, they are the core of the theory. Yet there are other often overlooked developments that provide equally convincing evidence that the economic system has undergone a lasting transformation. One of my favorite examples is the broken relationship between debt and interest rates, showing that the economic "laws" we were taught in school no longer apply.

Every economics textbook will tell you that the lower a borrower's creditworthiness, the higher the interest rate that borrower must pay. Imagine Chris and Emma both want to borrow €100 from the bank. Chris has €50 in his account at that same bank, while Emma has €500. The bank charges Chris a higher rate than Emma because the bank's confidence in his ability to repay is lower, with just €50 on deposit. The same reasoning applies when Chris and Emma both hold €500 at the bank, but Chris wants to borrow €500 and Emma €50: Chris will have to pay a higher rate on his loan.

That sounds obvious, doesn't it? For Chris and Emma, yes, but for countries and sovereign debt, this basic rule of economics no longer holds.

To illustrate this, let's take Japan as an example. It is by far the most indebted country on Earth, and at the same time also the one whose central bank goes to the greatest lengths to suppress interest rates. By the end of 2024, the Bank of Japan (BoJ) owned nearly half of all outstanding Japanese government bonds. In other words, the BoJ effectively finances almost 50 percent of a colossal public debt exceeding 250 percent of GDP, according to IMF data. That can safely be called monetization of debt.

To reinforce those bond purchases, the BoJ implemented yield curve control (YCC) between September 2016 and March 2024, more than seven straight years. YCC is a policy tool that allows central banks to steer the yields on government bonds: Under YCC, the central bank targets a specific interest rate or range and buys or sells bonds to keep yields pinned within that band. If yields rise too high, the bank buys bonds, driving the prices of those bonds up and, as a result, interest rates down. When rates are too low, the opposite occurs: The central bank sells bonds to nudge yields higher.

It is important to note that while YCC sits in the toolkit of central banks, it is rarely used. The only other pure application occurred between 1942 and 1951, when the Federal Reserve employed it to keep wartime debt affordable. That policy was anything but smooth.

To maintain YCC yields, the Fed had to buy bonds on a massive scale, which later fueled postwar inflation. In 1947, with inflation exceeding 17 percent, the Fed abandoned pegging short-term interest rates, and by 1951, the policy was fully scrapped.

Thankfully, the BoJ's YCC motives have nothing to do with war, but, as you will have expected, with debt. The next chart neatly underpins why our economics textbooks must be rewritten. The principle of relative creditworthiness, illustrated by Chris and Emma, no longer applies. Since 1994, Japan's total debt has increased by roughly 120 percentage points of GDP, according to BIS data. Over the same period, interest rates fell from 4.5 percent to below zero before rebounding slightly.

Note that in the chart, the interest rate on the right-hand vertical axis is inverted to better visualize the relationship. As rates fall, the gray line rises, and when they rise, the line moves down. As the chart shows, the relationship between debt and interest rates is unmistakably negative. As Japan's debt rises, interest rates decline. It is the Bank of Japan that made this happen through its massive bond purchases and years of rate fixing under YCC. With rates rising again in recent years, it is only a matter of time before the BoJ intervenes again.

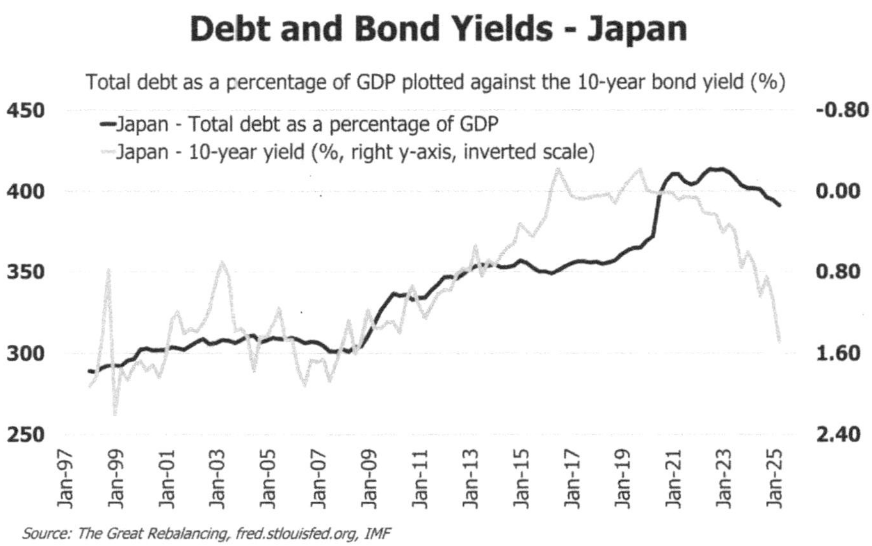

Behind the chart lie even stronger signs of fiscal dominance. The increase in Japan's total debt burden is explained entirely by higher government debt. In fact, over the past thirty years, corporate and household debt as a share of GDP have fallen. The surge in Japan's total debt burden comes entirely from a breathtaking 170 percentage point jump in government debt relative to GDP. As a result, the government's share of total debt has increased from 23 percent to a staggering 53 percent. A defining aspect of fiscal dominance is that the government becomes increasingly dominant in creating artificial growth. After all, only sovereign governments can issue unlimited debt and force their central banks to buy it. Japan's debt numbers confirm these fiscal dominance dynamics perfectly.

A Revealing Chart

Japan is the most striking example of a financial system where debt-financed GDP growth breaks conventional economic laws. At the same time, Japan is far from unique. Across all aging economies, the same pattern appears: The higher the debt climbs, the more interest rates fall.

The strength of this negative relationship becomes particularly clear when debt and interest rates across countries are plotted together. The chart on the next page shows total debt, expressed as a percentage of GDP, for the twenty largest economies in the world (excluding Russia and Turkey) on the horizontal axis (x-axis), set against each country's 10-year government bond yield on the vertical axis (y-axis).

The data show the same pattern: The relationship between debt and interest is inversely correlated. Countries with high debt generally have low interest rates, while those with low debt tend to have high rates, exactly the opposite of what economics textbooks teach us. Japan combines an exceptionally high debt-to-GDP ratio (IMF data) with an ultralow interest rate (consistent with IMF end-of-year figures). Spain, by contrast, has a total debt close to 300 percent of GDP and pays a yield of about 4 percent. The countries with the lowest debt-to-GDP ratios, in the upper-left corner of the chart, are the ones with the highest interest rates.

The chart again features a trend line, which is the line that best connects all data points. Remember R-squared, the statistic that shows how strong the relationship between two variables is? The R-squared value here is 0.67, meaning that debt levels explain about two-thirds of the variation (movements) in 10-year yields across countries. And this is not a one-off result. The negative relationship has persisted for years and has only strengthened since the pandemic; it's another straightforward sign that we have entered a structural shift toward fiscal dominance.

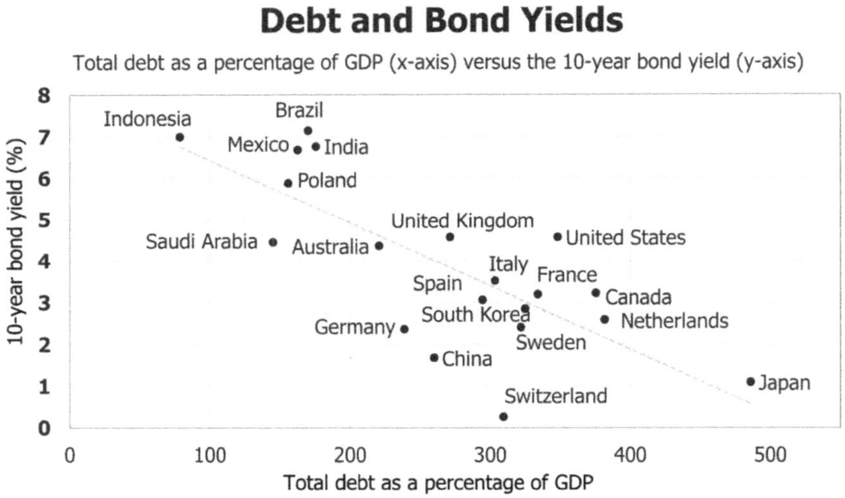

Source: The Great Rebalancing, fred.stlouisfed.org, IMF, Investing.com

This chart, mapping the inverse relationship between debt and bond yields across major economies, provides powerful evidence that fiscal dominance is a global phenomenon. And the conclusion is crystal clear: As global debt continues to rise, the probability of lower interest rates worldwide is very high.

Completing the Puzzle

The odds that you come across a debt-interest rate chart like the one above are slim. That's a shame, because it shows at a glance what the real relationship between debt and interest rates looks like: exactly the opposite of what standard economic theory would have you believe.

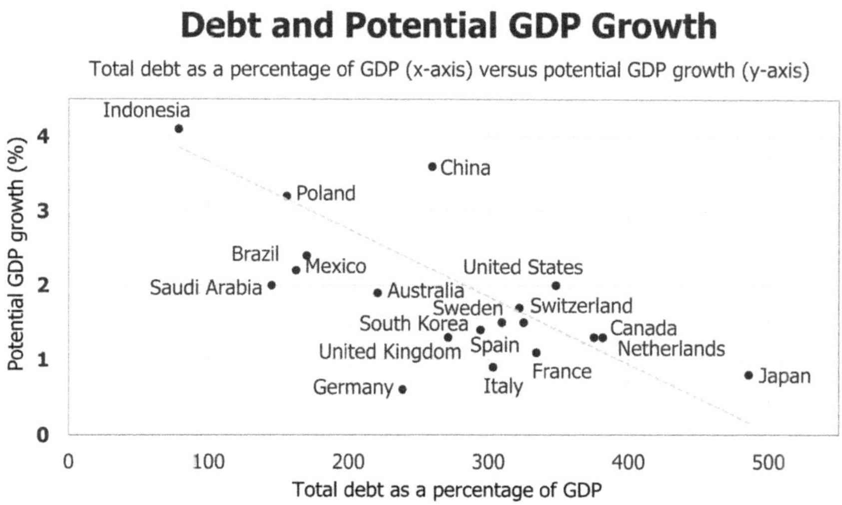

Source: The Great Rebalancing, Bloomberg, IMF

Let me take it a step further and tie the earlier themes together. If our economies are becoming ever more dependent on debt to sustain growth, and if this growing debt is contained through fiscal dominance via low interest rates, then the same dynamic should explain the relationship between debt and economic growth.

The chart above shows how this works. This time, debt-to-GDP ratios of the largest economies (horizontal axis) are plotted against their potential GDP growth (vertical axis). For this comparison, I use the projected potential GDP growth in 2030. Choosing estimated potential GDP growth for the year 2030 strikes a balance between precise current growth numbers, but distorted by temporary factors, and long-term forecasts, which are highly uncertain. The 2030 projection filters out today's noise while capturing demographic trends with reasonable accuracy.

As you can tell, the chart shows exactly the same pattern as the one depicting the relationship between debt and interest rates: The higher a country's debt, the lower its potential GDP growth. Or flipped around, the slower a country's expected growth, the heavier its debt burden. The chart tells us that countries with little growth potential must rely increasingly on debt to generate even modest

GDP growth, while those with abundant potential can grow with much less of it.

Where did India go? With a remarkable potential GDP growth rate of 9 percent, it lies beyond the chart's range, though it is included in the underlying data. Extending the vertical axis to 9 percent to display India would distort the clarity of the relationship. India's absence from the visible plot thus reinforces a key observation: The country will largely escape the debt-growth spiral and is poised for a major economic catch-up.

India's absence from the chart in no way changes its conclusion: As potential GDP growth in nearly all major economies declines sharply in the coming decades, their debts will continue to rise. And those higher debts will, in turn, drive interest rates even lower.

The relationship between debt and growth is undeniably negative, but the interpretation here directly contradicts the classical view of economists and central bankers. In that framework, monetary policy focuses solely on inflation, not debt. Lower GDP growth leads to lower inflation, allowing central banks to cut rates. And there lies the crucial difference with fiscal dominance, where low economic growth coincides with higher inflation.

Inflation as a Result

Inflation is inseparably linked to fiscal dominance. As Sargent and Wallace concluded back in 1981, when governments run structural budget deficits without covering them through taxes or spending cuts, central banks are sooner or later forced to finance those deficits. This monetization of debt expands the money supply and drives inflation higher. Cochrane added that people anticipate such monetary financing, further intensifying the inflationary spiral.

One could argue that fiscal dominance carries higher inflation as a built-in, structural side effect, a rather convenient one for those who aim to make debt more manageable. Within fiscal dominance, governments are now less constrained by traditional central bank policy, since it is no longer focused primarily on inflation, but on interest rates.

Imagine a world without central banks steering inflation through monetary policy. What would that world look like? To get an idea, we can do only one thing: return to a time when central banks did not yet exist.

The next chart shows US inflation by calendar year since 1774. Because the Federal Reserve was not created until December 1913, this gives us almost a century and a half of inflation data without central bank interference, the period highlighted by the dark gray area.

What jumps out right away: Without a central bank, inflation was far more erratic.

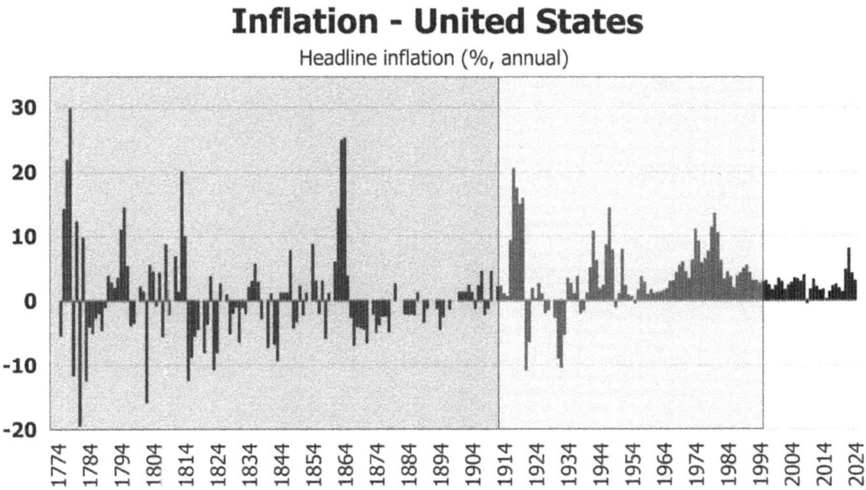

Source: The Great Rebalancing, Lawrence H. Officer and Samuel H. Williamson, 'The Annual Consumer Price Index for the United States, 1774-Present,' MeasuringWorth, 2025.

The light gray area covers inflation between 1913 and 1994, with the caveat that two of the three inflation spikes during this period were tied to the two world wars. The third was the US inflation crisis of the early 1980s, when Fed Chair Paul Volcker raised policy rates to as high as 20 percent to crush inflation that had climbed to nearly 15 percent. That episode marked the beginning of roughly three decades of unchallenged monetary dominance.

Unburdened by excessive debt (except during the two world wars), central banks successfully cemented their credibility as inflation fighters.

The final, unshaded period begins in 1994. That year, the Federal Reserve made inflation the primary focus of its monetary policy, though its inflation target was not formalized until 2012 under Bernanke. The result: From 1994 until the pandemic, US inflation was remarkably stable and predictable.

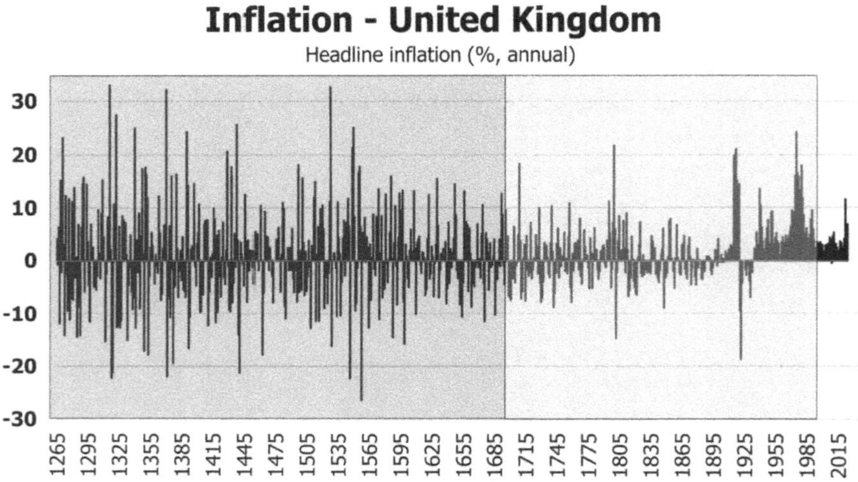

Source: The Great Rebalancing, Samuel H. Williamson "Annual Inflation Rates in the United States, 1775 - 2024, and the United Kingdom, 1265 - 2024," MeasuringWorth, 2025.

The United Kingdom provides an even better example of inflation's volatility in the absence of a central bank. The chart above traces British inflation all the way back to 1265. The Bank of England was founded in 1694, formally began targeting inflation in 1992, and adopted an explicit inflation target in 1997. As in the US, the impact of these decisions is obvious. Before 1694, inflation in England swung violently. After that, volatility diminished somewhat, but only with the introduction of a concrete inflation target did inflation truly stabilize.

In short, less inflation-focused central bank policy will almost inevitably produce more volatile, unpredictable inflation.

But is inflation also higher in a debt-driven economy, where monetary dominance is under strain? The answer to that question is harder to quantify because authentic examples of fiscal dominance are rare. This is precisely why this part of the book is titled "A New Paradigm."

Traditional assumptions about economics and financial systems no longer hold true, and most historical examples are tied to wartime financing.

Still, there is one classic case where fiscal dominance drove inflation completely out of control: Weimar Germany in the 1920s. After World War I, Germany faced a crushing debt burden: The reparations imposed by the Treaty of Versailles and the costs of reconstruction were unaffordable. The economy was devastated by war and the ensuing political chaos. Raising taxes or cutting spending was economically and politically impossible. The Weimar government, therefore, became entirely dependent on the central bank, the Reichsbank, which printed money on a massive scale to cover its deficits. It was, in effect, "monetary financing on steroids."

The outcome is well known and gave birth to a new economic term: hyperinflation. Between 1921 and 1923, the money supply exploded and by 1923, inflation was so extreme that prices were doubling within a single day. Within five years, the price of a loaf of bread rose from less than one mark to 200 billion marks. The Reichsbank, under total control of the government's fiscal emergency, destroyed the value of the Reichsmark through unprecedented money printing and plunged the economy into another deep crisis.

Weimar Germany is, of course, a rare case, but it illustrates vividly what happens when governments and central banks collude to finance debt without fiscal discipline. Inflation is given free rein to become an all-destructive force. Weimar's legacy explains why Germans remain deeply wary of inflation to this day, and why the president of the Bundesbank is invariably a hawk (a central banker with strict policies, singularly focused on keeping inflation in check).

Fresh in Memory

"When governments and central banks collude to finance debt." That sentence perfectly describes what happened after the COVID pandemic erupted. The outcome, unsurprisingly, fits the textbook pattern of fiscal dominance.

In the United States, between March 2021 and February 2025, inflation stayed at least half a percentage point above the Federal Reserve's 2 percent target for four consecutive years. The average inflation rate during that stretch exceeded 5 percent. In Japan, since April 2022, year-on-year inflation has remained at or above 2.5 percent almost every month, averaging 3.1 percent. At the time of writing, this streak is still ongoing. For comparison, between the global financial crisis and the pandemic, Japan's average inflation rate was a mere 0.3 percent. In the eurozone, post-pandemic inflation peaked at 10.6 percent, the highest level since the data series began in 1997.

Extreme Expectations

In line with Cochrane's argument that people anticipate monetary financing by central banks, rising inflation expectations are a direct reflection of fiscal dominance. A good example is the US inflation expectations survey from the University of Michigan.

The chart on the right page reveals a huge gap between the mean and median expectations from that survey. A quick reminder: The mean divides the sum of all, in this case, inflation expectations, by the number of respondents, while the median represents the middle value in the ranking of expectations. The widening gap between mean (black) and median (gray) expectations reveals that more Americans expect extremely high inflation, pulling up the average.

Perhaps they understand that central banks must keep buying government debt to stop their governments from running into trouble. Add to that the fact that the Fed ended hiking rates in July 2023, when inflation was still above 3 percent. Like the ECB, it was quick to pivot toward rate cuts. Has Fed Chair Jay Powell perhaps understood Sargent and Wallace's message all too well? Tighter monetary policy today leaves you with no chance to fight inflation later.

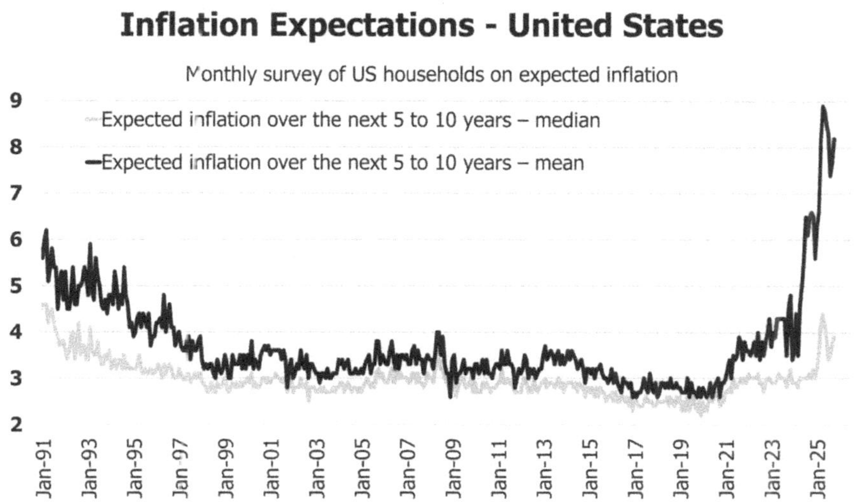

Source: The Great Rebalancing, University of Michigan

A Game of Bingo

Central banks inevitably place monetary policy at the service of governments once debt sustainability comes under threat. By now, that much is clear. The limits of central bank independence reveal themselves whenever a crisis erupts and debt levels explode.

Books, newspapers, and journals have been filled with writing on central banks. Many people believe they fully understand monetary policy, but in reality the sheer complexity of today's financial system makes it elusive. That explains why the endless debates never reach closure. I claim no special expertise here; in fact, there are aspects of central bank policy I can barely wrap my head around. So let me take an alternative, and hopefully more entertaining, route to show how the general dynamics of central banks really work: a game of bingo. Central bank bingo, to be precise.

Since the global financial crisis, central banks around the world have launched an avalanche of stimulus programs designed to stabilize their economies, steer them through crises, and above all, prevent the mountain of debt from delivering a fatal blow. Below is a summary of programs rolled out by four major central banks, packed with enough acronyms to fill a bingo card. And if I've missed one or two, my apologies.

The Fed was relatively quick off the mark during the 2008 crisis. It launched Quantitative Easing 1 (QE1). This was followed by another QE program in 2010 (QE2), one in 2012 (QE3), and again in 2020 during the pandemic (QE4), with the Fed purchasing trillions in government bonds and mortgage-backed securities to lower interest rates and stabilize markets.

In 2008, the Fed also introduced the Term Asset-Backed Securities Loan Facility (TALF) to provide loans backed by securitized assets, and the Primary Dealer Credit Facility (PDCF) to lend directly to market dealers. The Commercial Paper Funding Facility (CPFF), also reintroduced in 2020, and the Money Market Investor Funding Facility (MMIFF) provided lifelines to corporations and money market funds. The Fed also established swap lines with other central banks to make US dollars available worldwide.

After the Silicon Valley Bank collapse and regional bank crisis in 2023, the Bank Term Funding Program (BTFP) was launched, allowing banks to borrow against the face value of their bonds even when those bonds were trading at steep losses. Since then, banks have learned the hard way that paper losses on "safe" bonds can still bring them down. At the same time, the Federal Reserve knows it must always intervene to stop the domino effect.

The European Central Bank (ECB) began in 2010 with the Securities Markets Programme (SMP) to buy the debt of struggling countries such as Greece and Italy. In 2011 came the Long-Term Refinancing Operations (LTRO), followed by the Targeted LTRO (TLTRO) to give banks years of ultra-cheap funding. In 2012, ECB President Mario Draghi introduced Outright Monetary Transactions (OMT) with his now-legendary "Whatever it takes" pledge to save the euro. From

2015 onward, the ECB launched the Asset Purchase Programme (APP), a large-scale bond-buying scheme similar to QE in the United States, followed in 2020 by the Pandemic Emergency Purchase Programme (PEPP), an even more flexible response to the COVID crisis. Today, the ECB already has another, even more flexible and less transparent, program waiting in the wings: the Transmission Protection Instrument (TPI), designed to counter "unwarranted" bond-market movements that threaten the ECB's monetary policy. Take a moment to realize what the TPI is really designed to do: buy bonds from countries whose yields are deemed to be rising "unjustifiably." But who decides what is unjustified, and on what grounds? The ECB could just as easily have called it the "Fiscal Dominance Instrument."

The Bank of Japan (BoJ) has long been a pioneer of unorthodox monetary policy. It began quantitative easing in 2001 and intensified it after 2008. In 2013, the central bank launched Quantitative and Qualitative Easing (QQE), purchasing not only government bonds but also equities through ETFs. Today, the BoJ owns a significant slice of Japan's stock market. And as discussed earlier, in 2016 it revived yield curve control (YCC) to keep Japanese government bond yields artificially low, for nearly eight years.

The People's Bank of China (PBoC) is less transparent but no less active. Since 2014, it has used the Medium-term Lending Facility (MLF) and Standing Lending Facility (SLF) to provide short- and medium-term funding to banks, and the Pledged Supplementary Lending (PSL) program to finance projects such as infrastructure. Since 2019, the Loan Prime Rate (LPR) has been used to directly set borrowing costs. Alongside these came countless local stimulus programs, without official acronyms, many of which contributed to the debt overload of China's local government financing vehicles (LGFVs).

If that doesn't give you bingo, I don't know what will. Many central bankers and traditional economists will no doubt classify these actions as efforts to ensure that financial markets function as smoothly as possible. But the fact remains: Debt lies at the heart of almost every square on the central bank bingo card.

Too Late or By Design?

Let's return to the period after the COVID-19 pandemic, when inflation spiked to its highest level in more than four decades. The Fed raised rates for the first time in March 2022. Inflation in February 2022 stood at 7.8 percent and rose further to 8.5 percent in March. Since April 2021, almost a year before the first hike, US inflation had already exceeded 4 percent. For a central bank claiming to target 2 percent inflation, that first rate hike came embarrassingly late.

Beyond the late start, the cumulative rate increase isn't nearly as impressive as it initially appeared. During the inflation crisis of the late 1970s and early 1980s, the Fed policy rate ultimately rose by 14 percentage points, from 6 percent to 20 percent. US inflation climbed from 6.5 percent to 14.8 percent during that same period. In other words, rates rose far more sharply than inflation itself. Granted, crushing inflation near 15 percent required drastic measures.

But during the most recent inflation crisis following the pandemic, Fed policy looked very different. This time, inflation rose by 9 percentage points in total, from 0.1 percent to 9.1 percent, while the Fed policy rate increased by just over 5 percentage points. So, although the spike in inflation was comparable to that of the early 1980s, the cumulative rate hike amounted to barely a third of Volcker's tightening. To be fair, inflation did start from an exceptionally low base of 0.1 percent. Even so, the balance between inflation and interest-rate hikes flipped completely. Powell never once said it outright at his press conferences, but he seemed to realize that aggressive monetary tightening, with pandemic deficits still towering, would only make matters worse in the long run.

The ECB waited even longer to hike interest rates, until July 2022, by which time inflation was already above 8 percent. For ten consecutive months, inflation had exceeded 4 percent, yet ECB President Christine Lagarde stubbornly insisted inflation was "transitory." A colossal blunder for someone whose primary mandate is to safeguard price stability, at least on paper. In the end, the ECB raised rates by just 4.5 percentage points. And let's not forget: Those rates first had to be lifted out of negative territory. The ECB had kept them below zero for eight long years, with disastrous consequences for savers and bondholders.

Barely nine months after the policy rate peaked, the ECB reversed course, cutting its policy rate in half, from 4 percent to 2 percent, within a year. It's yet another reminder that when it comes to central banks, it is far more important to watch what they do than to listen to what they say. Their record over the past twenty years shows clearly that debt sustainability has become the top priority at the expense of fighting inflation. The result: a string of almost comic press conferences, where central bankers tie themselves in rhetorical knots trying to justify policies that flatly contradict their stated inflation targets.

Bazooka Balance Sheets

So, what about central bank balance sheets? These list central bank assets, including foreign reserves, gold, loans to banks, and, of course, government bonds. These balance sheets have followed the same trajectory as public debt: straight up. In fact, the relationship between the two variables is remarkably strong.

Next is another scatter plot to illustrate this. This one plots global debt as a percentage of global GDP on the horizontal axis. On the vertical axis is the size of the balance sheets of four major central banks, the Federal Reserve, ECB, Bank of Japan, and Bank of England, as a percentage of the GDP of their country or region. Each dot reflects the combination of the global debt-to-GDP ratio and the cumulative balance sheets of these four central banks, divided by the total GDP they represent, for every quarter since 2001. As can be seen, the correlation is even stronger than in earlier examples: Each time debt rises, central bank balance sheets expand right alongside it.

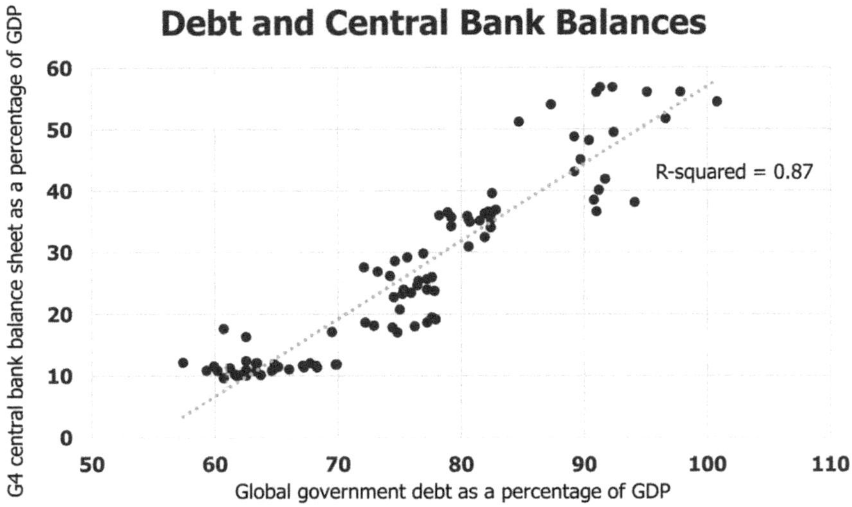

Source: The Great Rebalancing, Bank for International Settlements, Bank of England, Bank of Japan, ECB, Federal Reserve

Central banks that inflate their balance sheets as government debt climbs? That doesn't just sound like fiscal dominance, it *is* fiscal dominance. Unsurprisingly, central bankers are the first to deny it. They argue that expanding balance sheets are essential to ensure the smooth functioning of the economy and financial markets, and to meet their inflation targets. In a November 2022 speech, ECB President Christine Lagarde claimed that large balance sheets help "safeguard the transmission of monetary policy," thereby ensuring policy effectiveness.

That may sound plausible, but it's only half the truth. In practice, the driving motive is sometimes inflation control, but far more often debt sustainability. Liquidity, all the money circulating in the economy so that consumers, companies, and governments can borrow and refinance, is increasingly being used to support the mountain of debt.

Recall Michael Howell's statistic from Chapter 4: Three-quarters of all financial transactions involve refinancing existing debt. The modern financial world has become one giant refinancing machine. The larger the debt, the greater the share of refinancing, and the greater the turmoil if liquidity ever falls short to support it all. Central banks inject money to keep the refinancing machine running, and, increasingly, to buy government bonds themselves.

This dominance of refinancing explains why bloated central bank balance sheets provide liquidity and cause inflation, yet fail to produce economic growth. Only a small fraction of that liquidity ever finds its way into new investment in the real economy. And that's not all. Pressure on liquidity also builds through another channel: so-called "safe" government bonds, the backbone of global liquidity and a key buffer for the financial system, are becoming inherently riskier (as discussed later). That reality only reinforces the need for even more inflated central bank balance sheets.

The Interest Rate Paradox

Is there more evidence of fiscal dominance? Government interest expenses are often cited in this context. When debt-servicing costs explode, as the long-term projections of the Congressional Budget Office suggest, the pressure mounts on central banks to push rates down. In Europe, the ECB openly acknowledges that it will deploy the Transmission Protection Instrument (TPI) to suppress yields whenever markets drive them "too high."

Yet the paradox is that interest costs are not the most straightforward indicator of fiscal dominance, because to prove fiscal dominance, should they be high or low? If central banks succeed in forcing rates down, debt service costs fall accordingly. Japan once again provides the most telling example. Despite public debt equal to 250 percent of GDP, Japan's net interest payments in 2024 amounted to just 0.2 percent of GDP, far below levels in the United States or Italy. Not surprising, given that the Japanese central bank purchased nearly half of Japan's government debt and applied the rare tool of yield curve control for years.

Many forecasts warning that soaring interest costs will consume government budgets are based on historical interest rate data, which no longer apply. My view is that, in practice, fiscal dominance will keep those interest costs lower than most expect. Lower interest costs under fiscal dominance are not a sign of comfort. On the contrary, lower interest rates are a bitter necessity to prevent the debt system from collapsing, at the expense of inflation and the returns of traditional investors.

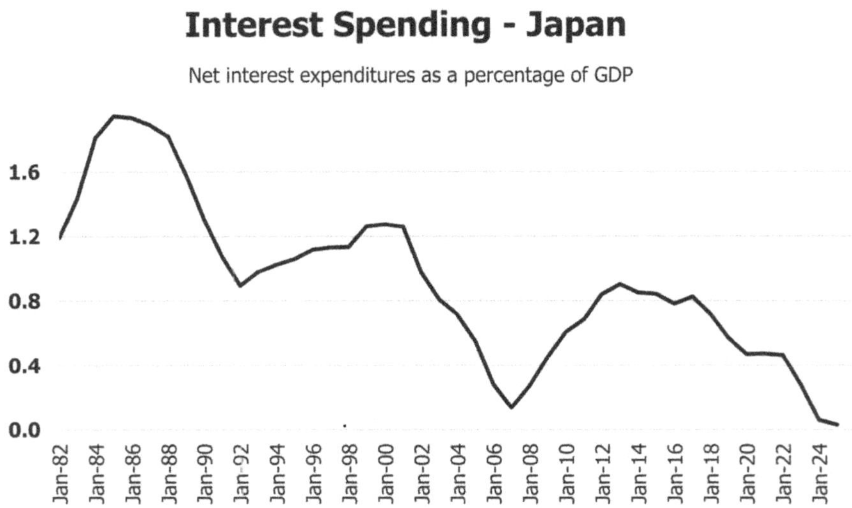

Source: The Great Rebalancing, OECD

Fiscal Dominance: Public or Private?

In addition to the traditional definition of fiscal dominance, structural deficits, low interest rates, and high inflation, there exists an alternative interpretation advanced by investor, economist, and writer Lyn Alden. According to this view, fiscal dominance arises when government budget deficits become more important than private-sector lending in driving economic activity. In other words, the government drives economic growth through persistent overspending, rather than through productive business investment or rising consumer demand. Central banks, charged with keeping the economy afloat, have little choice but to finance those chronic budget deficits.

The appeal of this definition of fiscal dominance is that it can be visualized easily by comparing private-sector lending, such as mortgages, credit cards, and corporate loans, with government budget deficits. The next chart does exactly that. The gray line represents the annual US government deficit (or surplus) in billions of dollars, while the black line tracks the annual change in loans to households and businesses. To make the comparison intuitive and easier to read, the budget deficit is shown as a positive number. A deficit is, by definition, negative, but since the aim is to measure its magnitude relative to private lending growth, I have inverted it into a positive value.

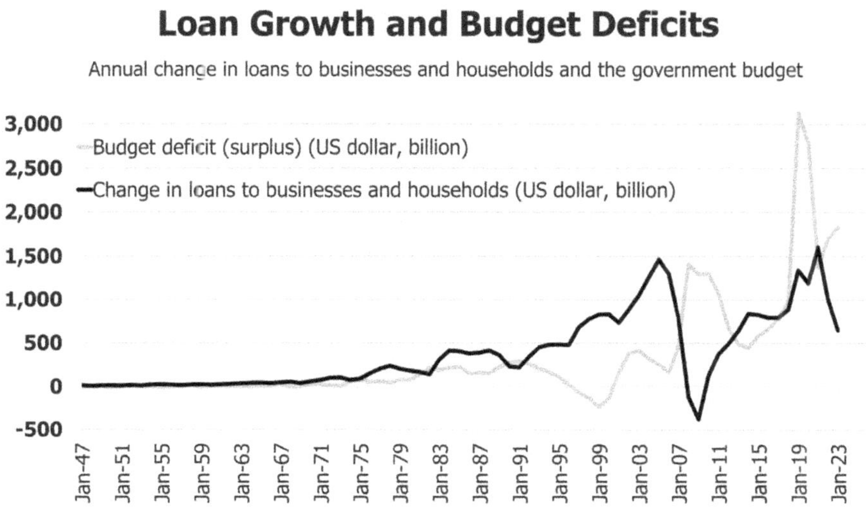

Source: The Great Rebalancing, fred.stlouisfed.org

Up until the global financial crisis, loans to businesses and households (black line) almost always exceeded the size of the US government deficit (the gray line). That is what you would expect in a healthy, debt-sustainable economy: Businesses and households are the primary engines of growth. After 2008, the pattern reversed completely; the budget deficit has been larger than the growth in business and household lending in nearly every year since. During the pandemic, the gap widened dramatically, and even after the strong post-COVID economic rebound, government spending kept outpacing private lending by a wide margin. It's very compelling evidence that fiscal dominance has taken hold.

A Matter of Trust

There is yet another way to expose fiscal dominance: trust. As John Cochrane argued, public trust, or mistrust, in governments directly affects both the economy and inflation.

When people expect governments not to repay their debts and anticipate that central banks will print money to cover them, inflation rises and the real value of debt declines.

So, where does that trust stand today? In an October 2024 survey by the CFA Institute of more than 4,000 investment professionals, nearly 80 percent expressed serious concern about the sustainability of US government debt. Nearly two-thirds believed the US dollar would lose its reserve-currency status within the next five to fifteen years.

And it's not just investors who are skeptical; ordinary citizens are too. According to the OECD's 2024 Survey on Drivers of Trust in Public Institutions, global confidence in governments' ability to tackle financial issues such as national debt is strikingly low across the globe. Fifty-four percent of respondents said that governments should prioritize debt reduction, but only 35 percent believed they were capable of doing so. Even worse, respondents questioned the integrity and effectiveness of their governments. Only 30 percent felt they had any voice in decision-making or believed that governments could resist corporate influence, while a mere 38 percent had faith in parliamentary oversight.

This erosion of trust, in both government policy and debt repayment capacity, intensifies the dynamics of fiscal dominance. A growing body of studies and surveys shows declining confidence not just in governments overall, but specifically in their ability to sustain and repay debt. As Cochrane noted, this is already enough to raise inflation expectations, a trend reflected in the University of Michigan's data: An increasing share of US consumers now expects unusually high inflation for years to come.

Compelling Evidence

Fiscal dominance has become impossible to ignore. Structural deficits are pushing public debt ever higher across the world. In the United States, the eurozone, Japan, and China, debt ratios have soared far beyond the once conventional 60 percent of GDP threshold.

The relationship between debt and interest rates had to be broken. Japan provides compelling proof: It combines the highest public debt with the lowest yields, thanks to a central bank focused not on inflation, but on controlling interest rates. Meanwhile, central banks have rolled out entire bingo cards of stimulus programs, massively expanding their balance sheets, not to fight inflation, but to rescue governments and facilitate debt refinancing. Budget deficits have taken over from business and household lending as the engine of growth, even as trust in government continues to erode. Businesses, consumers, and investors increasingly doubt debt sustainability, driving inflation expectations higher. This is the new regime: Debt rules, and central banks follow.

Inflation is the inevitable side effect of fiscal dominance, as became painfully clear after the pandemic. Global inflation soared to multidecade highs, while central banks responded both late and timidly. Weimar Germany remains the ultimate reminder of how monetary debt financing can spiral into disaster, culminating in hyperinflation. Whether we will face such extremes again is uncertain. What is not uncertain is that inflation will become more volatile and less predictable as central banks shift their focus away from price stability.

Despite this overwhelming body of evidence that fiscal dominance has taken hold of the financial system, some economists still insist that debt is not necessarily problematic, as long as inflation stays in check. Their theory takes center stage in the next chapter.

CHAPTER 11

MMT Won't Fix It

Introduction

The great risk of fiscal dominance is inflation. For one simple reason: Central banks have lost control of their official mandate, price stability. In Weimar Germany, it led to hyperinflation, and in post-COVID Europe to double-digit inflation above 10 percent.

But what if inflation were not a problem? What if governments could run perpetual deficits to buy economic growth without triggering runaway inflation? That is exactly what Modern Monetary Theory promises, a dream come true for governments worldwide struggling to keep the debt-fueled economy alive.

Or perhaps not.

Modern Monetary Theory: What Is It?

Modern Monetary Theory, or MMT, is an economic school of thought claiming that sovereign nations controlling their own currency, like the US with the dollar or Japan with the yen, can never really default. Such governments can always create more of their own money to pay the bills. The power to print unlimited money means governments no longer depend on taxes or borrowing. In fact, under MMT taxation, and not interest rates, is the primary tool to steer inflation. If inflation runs hot, governments raise taxes to curb consumer spending. People have less money left to spend after taxes take their bite. If inflation is too low, they cut taxes to boost consumer demand.

Within MMT, the decision to collect taxes or issue government bonds to finance the budget is purely a political one. Governments can simply finance spending by creating new money.

Interest rates matter far less within MMT dynamics. At least in theory, because MMT favors low interest rates so debt-service costs never get in the way of government spending. After all, interest expenses must also be financed, though for a sovereign government, that is technically no problem at all. Under MMT, the central bank, like the tax authority, is merely an institution that facilitates how governments choose to finance their spending.

Warren Mosler, a hedge fund manager and entrepreneur, developed the foundations of MMT in the early 1990s and officially published them in 1995 in a paper titled "Soft Currency Economics" (in 2013 it became a book titled *Soft Currency Economics II*). In it, Mosler argues that governments and central banks have long collaborated to finance public budgets. The term *Modern Monetary Theory,* however, was coined by Bill Mitchell, an Australian economist who, together with Mosler and Randall Wray, further refined the theory in the 1990s.

Here lies a key criticism: While MMT has attracted academic curiosity, it has never appeared in any leading economic journal. That stands in sharp contrast to the previously discussed work of

Solow (economic growth model, Chapter 2) and Domar (the r-g framework, Chapter 5), both of which shaped mainstream economic thought.

MMT only entered the mainstream when Stephanie Kelton, economics professor and former advisor to Bernie Sanders during his 2016 presidential campaign, popularized it in her 2020 book *The Deficit Myth.* Kelton argues that budget deficits are not a problem for countries issuing their own currency. Rather than obsessing over a balanced budget, Kelton states that governments should focus on economic and social goals, including full employment. In her view, inflation is not the enemy; political hesitation to pursue those goals is.

Money Creation and Inflation — A Journey Through Time

MMT is still a young theory. It remains largely untested academically and is often dismissed as unorthodox, though that's not necessarily a flaw, despite what traditional economists may think. The theory is partly descriptive: Governments cannot go bankrupt because they can always print more of their own currency. But it's also normative: Governments should spend as much as necessary to achieve full employment and other economic goals until inflation emerges. That last part makes MMT notoriously hard to test.

Most attempts to verify MMT therefore focus on the relationship between money growth and inflation. After all, MMT assumes that when governments print money through their central banks to finance spending, inflation does not have to follow, at least not until full employment of labor and productive capacity are reached.

Assuming that printing money does not cause inflation is a bold claim. It doesn't take much effort to compile an extensive list of leading economic studies showing, quite convincingly, that the link between money creation and inflation is, in fact, very real. Where money surges, inflation almost always follows. This principle is also central to fiscal dominance: When central banks monetize debt, inflation follows.

Because the relationship between money creation and inflation is decisive in determining whether we are dealing with fiscal dominance or MMT, I will highlight several groundbreaking and influential studies.

In 1911, Irving Fisher published his landmark book *The Purchasing Power of Money*. Fisher, one of the founders of modern economics, formalized what became known as the "quantity theory of money." The theory can be expressed in the following equation:

$M \times V = P \times Y$

Where:

- M = the money supply, the total amount of money circulating within an economy.
- V = the velocity of money, or how often each euro or dollar changes hands in a year.
- P = the price level.
- Y = GDP, the overall size of the economy.

In plain English, if the money supply (M) increases, prices (P) will rise, provided the other two factors, money velocity (V) and output (Y), remain constant. Fisher found in his US-focused research that a 6 percent increase in money supply produced roughly 5 percent inflation. Fisher's work remains influential to this day, celebrated for its elegant simplicity in linking money growth directly to inflation.

It is therefore no surprise that more than half a century later, in 1963, Nobel laureate Milton Friedman revived Fisher's ideas. In *A Monetary History of the United States, 1867–1960*, co-authored with Anna Schwartz, Milton Friedman made his timeless claim: "Inflation is always and everywhere a monetary phenomenon." According to Friedman, it is always central banks that cause inflation. Even when inflation stems from fiscal policy or structural deficits, central banks are still to blame. Friedman's book was groundbreaking for its empirical rigor, using historical data to prove that money growth drives inflation. During the 1920s, US money supply grew 4 percent annually and inflation averaged 3.5 percent. But when the money supply shrank by 10 percent during the Great Depression, prices collapsed by nearly 9 percent.

In 1972, fellow Nobel laureate Robert Lucas published his study "Expectations and the Neutrality of Money," in which he added a new dimension to the relationship between money growth and inflation: expectations. People do not passively wait to see what their government will do but anticipate policy. Lucas argued that only unexpected money growth causes inflation. In that case, people must adjust their expectations as they had expected something different. In 1960s America, an expected 3 percent rise in money supply barely moved the real economy, but it did push prices higher.

A few years later, in 1979, economist Robert Barro released "On the Determination of the Public Debt." Barro, a Harvard economist and one of the leading voices in macroeconomics, focused on how governments choose to finance their debt. Do they print money through their central banks or fund spending through taxes? His research showed that when governments finance deficits by printing money, as the US did in the 1970s, inflation inevitably follows. Barro directly linked government deficits to money growth and inflation. In doing so, Barro prefigured the theory of fiscal dominance, formally introduced a couple of years later by Sargent and Wallace in their 1981 classic "Some Unpleasant Monetarist Arithmetic."

In 1993, John Taylor published "Discretion versus Policy Rules in Practice." Taylor, a Stanford economist and creator of the "Taylor rule," showed that central banks can control inflation by adjusting interest rates in response to money growth. According to Taylor, the inflation crisis of the early 1980s was explained by money growth, which consistently exceeded 10 percent in the late 1970s. The crisis forced Fed Chair Paul Volcker to push interest rates up to 20 percent, after which inflation quickly collapsed. Taylor's work is important because it shows that central banks can use interest rates to control inflation (monetary dominance) and that problems arise when central banks cannot freely set interest rates (fiscal dominance).

In 1997, Michael Bordo and Anna Schwartz published *Monetary Policy Regimes and Economic Performance: The Historical Record.* Bordo, an expert on monetary history, and Schwartz, famed for her collaboration with Friedman, analyzed a vast historical dataset on the link between money and inflation. They showed that stable money growth, such as during the gold standard (1870–1914), kept inflation low, while excessive money growth drove inflation higher, as in the 1970s. This robust study demonstrated that the relationship between money and inflation is timeless.

Although Carmen Reinhart and Kenneth Rogoff may go down in history for an Excel error in their 800-year debt study focusing on financial crises, *This Time Is Different: Eight Centuries of Financial Folly*, several of their conclusions on government debt still stand tall despite their spreadsheet mishap. One of them is that highly indebted countries are often confronted with exceptionally high inflation. While MMT claims that countries controlling their own currency can never technically go bankrupt, hyperinflation creates an implicit form of default. Weimar Germany offers the textbook example: Hyperinflation destabilizes economies and destroys wealth.

With an entire library of studies linking money supply and inflation, major institutions such as the International Monetary Fund (IMF) and the Bank for International Settlements (BIS) have added the topic to their research agenda. An IMF analysis from 2008 found that excessive money growth can trigger inflation, particularly in emerging markets. In 2001, Turkey's money supply expanded by at a colossal 40 percent annual rate, accompanied by a spectacular 70 percent inflation rate. In recent years, we have seen a nearly identical pattern: average money growth of 50 percent since 2021, accompanied by 50 percent inflation. High inflation brings another problem, especially in emerging markets; the collapse of local currencies. Since 2021, the Turkish lira has plunged more than 80 percent against the US dollar.

The long catalog of empirical evidence and prominent studies is at the very minimum a stark warning that unlimited money creation causes inflation, with a high likelihood for inflation to spin out of control.

Well-Founded Criticism

MMT contains several features that, at least to me, raise more questions than they answer. Many of those same questions have also been posed by Harvard professor Greg Mankiw, author of *Macroeconomics,* a classic textbook that nearly every economics student (myself included) owns. Mankiw is one of MMT's fiercest critics, and in his 2020 paper "A Skeptic's Guide to Modern Monetary Theory," he explains exactly why.

Logically, Mankiw first revisits the historical relationship between money growth and inflation. He finds that since 1870, the correlation between the two has been strong and positive: 0.79. With a possible range from −1 to +1, this approaches a near-perfect positive relationship. More money almost always meant more inflation.

Mankiw's critique goes further, focusing on the rising interest costs that accompany higher debt. When central banks print money to monetize government debt, that "new money" ends up as reserves in the banking system. When banks have no alternative use for those reserves, they leave the surplus at the central bank. The central bank pays interest on those reserves, reducing the interest income it can remit to the government. In a regime of fiscal dominance, the rising interest burden forces the government to issue even more debt, much of which ultimately must be monetized, expanding the money supply all over again.

Mankiw argues that paying interest is nothing more than an alternative form of borrowing. MMT advocates acknowledge this mechanism but conclude that interest rates should therefore remain permanently low. In their view, it is purely a policy choice. But Mankiw strongly disagrees with this as well. If central banks pay too little interest on reserves, banks will push money into the real economy through new lending. A low interest rate makes parking cash at the central bank unattractive, again increasing the overall money supply. More money chasing goods fuels demand, and with it, inflation.

Another flaw, according to Mankiw, is MMT's proposed cure for inflation: government price controls. MMT assumes inflation results from the struggle between workers and companies over income, and that governments can resolve that struggle through wage and price regulations. That is hard enough to grasp, let alone measure. The idea is that workers always want higher wages while companies always want to raise prices to increase profits. When wages rise, companies raise prices even more to cover those costs, prompting workers to demand even higher wages to compensate for price increases, and so on. This creates a spiral of rising prices. MMT casts the government as the referee, breaking the spiral by imposing wage and price restrictions. That logic is far removed from mainstream economics, where supply and demand determine prices.

Mankiw sees the idea of governments acting as referees as entirely unrealistic, which is unsurprising since capitalism, dominant in most economies, is fundamentally opposed to government interference. Moreover, price controls have failed repeatedly in the past, breeding inefficiency and social unrest. In the United States of the 1970s, they brought shortages and black markets, not stability.

The same skepticism applies to taxes as a tool to control inflation. In practice, the idea is unworkable. Tax codes are too complex, and the bureaucracy is too large. In some countries, even minor tax reforms will take years. And as the Laffer curve in Chapter 7 illustrated, today's heavy tax burden risks triggering capital flight. Think back to the wealthy Norwegians relocating en masse to Switzerland. While governments under MMT technically don't *need* tax revenue to fund spending, the loss of human capital is always damaging, especially in aging societies with stagnant workforces.

MMT also underestimates politicians' relentless desire for reelection. Imagine an economy running at full capacity with everyone employed, social services generous, defense spending exceeding NATO's new target, and inflation starting to climb. Do politicians on the campaign trail on the eve of the elections say, *"We will stop spending and raise taxes because MMT tells us to"*? Of course not. As Kenneth Rogoff argued in "Modern Monetary Nonsense" (2019), MMT ignores the political reality that elected leaders, driven by reelection, prefer to keep spending and steer clear of unpopular measures like raising taxes.

A final criticism is that MMT inevitably breeds an ever-larger state. But how desirable is that? The larger the government, the smaller the space for businesses to take risks and for citizens to make their own choices. Competition and innovation become policy-driven rather than market-driven. Yet government, by nature, is not the most fertile ground for innovation; that's usually the domain of dusty attics filled with daring pioneers.

MMT, thus, undermines the last true engine of economic growth: productivity. A system built on controls, restrictions, and overregulation suffocates healthy economic incentives. The societal consequences of an oversized government should not be underestimated. It would not be the first time in history that people rebelled against exactly that. Bear in mind, this risk is not unique to MMT: France and Japan show how fiscal dominance can lead to governments of suffocating scale.

Nagging Questions

On paper, MMT looks tempting: Governments can print money to finance their deficits, never default, and avoid inflation. But how it actually works in the real world remains unclear to me. I'm left with nagging questions, most of them still unanswered.

Take inflation. MMT speaks of "conflict inflation," where workers demand higher wages and companies raise prices, setting off a struggle for income. The government, in theory, can end the conflict by raising taxes or fixing prices. But how is this inflation measured? And what counts as the "right" price level? The conventional basket of goods and services used to measure inflation (CPI, consumer price index) doesn't fit the framework. MMT effectively ignores supply and demand dynamics in retail prices. And how should we deal with inflation that does result from money creation, known as monetary inflation? In countries like Turkey, money supply growth produced hyperinflation, a risk MMT consistently underestimates. The theory's conflict-inflation concept quickly clashes with reality.

What exactly is the role of central banks under this theory? Under MMT, they are mere government agents, obliged to finance deficits and keep rates near zero. But most central banks are, often by law, independent. Can governments really force their hand? In Turkey, the government forced the central bank to slash interest rates when the situation called for the exact opposite, collapsing the currency and triggering hyperinflation. But if central banks resist and raise rates anyway, it sends a clear signal that inflation is on the rise. This causes turmoil in the markets, wiping out the value of savings and bonds alike.

Does MMT work everywhere? A solid theory should hold up universally. It may apply to countries with sovereign currencies, like the United States, China, and Japan. But in the eurozone, no country controls its own currency: The euro is shared by countries with vastly different economies. In addition, the question takes us right back to the introduction of this book. In the United Kingdom, Prime Minister Liz Truss lasted just forty-nine days in 2022, after a budget filled with massive unfunded tax cuts threw the financial markets into chaos. Also, in countries with weaker currencies, like Argentina, Venezuela, and once again, Turkey, hyperinflation is a recurring event. So, can MMT really claim to be universal?

Who is still willing to buy government bonds at zero percent interest? Today, governments borrow from banks, companies, households, and foreign investors. According to MMT, that is simply a choice. Yet in practice, governments put in a lot of effort to find enough buyers for their bonds. Why is this, if they supposedly can just turn on the money printer? In the case of US Treasuries, they benefit from artificial demand because they serve as the core buffers of the global financial system. But in other countries, that artificial demand simply doesn't exist.

In short, MMT raises more questions than it answers. It may sound like an ideal world, but in practice the interplay between deficits, central banks, money creation, and inflation is far more complex and stubborn. And if MMT fails, inflation explodes, and savers and bond investors still end up paying the price.

MMT: A Vague, Surreal Dream

Modern Monetary Theory envisions a world where sovereign governments in control of their currencies can spend without limit and without fear of inflation, ideal for any state struggling with debt sustainability. But I seriously doubt MMT holds in the real world. Many of its assumptions are partial, under-tested, or plainly unrealistic.

Moreover, the sheer weight of evidence linking money supply growth and inflation is overwhelming. The statistics are not on MMT's side. It's an intellectually elegant experiment on paper, but a dangerous gamble in practice. MMT overlooks too many real-world constraints, from market behavior to political incentives, and that leaves me deeply skeptical. In the end, MMT is less a solution than a seductive illusion of monetary wisdom.

CHAPTER 12
Repression as a Stopover

Introduction

Before this book turns fully to how you, as an investor, can navigate a debt-driven world of weak growth, structurally low rates, and higher, more erratic inflation, a brief interlude is in order. In practice, fiscal dominance is often confused with another economic phenomenon: financial repression. Although they are closely related, they are not identical. Yet they share one deeply unpleasant trait.

Fiscal Dominance and Financial Repression: What Is the Difference?

Fiscal dominance marks a regime shift in which central banks lose their independence, forced by the unsustainable fiscal policies of governments. Debt sustainability becomes the overriding goal, pursued at the expense of price stability. Central banks purchase government bonds on a massive scale, fueling inflation through rapid money supply growth. The central bank becomes, unwillingly, an executive arm of the treasury.

Financial repression, by contrast, is a deliberate act of policy design. It is a calculated collaboration between governments and central banks to suppress savers and investors through artificially low interest rates, elevated inflation, and capital controls. Here, the central bank's role is not subordinated but strategically aligned with fiscal policy to enforce debt sustainability.

The term *financial repression* was first coined in 1973 by Stanford economists Edward S. Shaw and Ronald I. McKinnon. That same year, each published a book: *Financial Deepening in Economic Development* and *Money and Capital in Economic Development.* Although they independently developed nearly identical ideas, the coincidence was less random than it appeared. McKinnon and Shaw belonged to the same school of economists, one that emphasized the crucial role financial systems play in economic development. Their core message was blunt: Financial repression stifles economic growth by penalizing savers and investors.

Financial repression was initially associated with emerging markets, but the concept gained wider attention in 2011. Carmen Reinhart and M. Belen Sbrancia brought the topic into the spotlight with their influential IMF paper "The Liquidation of Government Debt." They showed how governments, after World War II, cut down their towering debts through interest-rate caps, capital controls, and inflationary policies.

This brings us to the defining feature of financial repression: capital controls. For this policy to succeed, restrictions on the free flow of capital are key. Financial repression works only when investors are forced into government bonds and capital controls make sure their money can't escape abroad. Governments can do this in various ways. Citizens may face punitive taxes if they withdraw capital from bonds or transfer it overseas. Banks and pension funds are often obliged to hold "safe" government debt to meet regulatory buffer requirements meant to protect against financial crises.

Economists often describe financial repression as the milder cousin of fiscal dominance. They do so because, on paper, financial repression is temporary, whereas under fiscal dominance the loss of central bank independence is permanent. Yet the consequences for savers and bond investors, specifically due to those capital controls, are at least as harmful as under fiscal dominance.

Debasement: The Systematic Erosion of Money

Financial repression comes with a deeply damaging side effect. Savers and bondholders are trapped in a world of low yields, excessive money printing, and rising inflation. Heavy money creation combined with inflation steadily erodes the value of money, and with it the real worth of savings and wealth, leaving no escape hatch. This deliberate destruction of the (intrinsic) value of currency is the hallmark of financial repression. The word *intrinsic* sits in parentheses for a reason: Because today's money has no intrinsic value whatsoever. A €100 note costs just a few cents to print.

In Roman times, things were different. Roman emperors cut the silver content of their coins, literally reducing the intrinsic value, to mint more money and expand the money supply. The same playbook of monetary debasement reappeared in the sixteenth century, notably under King Henry VIII of England. The silver content of English coins fell from over 90 percent to as little as 25 percent, an episode later dubbed the "Great Debasement."

Today, currency debasement refers to the modern erosion of value caused by excessive money printing, artificially low interest rates, and higher inflation. There is no intrinsic value left in euros, dollars, or yen to dilute any further. Under financial repression, escape routes from this currency erosion are deliberately sealed off. Capital controls and regulations trap investors inside the system, even as their wealth steadily loses purchasing power.

The defining element of financial repression, suppression, also ties back to my earlier, nagging, and unresolved question about MMT: Who still wants to buy government bonds? Regulations worldwide compel banks to hold sovereign debt as capital buffers. In 2025, the Federal Reserve unveiled a plan to lower the amount of capital that systemically important banks must hold to survive a crisis. Systemically important banks are institutions so vast and interconnected that their failure would pull the entire financial system down with them. The Fed's primary reason for this plan, hardly concealed, was to give these banks more room to buy government bonds.

Meanwhile, the newly introduced *GENIUS Act* (Guiding and Establishing National Innovation for U.S. Stablecoins) in the United States provides clear rules that allow the stablecoin market to grow. Stablecoins are digital, blockchain-based versions of dollars, or other currencies, outside the realm of central banks, backed by what are traditionally viewed as stable, safe assets. That's how a stablecoin "guarantees" its value. In practice, those "safe" assets almost always mean US government bonds. The GENIUS Act is, above all, a clever mechanism to artificially boost demand for government debt. There is little intrinsic value to speak of.

China enforces far stricter and more explicit capital controls, while India imposes limits on the amount of wealth that can leave the country. If, under MMT, governments can simply print the money they need, why go to such lengths to coerce investors into buying bonds? To be clear: MMT does not offer room for capital controls. Because, as the theory dictates, since governments can print money freely such controls are unnecessary.

Both financial repression and MMT aim to finance chronic budget deficits and maintain debt sustainability. MMT relies on the idea that governments can print money without sparking inflation, whereas financial repression depends on coercion and control. In practice, the latter is far more common, which puts financial repression and MMT at odds with each other.

Which of the Three Fits the Bill?

So which is it, financial repression, fiscal dominance, or MMT? By now, it should be clear that MMT, in my view, is no serious contender. It leaves too many loose ends. The symptoms of fiscal dominance, described in Chapter 10, are visible almost everywhere you look. At the same time, it's hard to ignore the growing web of rules that force investors into government bonds and the rising number of measures designed to prevent capital flight.

An "exit tax" levied when someone emigrates is a particularly chilling example. Residents leaving Australia, Canada, France, or the United States face such taxes, while wealthy Norwegians must even pay tax on unrealized gains when they depart. This undoubtedly relates to the massive capital outflows seen in 2022, described earlier in this book.

My answer to the question of whether this is financial repression or fiscal dominance: somewhere in between. The system is mid-transition toward full fiscal dominance, with financial repression serving as a potentially long-lasting intermediary stage. The global financial crisis, and especially the COVID-19 pandemic, displayed unmistakable signs of fiscal dominance: massive budget deficits largely financed by central banks that sacrificed their goal of price stability. The years that followed those crises, however, bore the marks of repression, with governments trying to preserve the status quo by forcing investors to buy government bonds even at absurdly low yields. The fact that the ECB held policy rates below zero from 2014 until COVID, without any new crisis in sight, speaks volumes.

For investors, it matters little where we stand in this transition. Both fiscal dominance and financial repression loom like dark clouds over future returns, compounded by the relentless erosion of purchasing power in euros, dollars, and yen alike.

Whether it's fiscal dominance or financial repression, the takeaway for investors is the same: Traditional investment portfolios must be radically rebuilt to generate positive real returns. That holds true for asset managers, insurers, pension funds, family offices, hedge funds, and your investment portfolio. Fortunately, you hold one key advantage over those conservative, rigid, traditional professional investors: You can escape the extreme policies of governments and central banks that keep the debt-driven system alive.

In the remainder of this book, I will show you exactly how.

Part IV

The Solution

CHAPTER 13
Scarcity as Escape

Introduction

A significant part of this book is devoted to explaining how our growth model functions and what it takes to keep it afloat. I have shown that ultralow interest rates, persistent inflation, and the steady debasement of money are defining features of this system, which ultimately serves one single purpose: to ensure that the final engine of growth, debt, keeps running.

The better you understand how the world around you works, the clearer it becomes where the solution must come from. The more you recognize the profound influence of fiscal dominance on today's financial markets, the more obvious it becomes that almost every investment portfolio must be fundamentally restructured.

That is a massive challenge, one that will take years, if not decades, to complete. But it goes deeper than that. The solution that allows us to escape low rates and high inflation can also prevent the financial system from collapsing altogether. Collapse may happen, but it is not inevitable. This is a crucial nuance I find too often missing in the arguments of investors, economists, and other so-called experts who rail against the current system. In the end, finding the solution is what truly makes the difference.

So what does that solution look like? It is remarkably simple: In a world awash with debt and devalued money, invest in the exact opposite. Do not invest in abundance; invest in scarcity. Scarce assets protect against the toxic mix of low interest rates, high inflation, and currency debasement. And equally important, they help rebalance the financial system itself.

What Is Scarcity?

Scarcity is the foundation of economics and revolves around one key principle: choice. Because resources such as capital, labor, and raw materials are limited, while human needs are endless, our appetite for growth knows no bounds; choices must be made continuously.

"Economics is the science which studies human behaviour as a relationship between ends and scarce means which have alternative uses." This elegant definition was introduced by British economist Lionel Robbins in 1932, anchoring scarcity firmly within modern economic thought. But the roots of scarcity as an economic concept stretch back much further. For thousands of years, scarcity has fascinated the world's most influential thinkers. In Ancient Greece, thinkers such as Plato and Aristotle wrestled with the question of how scarce resources should be distributed within a broader philosophical framework. Centuries later, in the eighteenth and nineteenth centuries, economists like Adam Smith, David Ricardo, and Thomas Malthus sought to understand and map the influence of scarcity on human decision-making.

As capitalism gained ground as the dominant economic model, the interpretation of scarcity subtly evolved. Scarcity increasingly came to be seen as the invisible force behind free markets, value, and prices. Scarcity means that resources are limited relative to human wants, so demand would exceed supply at a zero price. Consequently, scarce goods command a positive price, provided that something also reflects utility. Lunar dust, for instance, is extremely scarce on Earth, but of little use to most people.

By linking value to scarcity, a direct connection to investing emerges. Scarce assets derive their value from the fact that they cannot be produced, issued, or printed without limit. Their supply is inherently constrained. Scarcity also reflects an asset's ability to preserve or even increase its value, whether in absolute terms (its nominal price in, for example, euros) or in relative terms (compared to inflation or other assets).

Scarcity is therefore a vital characteristic in a regime of fiscal dominance. Scarce assets shield investors from the poisonous cocktail of excessive money creation, high inflation, and low interest rates. Some even help you escape from financial repression because they exist outside the traditional financial system. The supply of scarce assets cannot be infinitely diluted by governments desperate to sustain a debt-driven growth model.

In Abundance

While the theory of scarcity is hard to dispute, one big question remains: Which assets truly qualify as scarce, and which have proven their ability to protect wealth? Which assets allow you to escape fiscal dominance? And just as important, though often overlooked: How do you build a balanced investment portfolio around them?

To answer those questions effectively, I again take a pragmatic approach, starting with the enormous impact fiscal dominance has on the two assets that are anything but scarce: bonds (debt) and currencies (money).

This impact is illustrated in the chart on the next page. The black line tracks how a €100,000 investment in global bonds has performed over the past 25 years. To be clear, the black line reflects the value of that investment after accounting for inflation, the rise in the general price level. In other words, it depicts the real value of a €100,000 global bond investment since 2000.

Real value is the only measure that matters, as inflation ensures that everyday life almost always becomes more expensive. To preserve your purchasing power, an investment must at least keep pace with inflation. Yet asset managers, banks, financial media, investment books, and pension funds almost never present real, inflation-adjusted returns, which is remarkable, given that rising prices are a constant reality. By the way, for this analysis, I assume a euro-based investor and use eurozone inflation to calculate the real value of the bond investment.

Source: The Great Rebalancing, Bloomberg, ECB, Eurostat

The gray line represents the real value (again after adjusting for inflation) of a savings account starting with €100,000 and opened in 2000, earning interest equal to the European Central Bank's policy rate. In the eurozone, savings rates vary across countries, reflecting differences in credit risk. Italy, for example, with government debt well above 100 percent of GDP, typically must offer higher rates than Germany, whose debt ratio is far lower. Still, rate comparison sites show that the ECB's policy rate, the benchmark for bank deposit rates, is a reliable proxy for assessing how savings have performed in real terms.

Saving Is No Virtue

And the results are dismal. On both "investments," bonds and savings, you would have lost value after accounting for inflation. Bonds declined by an average of 0.5 percent per year in real terms, while savings lost as much as 1.3 percent annually. Over the past 25 years, saving and investing in bonds have steadily eaten away at your purchasing power.

By October 2025, the gray line ends at roughly €71,000. In other words, after 25 years of disciplined saving, you would have lost €29,000 in purchasing power (€100,000 minus €71,000). The real value of your savings will buy you €29,000 less in goods and services. Compared with the initial €100,000, nearly 30 percent of your purchasing power has evaporated. That is a staggering loss.

Most savers are completely unaware of this because their accounts display only nominal balances, not the inflation-adjusted reality. In this example, your account would show a nominal balance of €127,000 after 25 years. That is the actual number you see on your bank statement or banking app. You think you are €27,000 ahead after 25 years of saving, but in real life, you've lost €29,000 in purchasing power. With €127,000 today, you can buy far less than you could in 2000 with €100,000. That is the silent, corrosive effect of inflation.

Now imagine you hadn't earned the ECB rate on your savings but a full percentage point more every single year. Even then, 25 years later, you would still have lost around €10,000 in purchasing power due to inflation. Saving is especially popular in Europe. It is widely viewed as something virtuous, a mark of prudence and financial discipline. In truth, it is a loss-making strategy that consistently and significantly erodes purchasing power. You only see that truth when you view your savings through the lens of inflation-adjusted value.

The same logic applies to your investments. Those who understand that saving is futile and "put their money to work" still end up investing in bonds, assuming they are the "sensible" option. But as the chart makes painfully clear, bonds too have collapsed under the weight of low yields and high inflation. A single inflation shock was enough to devastate their real value for decades. The real value of a €100,000 global bond investment made in 2000 has dropped by roughly 12 percent by October 2025. Having lent your money to governments around the world for 25 years, a venture not without risk, you still lost purchasing power. In return for that risk, you've received no positive reward after 25 years.

A global government bond portfolio has failed miserably to keep up with inflation. That alone should raise serious questions about whether this asset class still fulfills its purpose of growing and protecting wealth.

The chart also neatly highlights the impact of fiscal dominance during and after the COVID pandemic. The ECB kept interest rates pinned near zero well into 2022, while massive budget deficits drove inflation above 10 percent. In a regime where central banks are forced to abandon their mandate of price stability, the real value of interest- and inflation-sensitive assets and savings is crushed. How else can we explain the ECB waiting until inflation had already blown past 8 percent before lifting rates? ECB President Christine Lagarde's now-famous remark, "Inflation is largely transitory," was little more than a rhetorical shield, an attempt to avoid admitting that the inflation target had been abandoned.

Communication Problem

In many countries, laws require that advertisements for investment products include a warning such as: *"Investing involves risks. You may lose your capital."* Fair enough, regulators want to remind people that investing does not always lead to positive outcomes. But why are banks selling savings products almost never required to include a similar disclaimer? Something like *"Saving involves risks. You will lose purchasing power"* would be quite appropriate, especially if those same regulators were to look at my chart.

The problem, once again, is that information on savings and investment products almost never mentions real returns or real value. The focus tends to lie elsewhere. For example, in many countries, savers enjoy protection up to around €100,000 should their bank collapse, a feature that providers of savings products eagerly promote to attract deposits. Some savings platforms even go so far as to highlight the creditworthiness of the country where the provider is based, rather than that of the provider itself. Yet none of these "attractive" features offer any protection from the steady erosion of purchasing power. Inflation relentlessly devours real wealth, and it feasts most when rates are low.

Saving is no virtue in an environment of fiscal dominance, particularly when it is accompanied by financial repression, where capital cannot easily escape the grip of low rates and high inflation. The same is true for investing in bonds, a conclusion that runs directly counter to conventional wisdom and prevailing investment practice.

Race to the Bottom

The figures above expose a sobering reality: Two of the most widely accepted ways to build wealth, holding money in a savings account and investing in bonds, actually destroy value once inflation is taken into account. The interest earned on savings and bonds is nowhere near enough to offset the decline in purchasing power. This is an extraordinarily important message, given that trillions of euros, dollars, and yen sit idle in savings accounts or bond portfolios. All those trillions are now worth far less in real terms than at the time they were deposited or invested.

If you strip away interest entirely, the impact of inflation on purchasing power becomes even more devastating. The next chart shows the real value of 100,000 held in US dollars, euros, Japanese yen, and Chinese yuan since 2000, if you had simply placed the cash under your mattress, earning no interest at all.

The results are striking. 100,000 in US dollars from 2000 is worth only about half as much today in real terms, after deducting US inflation, a 50 percent loss of purchasing power. Over the past twenty-five years, the US dollar has lost half its value, simply because prices kept rising. Euros have lost roughly 45 percent, the yuan nearly 40 percent. Even in Japan, famous for its long stretches of deflation, the yen's purchasing power has declined by about 12 percent. It is a simple chart, but with an extremely powerful message: Over time, inflation systematically destroys the value of money.

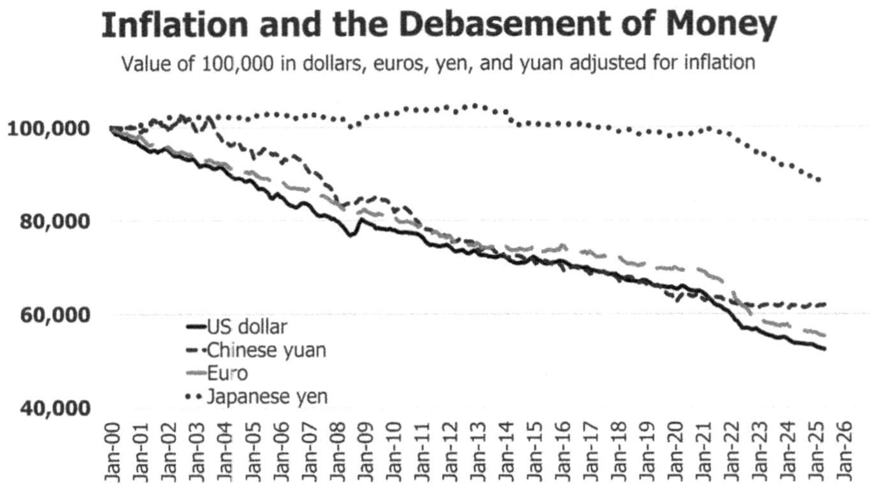

Source: The Great Rebalancing, Bureau of Labor Statistics, Eurostat, Ministry of Internal Affairs and Communications, National Bureau of Statistics of China

What most people fail to grasp is that this long-term erosion in the value of money is not a by-product; it is very much intentional. Every central bank on the planet shares a similar objective: To make sure, through monetary policy, that prices never stop rising. For most central banks, the official inflation target is set at 2 percent.

Central bankers, economists, and policymakers assume that this arbitrary percentage benefits the economy and the functioning of financial markets. The simplistic idea is that if prices rise steadily, people are encouraged to spend and invest. If prices stop rising, businesses and consumers might delay their purchases, which would harm the economy. Inflation is the lubricant of the economy, at least according to conventional theory.

But would you really cut back on spending if prices remained stable? I doubt it. Yet the notion that inflation is somehow *necessary* for the economy to thrive remains the cornerstone of every central bank's mandate. Their policies are explicitly designed to push inflation toward 2 percent, supposedly the sweet spot that keeps the economy humming. The irony is hard to miss: The official mission of central banks is to reduce the purchasing power of their own currency, even as they claim to protect it.

To emphasize just how paradoxical central bank policy really is, I often start my presentations with the definition the ECB itself created to describe its mission. It reads as follows:

"The ECB's primary objective is to maintain price stability, that is, to preserve the purchasing power of the euro. The ECB's Governing Council considers that price stability is best maintained by aiming for 2 percent inflation over the medium term."

Every time I read this, I fall into a mental trap. The ECB claims to "preserve the purchasing power of the euro." Not merely the euro itself, but its *purchasing power.* It is primarily the value the ECB seeks to protect, even though a single euro holds little intrinsic worth. To achieve this, the ECB must maintain price stability, which is achieved by "aiming for 2 percent inflation over the medium term." How does any of that make sense? I simply cannot reconcile those sentences. A steady rise in prices is the opposite of stability; it is devaluation with 100 percent certainty.

As discussed in Chapter 9, ten years of 2 percent inflation cut the real value of debt by about 18 percent. Obviously, the same logic applies to the euro. After a decade, it has lost nearly a fifth of its value. That is not stability by any reasonable definition. I read the ECB's objective as follows: The central bank will do everything in its power to make our euros lose 2 percent of their purchasing power every single year.

Gresham's Law

All central banks share this paradoxical goal: Under the banner of "price stability," they aim to devalue money by deliberately creating inflation. With nearly 180 currencies worldwide, each issued by its own central bank, the result is inevitable: a global race to the bottom. Which currency will be debased by its central bank the fastest?

That race triggers a defining reaction, an intuitive response to the ongoing destruction of the value of money, and one that decides which assets thrive and which don't. As the value of all 180 currencies declines, people instinctively search for the currency that loses the least. The real contest is not about who reaches the bottom first, but who stays furthest away from it.

Thomas Gresham, an English merchant and financier, understood this dynamic better than anyone. Gresham played a crucial role in restoring confidence in the English currency in the sixteenth century, following the disruptive devaluations under Henry VIII and later Edward VI. He advised Queen Elizabeth I to restore the silver content of English coins in order to stabilize the value of money. He observed that "bad money," coins with less silver, drove out "good money," the higher-silver coins, from circulation.

The idea that "bad money drives out good" later became known as Gresham's Law. The phrase itself was coined in 1858 by economist Henry Macleod, who formalized and popularized Gresham's three-century-old observation.

Gresham's Law states that when two forms of money circulate at the same nominal value (say, one euro) but with different intrinsic values, the more valuable one, referred to by Gresham as "good money," will eventually disappear from circulation. People hoard the good money, while spending the less valuable, or bad money.

As David McWilliams aptly explains in his book *Money: A Story of Humanity*, governments and central banks have spent centuries stretching the "value" of their monetary systems. One proven method was to reduce the intrinsic value of coins, for instance by lowering their silver content, allowing more coins to be minted from the same stock of silver and the economy to grow faster. This is currency debasement in its purest form.

McWilliams also demonstrates convincingly that whenever central banks and governments pushed debasement too far, the system collapsed. Confidence in the currency evaporated and financial markets broke down. Then the cycle started all over again, with policymakers hunting for more money, often ending with a different global reserve currency.

Gresham saw this centuries ago: Debased coins, the bad money, flooded the market, while the more valuable coins, good money, vanished. Which coin would you spend if you had one made of 100 percent silver and another of only 25 percent, yet both bought the same in the grocery store?

This brings us to our modern monetary system. Our coins contain no intrinsic value whatsoever. That can hardly be called "good money." Add to that the official policy of central banks to deliberately weaken their currencies through inflation, doesn't that make it bad money by definition?

Under fiscal dominance, the purchasing power and value of money come under even greater pressure. Central banks are forced to abandon their inflation targets in favor of debt sustainability. What happens next is decisive. When a currency lacks intrinsic value and inflation is high, trust in money itself begins to erode. The result is obvious: instability across economies and financial markets alike.

Just as importantly, fading trust drives people to seek out money that cannot be endlessly printed, diluted, or debased, money that protects against inflation. Fortunately, such money exists and has done so for thousands of years.

I'll give you one guess what that money is.

CHAPTER 14
Gold - The Standard

Introduction

The most well-known, trusted, widely accepted, and enduring form of value tied to scarcity is gold. Over the five thousand years that gold has served as money, hundreds, if not thousands, of books have been written about it. The risk here is obvious: that I merely repeat what has already been said countless times.

This book, however, builds toward a conclusion about how we should invest in a world where traditional economic laws no longer apply, and where large-scale rebalancing of existing investment portfolios is needed.

That is why I focus primarily on the role and characteristics of gold within the new financial order shaped by fiscal dominance and a shifting global balance of power. These are:

- Gold as the standard of the monetary system.
- Gold as an escape from the dollar.
- Gold as a shield against inflation and relentless money printing.

In the final part of this book, I will add to this list the many attractive qualities of gold as an investment within a well-diversified portfolio.

Gold as Money

For thousands of years, gold formed the foundation of the financial system and represented the intrinsic value of money. For a long time, the connection to intrinsic value was direct: People paid with gold (and silver) coins, meaning that value literally passed from hand to hand.

Today, gold sits in the vaults of central banks, originally intended to serve as reserves backing the currency in circulation. Gold is scarce; its supply grows only modestly each year. It is indestructible, it does not corrode, and it is virtually accepted everywhere on the planet.

Gold is universally recognized as valuable and, in many countries, can still function as a medium of exchange. But its most defining feature is, without question, trust. Few people doubt the intrinsic value of gold. That is precisely what makes it so uniquely suited to function as money.

Gold is money that does not rely on governments, central banks, or other institutions to enforce or guarantee its value.

This stands in stark contrast to fiat money. The term "fiat" signifies that its value is not derived from intrinsic value but from decree. Fiat money has value only because governments and central banks declare it does and we trust the issuer and therefore accept it as a means of payment. In today's digital age, fiat money can be created at the push of a button, increasingly by central banks compelled to finance government debt.

The breakthrough of gold and silver as monetary standards came around 600 BC, when King Croesus of Lydia minted the first coins, a blend of gold and silver. This innovation simplified trade, a field in which the Lydians already excelled. Centuries later, China combined gold and silver with copper coinage, while early experiments with paper money failed because they lacked the trust that real metal inspired.

Gold's eventual rise as the sole standard was, at first, partly a matter of chance, unexpectedly aided by a famous historical figure:

Sir Isaac Newton. Better known for his three laws of motion, Newton also served as master of the Royal Mint. In 1717, he inadvertently fixed the exchange rate between gold and silver in a way that undervalued silver relative to gold. As a result, silver coins were worth less in everyday trade than the silver they contained. And so Gresham's Law took hold, meaning the silver coins vanished from circulation.

A century later, gold's superiority was confirmed anyway. In 1816, the influential British economist David Ricardo argued for a gold-only standard, explaining that a "bimetallic" system based on both gold and silver was inherently unstable. Once again, Gresham's Law was the culprit. Because gold and silver prices fluctuated, even a perfectly fixed exchange rate meant one metal would inevitably vanish from circulation as prices shifted.

Ricardo viewed gold as superior because of its greater scarcity, higher value per unit, and more stable supply, which offered better protection against inflation. He proposed linking banknotes exclusively to gold to create a reliable and robust monetary system. His argument was adopted through the Coinage Act of 1816, which formally introduced the gold standard in Britain.

The best-known example of gold serving as the monetary standard is, of course, Bretton Woods. In 1944, as World War II was drawing to a close, delegates from forty-four countries gathered in the small American town of Bretton Woods, New Hampshire, to design a new monetary order, with none other than John Maynard Keynes among its chief architects. The goal was to restore global stability to the monetary system after years of war and depression.

The result was simple though, in hindsight deeply flawed. The dollar was crowned the world's reserve currency, the linchpin of the international financial system, and pegged to gold at $35 per troy ounce. Other currencies were then pegged to the dollar, effectively creating a global gold standard.

This brief history shows that of the more than five thousand years in which gold has served as money and a medium of exchange, it has acted as the monetary standard for at least half that time. Even after the establishment of the first central bank, Sweden's Riksbank in 1668, gold, sometimes alongside silver or copper, remained the backbone of the global financial system.

Breaking the Standard

Yet throughout history, the gold standard has collapsed more than once, at times in a spectacular way. From the very start, Bretton Woods rested on fragile foundations. History soon repeated itself: Driven by an insatiable appetite for growth, global demand for money soared. As issuer of the world's reserve currency, the United States was forced to print ever more dollars to meet that demand, placing an unsustainable strain on its gold reserves.

As more dollars entered circulation and the dollar was directly tied to the gold price, potential claims on US gold reserves increased. Because each dollar was convertible into gold at the fixed rate of $35 per ounce, foreign governments began to wonder how much gold actually backed the growing mountain of dollars.

This contradiction, that the issuer of the world's reserve currency must provide ample liquidity while simultaneously undermining confidence in that same currency, later became known as the Triffin Dilemma, after economist Robert Triffin.

By 1961, cracks in the Bretton Woods system were becoming visible. Faith in the dollar wavered under the weight of huge US budget deficits and the escalating Vietnam War. Foreign central banks started exchanging their dollars for gold, well aware that an expanding supply of dollars was losing value against the scarce stock of gold.

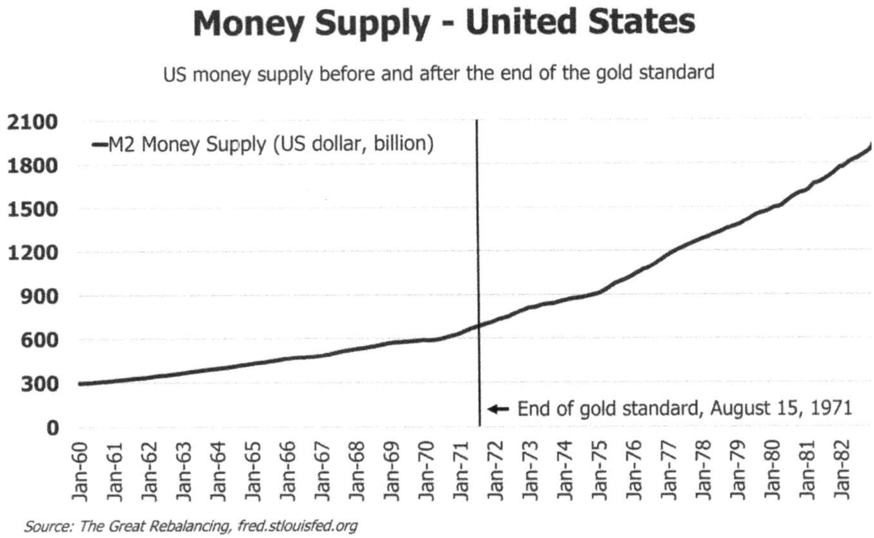

By the late 1960s, the situation had become untenable. Central banks demanded back their gold on a massive scale. France, which got back some of its gold throughout the decade, supposedly even dispatched a naval vessel to New York to collect its gold, a dramatic symbol of waning trust.

US gold reserves plummeted from 20,000 metric tons in 1950 to just 8,500 metric tons by 1971. On August 15, 1971, President Nixon ended the convertibility of the dollar into gold. In a televised address, he suspended the "gold window," severing the last link between the dollar and physical gold.

Most readers will have some idea of what caused the end of Bretton Woods; Nixon's televised speech still surfaces on social media from time to time. Fewer people realize that the collapse of the gold standard marked the beginning of an era of unparalleled debt creation and accumulation.

Freed from the unsustainable decline in gold reserves, the United States began printing unlimited dollars. Fiat money took over the financial and monetary system. And just as Gresham's Law would predict, gold vanished from circulation. Fiat transformed the system.

After 1971, the "value" of money rested solely on trust and no longer on intrinsic value.

To underscore this pivotal moment in monetary history, the chart on the previous page shows the US money supply from 1959 to 1983. It takes little imagination to see where Nixon pulled the plug on gold. After 1971, the US money supply shot up faster than ever before.

Exter's Pyramid

One of the most intuitive ways to understand how a gold standard operates is by looking at John Exter's "Inverted Pyramid." Exter, an economist at the Federal Reserve and later the founding governor of the Central Bank of Sri Lanka, created the concept of the pyramid to illustrate the hierarchy of financial assets. In its simplest form, the inverted pyramid looks like this:

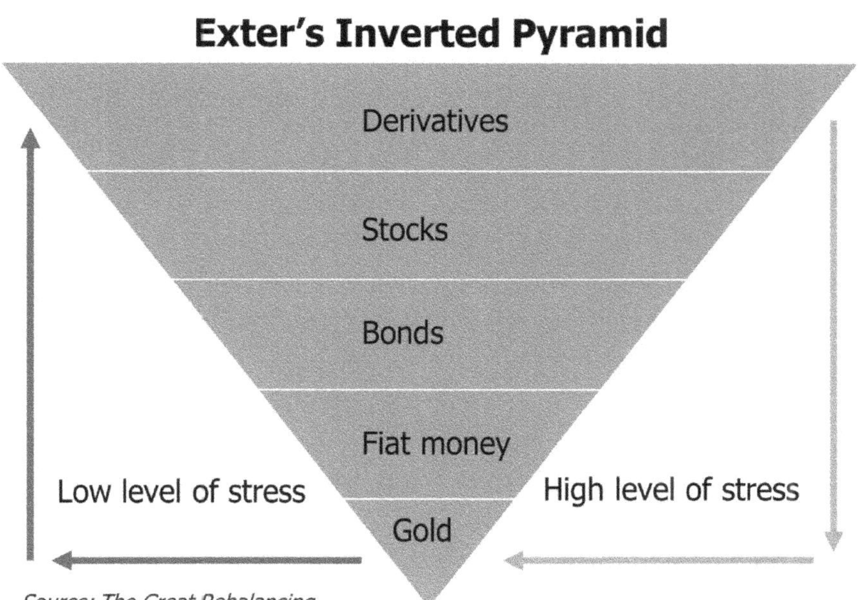

Source: The Great Rebalancing

At the top of the pyramid, and therefore at the bottom of the figure, sits gold, serving as the anchor of the financial system. Gold holds this position because it possesses intrinsic value, is indestructible, carries no counterparty risk, and is uniquely scarce. Gold does not merely rely on trust; it commands it.

Above gold sits fiat money. In Exter's view, fiat money is not an asset, but a liability, or an "I owe you" (IOU). This money has value only as long as people trust that the issuing government will honor its promise that the currency will be accepted and that its purchasing power will hold. Fiat money is, at its core, a social contract built on trust. That becomes deeply problematic when inflation breaks that promise and purchasing power declines: a recipe for trouble.

Next come bonds, loans whose creditworthiness depends on the issuer. Above bonds are equities, ownership stakes promising future dividends and profits, provided the company survives. Stocks rank below bonds in the hierarchy because, when companies fail, shareholders are paid only after bondholders have been compensated, if anything remains.

At the very bottom of the pyramid, hence at the top of the figure, are derivatives, which are financial contracts whose value depends on the price of something else, such as a stock, bond, interest rate, or commodity. Derivatives are often described as the grease of financial markets, but it's worth remembering that they exist solely by virtue of trust and liquidity. Not least because derivatives are often accompanied by leverage, borrowing to magnify potential gains or losses. This means that not all derivatives are necessarily backed by the underlying asset on which they are issued. The lack of intrinsic backing relegates them to the bottom tier of Exter's inverted pyramid.

Exter developed the idea of an inverted pyramid to show what happens when financial markets come under stress. The lower you move within the pyramid (the higher up in the chart), the more sensitive the assets to uncertainty and volatility, and the more critical liquidity, trust, and counterparty risk become. In times of calm, capital flows from low to high in the diagram, from gold toward more speculative assets. But when confidence cracks and fear takes over, these flows reverse almost instantly.

Exter's pyramid thus offers a visual explanation of gold's timeless role as the ultimate safe haven. When panic strikes, capital rushes back to gold, explaining why it so often outperforms when economies falter, geopolitical tensions flare, or stock markets become turbulent.

Turning the System Upside Down

Exter conceived his pyramid with a single question in mind: What happens when stress hits the system? Consequently, attention is usually focused on the lower layers of the pyramid, where assets are most exposed to uncertainty. Reports from institutions such as the BIS and the IMF on systemic risk tend to concentrate on the bottom part of the pyramid as well, mapping where financial institutions' debt sits, how much leverage exists, and how these derivatives connect banks to one another. History has repeatedly shown that it is often this deep interconnection among banks and financial firms that ignites crises.

Yet this is no reason to neglect the upper portion of the pyramid, the bottom in the chart. What happens when the foundation of the system, gold, rises in value? Or when that foundation broadens and strengthens? Such a shift automatically stabilizes the current financial structure. There would still be mountains of money, debt, and derivatives piled on top, but the pyramid as a whole would stand firmer.

That is, to a large extent, the line of reasoning I follow: It does not have to take an implosion at the top of the inverted structure to reset the system and force a new equilibrium. A stronger foundation can emerge when policymakers, governments, corporations, and individuals rediscover and embrace gold's role as the true standard.

Scarcity, Visualized

Because gold is a physical asset, the foundation of our financial system can be visualized in a powerful way. All above-ground gold, that is, gold mined throughout history, is estimated at around 220,000 metric tons. It sounds like a lot, until you start stacking it. Combine it all into one solid block, and you get a cube measuring roughly 22 by 22 by 22 meters.

For perspective: that cube would occupy less than 2 percent of the cargo capacity of the world's largest container ships. For comparison, you could easily fit that cube on Wimbledon's Centre Court without anyone losing their seat. Admittedly, the roof would have to remain open, since it hangs only 16 meters above the court.

A cube of 22 meters per side, according to Exter's pyramid, represents the very foundation of the global financial system. Not debt, not paper, not ones and zeros in a computer, but a tangible, scarce asset. It is a striking illustration of just how extraordinarily scarce gold truly is.

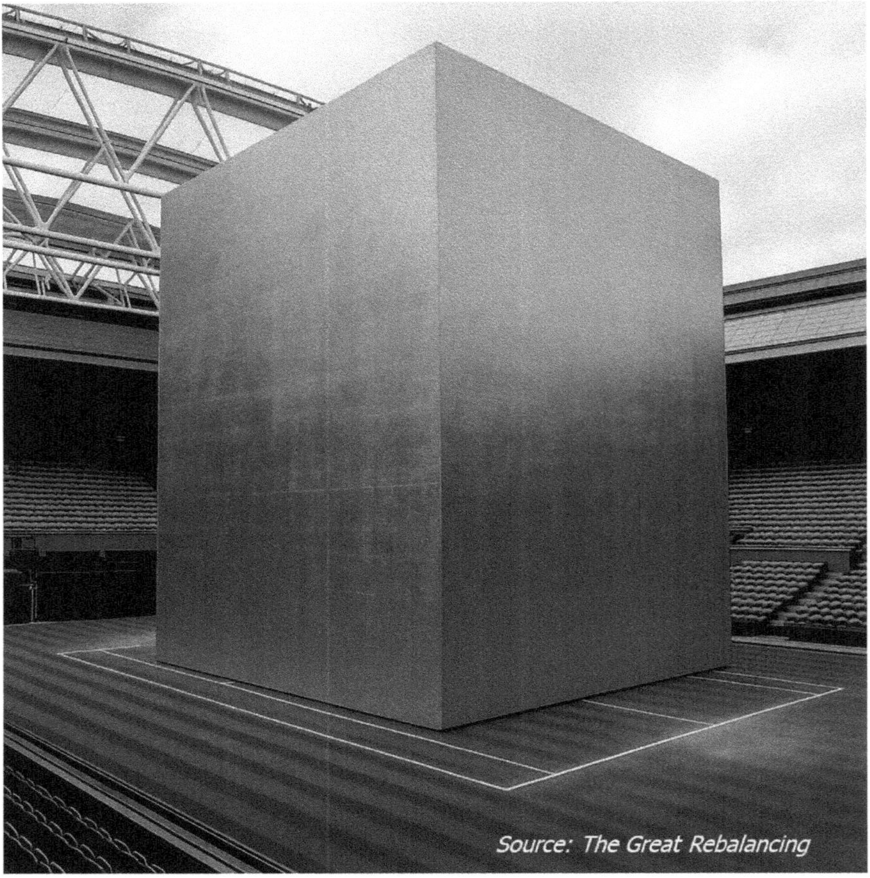

Source: The Great Rebalancing

That cube consists solely of physical gold. Not "paper gold" or synthetic gold products such as derivatives. The distinction is pivotal. Many investors who believe they own gold in fact hold only a derivative claim to future delivery. But paper gold, like futures contracts, is not gold. These instruments belong at the bottom of Exter's inverted pyramid, alongside other derivatives.

When panic grips the markets and capital floods upward through the pyramid (downward in the figure), the risk grows that the promise of gold ownership cannot be fulfilled. You cannot build a financial system on paper gold. It is not intrinsically scarce.

Escaping the Dollar

Many traditional investors I speak with see the notion of gold as the foundation, and ultimate store of value, of our monetary system as little more than a theoretical curiosity. Often, they dismiss it as something relevant only to a bygone era, when coins contained actual gold.

To be fair, I used to think that way myself. I understood gold as a scarce asset and a store of value, yet I never fully grasped its role within a system where every other form of money is inherently worthless. Nor its crucial role within a debt-driven system where ever more (worthless) fiat money is printed to finance soaring government debt.

But that is not the whole story. With geopolitical tensions intensifying and an expanding coalition of nations seeking to escape the grip of dollar hegemony, I believe gold is now more relevant than at any time since 1971, when President Nixon ended the gold standard. To understand gold's renewed role in the attempts of governments to break free from US dollar dominance, we must first return to the origins of the dollar itself.

As mentioned in Chapter 4, Alexander Hamilton, in the late eighteenth century, advised President George Washington, the first president of the United States, to link the fledgling US dollar, albeit indirectly, to the Spanish silver dollar. This connection gave the new currency, lacking both history and international trust, a solid foundation and the young nation economic stability.

The Spanish coin, known as the *piece of eight*, was made of silver, worth eight reales, and could easily be divided into smaller pieces. A practical feature, especially for Spain, whose empire revolved around international trade. For Hamilton, what mattered most was that the Spanish dollar was then so dominant that it effectively functioned as the world's reserve currency. His vision, enshrined in the Coinage Act of 1792, instantly tied the dollar to stability, trust, and intrinsic value, precisely what the young American currency was missing.

"A Small Group of Countries"

In 2024, the official blog of the Federal Reserve Bank of New York, *Liberty Street Economics*, published a post that perfectly illustrates how Western economies, and their central bankers, continue to underestimate the determination of certain nations to challenge US dollar hegemony.

The post concluded that the declining role of the US dollar as the world's reserve currency was being driven by, and I quote, "a small group of countries." The authors further noted that it was the central banks of this very group of nations that had been aggressively purchasing gold and adding it to their reserves, at the expense of the dollar.

You might think: "So, what?" But that reaction may quickly fade once you discover which nations belong to this so-called "small group." The group consists of China, India, Russia, and Turkey. The authors used the actual number of countries involved, the mere count, as justification to claim that the dollar's reserve status remains secure.

That conclusion is, to put it mildly, bewildering. Together, these four countries account for nearly 40 percent of the global population, around 25 percent of world GDP, and close to 20 percent of global trade. How can anyone argue that the dollar's position as the global reserve currency is safe when such a vast share of the world is clearly moving in another direction? Moreover, China's influence is now felt across Asia and extends well beyond.

The chart below from the World Gold Council reveals the largest official net gold purchases by central banks in 2024. Is it really a coincidence that three of the four nations in that supposedly "small group" also rank among the top four gold buyers? All evidence points to the same conclusion: China, India, Russia, and Turkey are actively working to loosen the dollar's grip by heavily expanding their gold reserves.

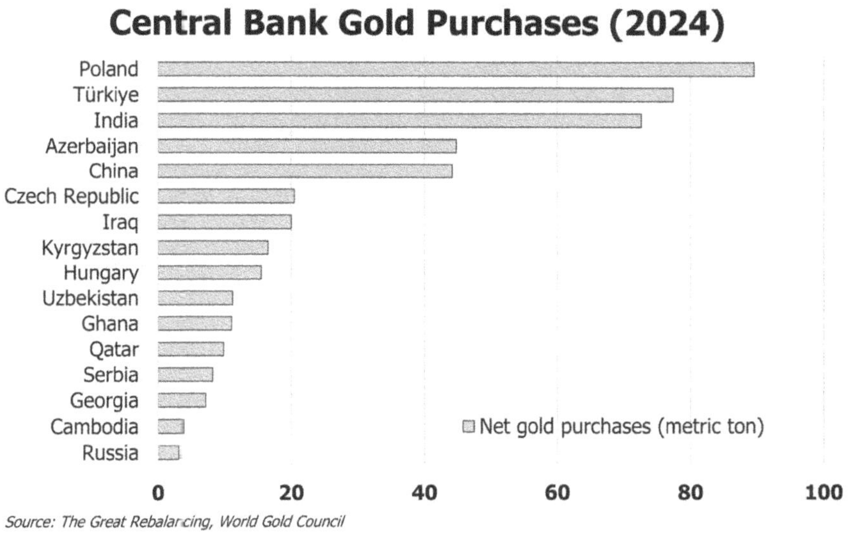

These nations, however, share a fundamental problem: hardly anyone wants their currencies. China manages to get by with the yuan within Asia to some degree, and part of its trade, such as oil imports from Saudi Arabia, is settled in China's currency.

Still, only a small fraction of global trade is invoiced in yuan, with estimates ranging from 4 percent to nearly 10 percent. The yuan's share of global foreign exchange reserves is even smaller: barely 2 percent, according to the IMF.

Yet China's ambition is unmistakable. Beijing makes sure that the trade settled in yuan isn't quietly converted back into dollars. Instead, those trade proceeds go straight into gold. Former Goldman Sachs commodities chief Jeff Currie has dubbed this approach the "gold recycling theory." It represents a departure from the traditional "dollar recycling theory," in which trade surpluses in local currencies are funneled back into US dollars. Now, China's trade surpluses are being redirected from dollars into gold.

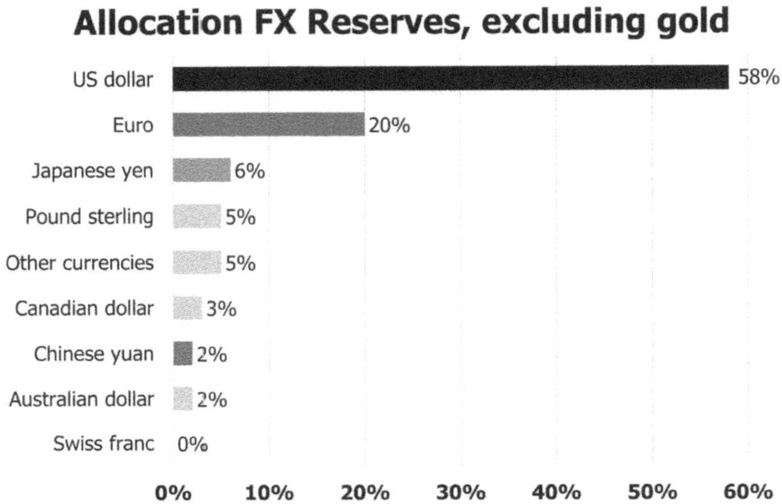

Source: The Great Rebalancing, IMF

For the other three countries, their currencies barely register on the international stage. Beyond their borders, few want to be paid in Indian rupees, Russian rubles, or Turkish liras, let alone hold them as reserves. What remains for China and these countries is to follow the strategy Alexander Hamilton pioneered more than three centuries ago: to instill stability, trust, and value in their currencies by anchoring them to something of real value, namely gold. Only then might they persuade others to accept their money on a broader scale.

The role of gold as the foundation beneath fiat money in a rapidly shifting global economic and political order is very much alive and growing. This is evident from the continuing gold accumulation by central banks, particularly in emerging economies. Importantly, their demand for gold is largely insensitive to price. China does not care how high the gold price climbs; expanding its reserves remains the only long-term path to reducing dependence on the dollar. Or, as economists would put it, the gold demand of central banks seeking to end dollar hegemony is price inelastic.

Add to this the fact that gold accounts for less than 15 percent of China's vast foreign exchange reserves, and you know exactly what China will continue doing in the years ahead.

Gold as a Shield Against Inflation

Governments and central banks striving to liberate themselves from the US dollar are creating a relentless, price-insensitive source of demand for gold. Central banks, however, are not the only ones generating structural demand for gold. Investors looking to protect their wealth from the erosive effects of inflation would do well to include gold in their portfolios.

In a world of fiscal dominance, where central banks lose their independence, and of financial repression, where governments and central banks cooperate to sustain massive debt loads, inflation risks rise sharply. As the previous chapter demonstrated, the consequences for real returns on savings and bonds are devastating.

But just how effective is gold as a hedge against inflation? The conventional approach, used in most academic and market research, is to compare inflation data with changes in the gold price. Inflation is typically measured by the consumer price index (CPI).

The next chart shows the relationship between US inflation (CPI) and changes in the gold price in US dollars, expressed as the average correlation since 1970. Two correlation figures are presented. On the left is the relationship between gold and the already reported inflation, in this case, the average inflation rate over the past twelve months. Yet, what is often overlooked is that investors primarily anticipate what lies ahead. Reported inflation numbers are basically old news. It is expectations about future inflation that drive investors to buy or sell gold.

That is why the right-hand side of the chart shows the correlation between changes in the gold price and inflation in the twelve months ahead; it's as if investors could peer into a crystal ball, telling them exactly what inflation will be in the coming twelve months.

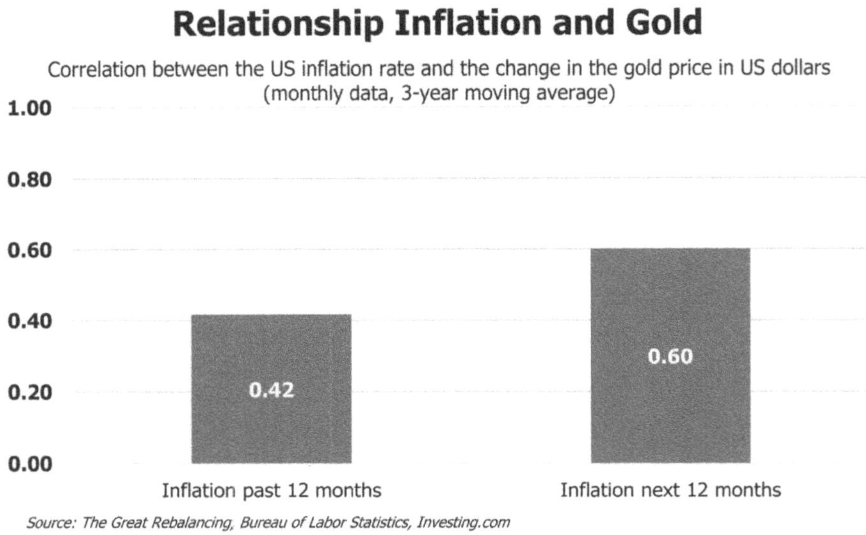

Since 1970, the average correlation between gold and past twelve-month inflation has been 0.42. The correlation with inflation over the following twelve months is higher, at 0.60. Economists and statisticians would interpret this as solid evidence that gold is a reliable inflation hedge. Especially because the gold price shows a stronger relationship with inflation that is yet to come. Higher expected inflation tends to go hand in hand with rising gold prices.

Yet this evidence of gold as an inflation hedge should be interpreted with some caution. The next chart shows how this correlation has behaved since 1970. The lines plot gold's correlation with past (gray) and future (black) twelve-month inflation. The striking takeaway is their volatility. The correlations between gold prices and past and future inflation swing widely. Often the relationship is positive, gold and inflation move in the same direction, but it frequently turns negative as well, with gold moving opposite to inflation. In that case, the hedge breaks down when inflation climbs and gold drops, not exactly what investors expect from gold representing inflation protection.

Relationship Inflation and Gold

Correlation between the US inflation rate and the change in the gold price in US dollars

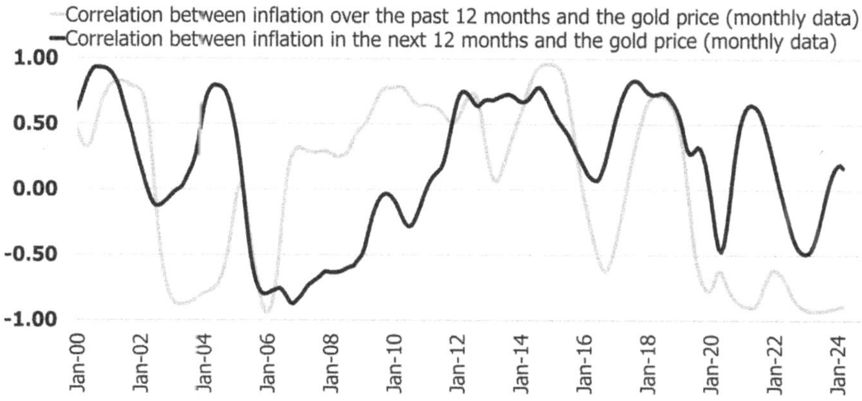

Source: The Great Rebalancing, Bureau of Labor Statistics, Investing.com

However, my broader point is this: Comparing gold prices to official inflation metrics, the CPI, makes less sense than it appears. What do these inflation figures actually measure? The CPI is a subjective and ever-shifting basket of goods and services, supposedly representing what the "average consumer" buys. But the average consumer does not exist. In addition, the basket is constantly being adjusted. Where food for decades dominated the CPI index, today energy, housing, and healthcare carry much greater weight. Even with sophisticated statistical adjustments, comparability of inflation data over time remains limited.

Moreover, reported inflation data are revised multiple times. First comes a preliminary estimate, followed by adjustments as new information becomes available, and finally a "definitive" figure. Weeks, or even months, may pass between the first and final inflation release. Yet investors react almost exclusively to the first number, or, more precisely, to the surprise the first inflation estimate delivers. When inflation prints far above expectations, fears of structural inflation surge and demand for gold jumps. In many cases, the precise number matters less than the magnitude of the surprise.

Inflating

Looking at the historical meaning of inflation quickly reveals why a subjective price index is not the best variable to begin with. The word inflation derives from the Latin *inflatio*, meaning "swelling" or "blowing." From the eighteenth century onward, the term was primarily used in an economic context to describe the growth of the money supply. Thus, inflation originally referred to the expansion of money itself. Only later did it become synonymous with rising prices, even though these are merely a symptom of the deeper cause: money creation.

One of the first to articulate the link between money growth and inflation was the Scottish philosopher and economist David Hume. In his 1752 essay "Of Money," he described how an expanding money supply ultimately raised prices without generating lasting economic growth. A century later, American economist Francis A. Walker helped popularize the term further. In his 1878 book *Money* (economists, after all, love writing about money), he described how "greenbacks," paper money issued during the American Civil War without any value backing it, drove inflation by circulating in abundance. Greenbacks were, once again, bad money.

Gold and Money Supply

With the original meaning of inflation in mind, it is worth asking whether gold provides protection against excessive money creation. Ideally, that question should be asked on a global scale, because the twin forces of demographic aging and fiscal dominance are global phenomena. And while the extreme money printing in the United States grabs most of the headlines, other nations have gone even further.

Just look at China's money supply on the next page. When measured in US dollars, its money supply is now more than twice that of the United States, even though the Chinese economy is roughly 40 percent smaller. If you still doubt that China, with its rapidly aging population, must buy its growth, the following chart should dispel that illusion.

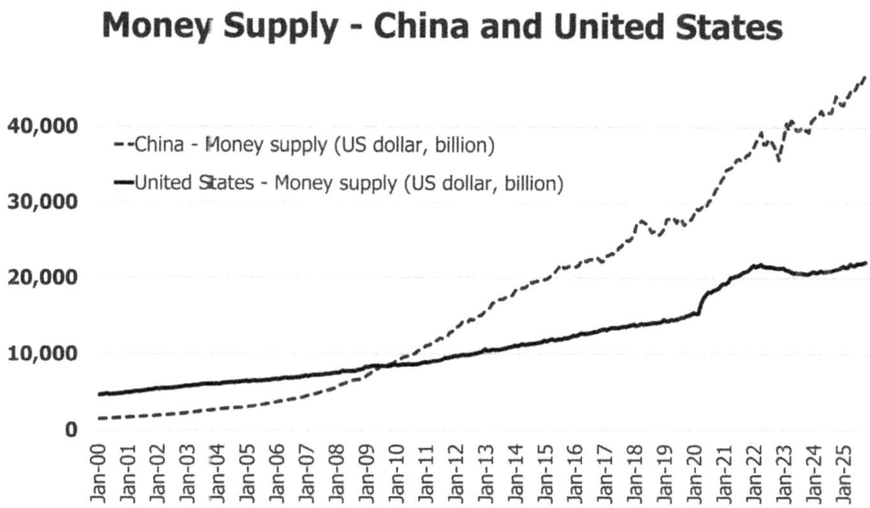

Source: The Great Rebalancing, fred.stlouisfed.org, Centrale Bank van de Volksrepubliek China

The chart on the next page shows the correlation between changes in global money supply growth and the price of gold. The data series are shorter due to limited availability, but the analysis is comparable to that for inflation. Just like with inflation (CPI), the relationship between gold and past twelve-month money supply growth (gray line) is significantly positive (0.52), but also volatile and unstable. The relationship with future money supply growth (black line), however, tells a very different story. Since 2012, that correlation has been consistently positive, relatively stable, and trending toward +1. At that level, the relationship between money supply and gold becomes perfect: The faster the money supply expands, the more often gold rises.

This exceptionally strong relationship is precisely what you would expect in an era of growing fiscal dominance. Central banks are running the printing presses en masse to finance structural budget deficits, producing higher inflation as a direct consequence. It is no coincidence that this relationship between money supply and gold has become almost perfect since the COVID pandemic, when public debt exploded worldwide.

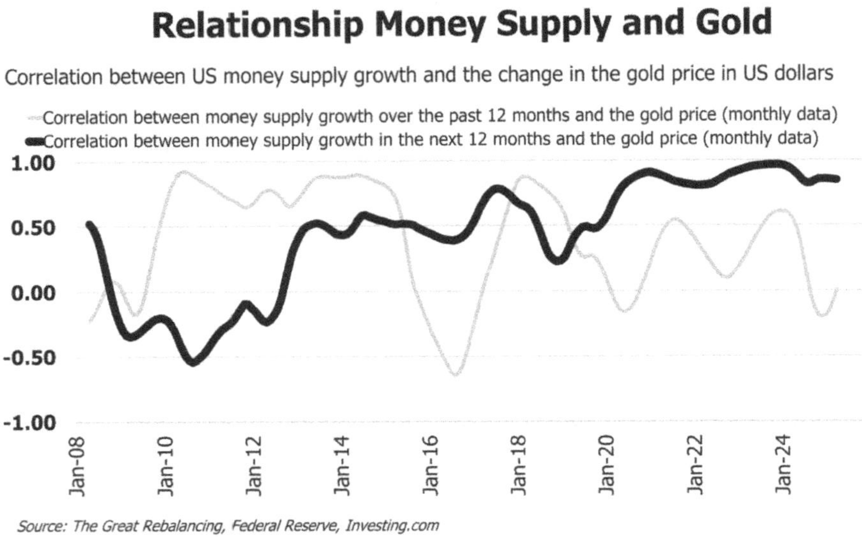

Gold Versus Fiat

Calculating correlations is a well-established way to measure the relationship between two variables. Nevertheless, it remains a rather abstract exercise. A correlation does not tell you how much gold rises when inflation or money supply growth accelerates. It gives the direction of the relationship, not the magnitude, therefore not whether your purchasing power is preserved.

To make gold's protective power more tangible, I calculate the real value of a gold investment in the same way as I did for bonds, savings, and money (cash) in the previous chapter. To be specific: What has happened to the real value of a €100,000 investment in gold since 2000? By expressing gold's real value in euros, dollars, yen, and yuan, we can directly compare it with fiat money. Keep in mind that the previous chapter already showed that fiat currencies lost up to 50 percent (the US dollar) of their purchasing power over the past 25 years.

What follows is a particularly impressive chart (see next page). The real performance of gold looks nothing like that of savings or bonds. For savers, bondholders, and traditional 60/40 investors, the chart must be painful, both to the eye and to the wallet. The gain in purchasing power from holding gold rather than fiat money is nothing short of spectacular.

Depending on the currency, gold would have multiplied your purchasing power between fivefold (eurozone) and sixteenfold (Japan). A €100,000 gold investment in 2000 would today be worth over €1,000,000, and, more importantly, nearly €600,000 after adjusting for inflation. For the other currencies, the gains are even more impressive.

Notice that gold's surge in purchasing power relative to fiat occurred right after major crises (2008, 2020). Those were the moments when fiscal dominance fully overtook the financial system and central bank policy, as governments issued massive amounts of debt to contain the crisis.

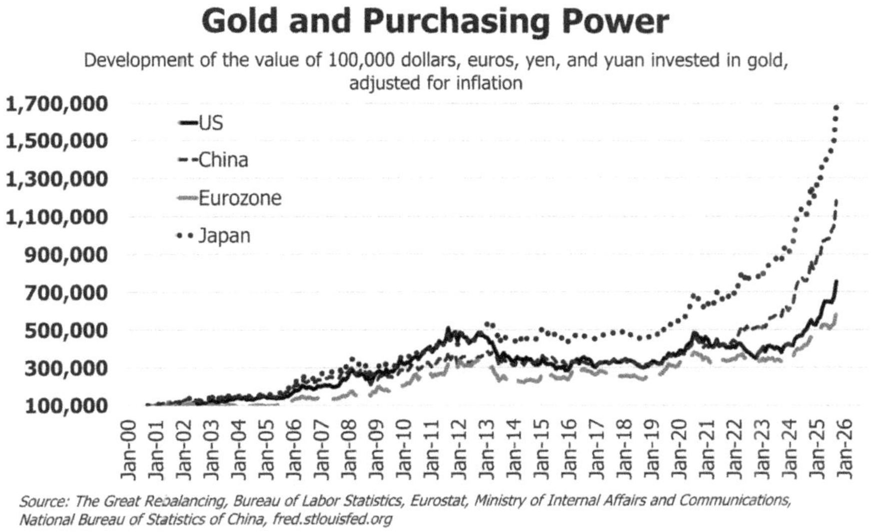

It is also no coincidence that gold's purchasing power appreciated most against the yen and the yuan. In Japan, the Bank of Japan implemented yield curve control for eight straight years and purchased nearly half of the country's sovereign bonds to keep rates artificially low, crushing the yen in the process. In China, we saw that the money supply exploded after the global financial crisis as policymakers chased increasingly unrealistic growth targets.

A longer historical perspective tells the same story, though sometimes less dramatically. Since the collapse of the gold standard in 1971, gold has preserved or increased purchasing power in almost every period. The more recent the data, the sharper gold's gains, perfectly mirroring aging populations, ballooning debt, and entrenched fiscal dominance.The relationship between gold and money creation is undeniable.

Back to the Standard

For five thousand years, gold has been the standard providing stability and confidence to the financial system through its scarcity and intrinsic value. As governments and central banks print unlimited amounts of fiat currency to sustain the debt-fueled growth model, gold offers a proven and remarkably robust hedge against inflation.

For a growing number of countries seeking to break free from the US dollar, gold is (re)emerging as the standard. The monumental gold purchases of central banks in China, India, Russia, and Turkey, nations whose currencies few are willing to hold, signal a transition toward a new world order where dollar dominance is no longer a given.

For investors, the conclusion is both simple and sobering. Those who continue to rely on savings and bonds in a world of permanent monetary expansion lose twice: first, their returns, then their purchasing power. That reality is now the catalyst for a global search for assets that *do* provide wealth protection, and for a great rebalancing of investment portfolios around the globe. And gold unquestionably belongs in those portfolios.

But it is not the only scarce asset that deserves a place in the portfolios of the future.

CHAPTER 15
Digital Gold

Introduction

Unfortunately, the phrase "digital gold" has become so overused to describe Bitcoin that it has lost much of its force. Today, digital gold is usually shorthand for the familiar list of technological advantages that Bitcoin enthusiasts recite endlessly: portability, divisibility, accessibility, durability, and verifiability.

Don't get me wrong, those qualities are real, but they fail to capture the essence of what digital gold truly means. Bitcoin has the potential to embody digitally stored value, comparable to the analog role gold has long played in the financial system: value that strengthens the upper layer of Exter's inverted pyramid, making the system more stable as a whole. In that capacity, bitcoin serves as a form of protection against the unrestrained creation of fiat money.

I deliberately speak of Bitcoin's "potential." While Bitcoin is certainly moving in the right direction, it has yet to fulfill that fundamental role as the monetary system's anchor, like gold has done for thousands of years. In my view, this distinction should be reflected in any next-generation, resilient, future-proof investment portfolio.

The Right Bitcoin Framework

Like gold, Bitcoin poses a tempting trap: You could easily fill an entire book with it. It is new, a rare event in itself, the birth of a truly new asset class. It is highly volatile, unpredictable, and surrounded by a near-religious community of believers. On top of that, Bitcoin combines its potential role as an additional pillar beneath the financial system with a revolutionary technology: blockchain.

Put simply, blockchain is a decentralized digital ledger, a public log that registers and stores all transactions. These transactions are not recorded by one central authority but by thousands of computers around the world, the nodes. Each of these nodes cryptographically verifies new transactions before adding them to an irreversible chain of data. If those terms don't immediately paint a clear picture, that's fine; each of these features will be explored later in this chapter.

Bitcoin was built to replace trust in central banks and governments with trust in technology. This distinction is crucial, yet often misunderstood. Many people describe Bitcoin as a manifestation of mistrust, but that misses the point. Traditional monetary systems rely on trust in centralized institutions, such as banks and governments. Bitcoin offers an alternative where trust is shifted to a decentralized, digital network.

This network has no leader, board, or owner that people must trust. Trust rests instead on mathematics, technology, and transparency. When the network functions properly, this coded trust can be stronger than the institutional trust enforced by entities with a monopoly on money creation. That should not be surprising, given earlier chapters showed how governments and central banks repeatedly break their promises about money, including preserving its purchasing power.

The essence of blockchain technology is to ensure that transactions, recorded in "blocks" (hence the name blockchain), are permanent, transparent, verifiable, and, perhaps most importantly, irreversible. Computers compete in a kind of giant digital lottery, trying to guess ultra-large numbers in order to add new blocks to the chain, a process known as proof-of-work. As these guesses grow harder and require more computing power, and as more computers join, the Bitcoin network becomes progressively stronger and more secure.

Obviously, these computers do not participate for free. Whoever succeeds in winning the lottery is rewarded with newly minted bitcoin, thereby increasing the total number of bitcoin in circulation. Hence the term proof-of-work: The computational effort must come first; only then is the reward granted. This mechanism creates a continuous incentive to strengthen and secure the network. Every 210,000 blocks, roughly every four years, the reward is cut in half. This process, called the halving, gradually slows the issuance of new bitcoin, embedding scarcity directly into the system's design.

These are the basics, but the story goes much deeper. Bitcoin's blockchain is, to a certain extent, programmable, allowing for additional applications. Examples include smart contracts (agreements that automatically execute when specific conditions are met) and NFTs (non-fungible tokens), which serve as unique digital collectibles or proofs of ownership. On top of the main Bitcoin chain, second-layer solutions such as the Lightning Network are being developed to enable faster and cheaper transactions.

This versatility allows Bitcoin to be analyzed through many lenses: as money, as infrastructure, as a network, as technology, and as a scarce asset. Many of these perspectives are too technical and complex to explore fully in this chapter. Moreover, I am not technically equipped enough to analyze these aspects in depth or with full precision. This is not a trivial disclaimer, as the Bitcoin community is notoriously sensitive about how Bitcoin is portrayed. Some "Bitcoin maximalists" will no doubt subject my explanation to their rigid and often uncompromising scrutiny. As an investor, I can't help but look at that dynamic with a mix of curiosity and amusement.

Within the scope of this book, however, what matters most is Bitcoin's potential impact on the soundness of the traditional financial system, comparable to the historical role of gold. So, to stay aligned with the central theme of this book, the appeal of scarce assets in a world dominated by debt, low interest rates, and persistent inflation, I will focus on three core questions:

- Will Bitcoin also become a standard?
- Does Bitcoin protect against fiscal dominance?
- How far has Bitcoin come?

That last question should not be underestimated. Investing is ultimately about weighing opportunity against risk. Nothing is ever certain, not even Bitcoin's future. Although my investment fund holds a deliberate and thoughtful position in bitcoin, uncertainty, volatility, and diversification must always remain center to any portfolio. A portfolio should therefore never consist solely of bitcoin or any single scarce asset. Absolute certainty simply does not exist.

A Brief History

Before addressing those three questions, I will first provide a brief history of Bitcoin. To many, Bitcoin seems like a sudden "invention" from 2008, born out of the global financial crisis. But that is only part of the story. Bitcoin's roots trace back to the 1970s, when cryptographers, people devoted to securing and encrypting information, dreamed of digital money that could ensure privacy and freedom beyond central control. Carried by the cypherpunk movement, a group of activists who sought to protect autonomy and privacy through cryptography, Bitcoin was no accident. It was the culmination of decades of innovation.

In the 1970s, David Chaum, an American cryptographer, developed a form of digital money. His eCash, launched in 1983, used encryption to enable anonymous payments by turning data into unreadable code that could only be unlocked with the correct key. Chaum's emphasis on privacy profoundly influenced later generations of digital money systems, including Bitcoin, and underscored the importance of decentralization, the deliberate distribution of control and data across multiple participants.

The 1990s saw the cypherpunk movement gain real momentum, inspiring new approaches to and solutions for digital money. E-gold came in 1996, a gold-backed payment system developed by Douglas Jackson. Two years later, Wei Dai proposed b-money, a decentralized ledger where all transactions were visible across a network of computers. That same year, 1998, Nick Szabo introduced Bit Gold, later refined in 2005, which incorporated both scarcity and proof-of-work. Notice that gold has already been mentioned several times. These early crypto pioneers understood all too well that gold provided a valid foundation on which to build a new monetary system.

In 1997, Adam Back created Hashcash, which used proof-of-work to combat email spam. It required users to spend computing power to create a kind of digital stamp before sending an email, which made mass spamming expensive, and therefore impractical.

Finally, Hal Finney's RPOW (Reusable Proof of Work), introduced in 2004, allowed users to create digital tokens by solving cryptographic puzzles, a direct precursor to Bitcoin's proof-of-work system. Fittingly enough, Finney became the recipient of the very first Bitcoin transaction in 2009.

The Bitcoin Whitepaper

In 2008, as the global financial system teetered on the brink of collapse and governments and central banks intervened on a massive scale to save it, someone, or a group of people, under the pseudonym Satoshi Nakamoto, published the Bitcoin whitepaper. To this day, the true identity of Satoshi Nakamoto remains a mystery. What we do know is that the Bitcoin whitepaper presented a radical alternative to the existing monetary order.

The paper outlines a decentralized system of digital money that operates without banks or intermediaries. It allows individuals to transfer payments directly to one another via the blockchain, a public, immutable digital ledger. The system's integrity is secured by proof-of-work, the collective computing power that prevents transactions from being forged or the same money from being double-spent. There exists no central authority to control, censor, or manipulate the network. Anyone with a computer can join or leave at will.

This brief summary of Satoshi Nakamoto's alternative monetary system, ending with "his" disappearance from view in 2011, demonstrates again that Bitcoin did not appear out of thin air. It was a direct response to the fragility of the existing system and the central power governments and banks have within it. The long chain of earlier innovations reveals that the technology Satoshi built upon had a deep and well-documented history. What made Bitcoin revolutionary was the synthesis of those building blocks into one coherent, self-sustaining monetary network.

Briefly, I considered expanding this section to explore Bitcoin as a network and a technology. Aside from the fact that Bitcoin purists would probably deem my attempt inadequate, I quickly realized that would not only invite endless repetition, but, more importantly, it would also dilute the core message of this book. Many excellent works already explain Bitcoin's technical architecture, its decentralized network, and blockchain's transformative potential. For the purpose of this book, the focus must be on: bitcoin's unique scarcity, its effectiveness as protection against inflation, its growing acceptance among investors, and how these qualities add value to an investment portfolio.

Bitcoin as a Standard

To assess whether bitcoin can truly evolve into a new standard within the current financial system, it makes sense to begin with its similarities to gold rather than its differences. Beyond the technology, bitcoin's potential ultimately depends on the same core principles that underpin gold's role: proven scarcity, independence from central authority, and broad-based trust.

Scarcity

Bitcoin's scarcity is unlike that of any other financial asset. It is the first asset whose limited supply is not dictated by natural constraints or human discretion, but embedded directly in code. Satoshi Nakamoto hard-coded a rule into the system stipulating that the total number of bitcoin will never exceed 21 million.

That limit is fixed. In theory, the limit could be changed by consensus within the network, but as several studies have noted (Ammous, *The Bitcoin Standard*, 2018; Hasu, *Unpacking Bitcoin's Social Contract*, 2018), doing so would almost certainly trigger a network split, erode trust, and destroy value, making such a change practically impossible. For the attentive reader: "Bitcoin" with a capital B refers to the network, protocol or system, while "bitcoin" in lowercase refers to the asset or investment itself.

The last bitcoin will not be mined until around the year 2140, yet the vast majority, roughly 20 million coins, have already been issued by the network. However, not all of these are still in circulation. An estimated three to four million bitcoin are believed to have been permanently lost due to forgotten passwords, broken hard drives, or misplaced private keys. Private keys are encrypted digital codes that grant access to your bitcoin and secure your ownership. In Bitcoin's early days, when infrastructure was primitive, such losses were common. There are countless news stories of early users who lost fortunes when old laptops or hard drives were tossed out during a spring cleaning.

Bitcoin is even scarcer than gold. The global above-ground stock of gold grows by about 1.5 percent per year. According to the World Gold Council, proven underground reserves amount to around 50,000 metric tons, roughly one-quarter of all gold ever mined. There are also unproven gold reserves, such as deposits deep beneath the ocean floor or dissolved in seawater, but extracting them is economically unviable and technically impossible at this stage. And although space scientists speculate that asteroids may be rich in precious metals, mining them remains science fiction.

And should such an asteroid ever strike Earth, our worries would lie more with avoiding the fate of the dinosaurs than with how much gold it delivered. Gold's role as protection against central bank policy and fiscal dominance would, at that point, be the least of our concerns. More relevant is that the approximately one million bitcoin still to be mined represent only about 5 percent of the total supply, making bitcoin decisively scarcer than gold.

A final note on bitcoin's scarcity. Some skeptics question whether bitcoin is truly scarce because each bitcoin can be divided into 100 million units, known as satoshis. Some economists argue that such divisibility undermines scarcity. But that reasoning is flawed: Splitting something does not make it less scarce. The classic pizza analogy illustrates this point: You can slice a pizza into a million pieces, but it remains one pizza. And if you need to feed a million hungry people, you will quickly understand just how scarce that pizza really is.

What these economists mean is that since bitcoin can be split into tiny parts and transactions can continue indefinitely even with a fixed supply, its effective scarcity decreases. Economists call this functional scarcity. But in the context of bitcoin's role at the top layer of Exter's inverted pyramid, as a store of value and the foundation of the financial system, only absolute scarcity truly matters. It makes no more difference whether a central bank holds its gold in grams or in kilobars, the total quantity remains the same.

Independence

In the financial system, independence means that an asset can exist and function without reliance on any central authority. It operates without intermediaries, without issuers, and, crucially, without the risk of being diluted, frozen, or confiscated. No government, central bank, or corporation can access or create more of it at will. That is, as long as you genuinely own that asset yourself.

A recent example highlights just how vital the absence of centralized control for financial assets can be. Following Russia's invasion of Ukraine in February 2022, Western nations froze approximately $300 billion in Russian foreign reserves. These reserves, held by the Russian central bank, were blocked by the United States and its allies. In a fiat-based system, governments and central banks issuing their own currencies ultimately control money. Russia's gold reserves, however, could neither be frozen nor seized.

In times of crisis, whether war, political upheaval, economic depression, or a collapse of trust in public institutions like central banks, people seek independent stores of value outside the system. Gold's independence stems from its physical nature. You can store gold in a vault, bury it, trade it without intermediaries, or use it as payment. It is difficult to confiscate, though not impossible. On April 5, 1933, President Franklin D. Roosevelt signed an executive order banning US citizens from owning gold coins, bullion, and certificates in an attempt to stabilize the dollar during the Great Depression. Keep in mind, however, that this did not destroy gold's value, a fact often overlooked when that episode is cited as an argument against gold.

Bitcoin's independence also stems from its decentralized architecture. Like gold, it operates outside the reach of central authorities, but in digital form. The blockchain, an immutable public ledger, records every transaction in a way that no one can alter, block, or censor. Bitcoin has no CEO, no governing board, no owner, and no one who can dictate what happens to the network or its transactions. No one can switch off Bitcoin or seize your funds, so long as users protect their private keys, the encrypted codes granting access to their holdings. This makes bitcoin not only censorship-resistant, but also appealing in countries where bank access is limited or accounts can be frozen at will.

The latter may sound like the kind of thing that happens only in small, fragile economies, but nothing could be further from the truth. Across a growing number of Western nations, bank accounts are being closed en masse under the weight of excessive regulation. During the 2022 trucker protests in Canada, for example, the government froze the bank accounts of those involved. Preserving and maintaining access to your wealth should be among the highest priorities for anyone preparing for a potential crisis.

Trust

Trust decides whether a monetary standard endures or collapses. It is the belief that something will retain its value, even amid economic turmoil, geopolitical conflict, or even war, and also will do so within a financial system dominated by debt, a system that requires artificially suppressed interest rates even as inflation risks climb. It is precisely in such a system that scarce assets can earn and maintain trust. Just as savings and bonds have lost that trust through their structural loss of purchasing power.

As noted earlier, Bitcoin's trust arises from technology. It is the conviction that your holdings cannot be stolen or double-spent, and that no one, neither governments nor central banks, can reverse or block your transactions. Bitcoin also relies on the trust that it will not be banned, though the likelihood of such a ban is steadily diminishing.

Since its launch in 2009, the Bitcoin network has never gone offline. The same cannot be said for many other digital systems. The Bitcoin blockchain itself has never been hacked or tampered with. Other blockchains, crypto exchanges, and digital wallets have been compromised, hacked, or stolen from, but not the Bitcoin network itself. That distinction is often overlooked in traditional finance debates. The fact that the network has run flawlessly for over fifteen years earns it at least some degree of trust.

When I think of trust, I am reminded of Yuval Noah Harari, author of *Sapiens: A Brief History of Humankind*, discussed earlier in Chapter 1. In that book, Harari compellingly explains how humanity rose to dominance through its unique ability to enable large-scale cooperation built on shared trust. Which makes it all the more striking that Harari, in a video on X, describes bitcoin as a "currency of distrust," claiming it rests solely on the rejection of human institutions.

But is that really true? Certainly, an increasing number of people question how governments and central banks conduct policy. And rightly so, given what's happened to their purchasing power. Bitcoin gives these people a genuine alternative. Bitcoin is not about rejecting trust; it is about redirecting it. It replaces trust in centralized authorities like central banks and governments with trust in a decentralized network immune to manipulation.

As Harari himself describes in *Sapiens*, humans create systems that allow strangers to cooperate. The parallel with Bitcoin could hardly be more fitting.

Bitcoin and Fiscal Dominance

One of the challenges in studying bitcoin is its limited data history. Although the network went live in 2009, meaningful trading didn't start until years later. That explains why many price series start in 2010 or beyond. In addition, early trading volumes were tiny, contributing to bitcoin's extreme price swings and volatility. Though volatility has declined sharply in recent years, it's still four to five times higher than that of equities, which were long considered the riskiest asset class.

This is understandable, given Bitcoin's short lifespan, but it also means that correlations and relationships carry far less statistical weight. By contrast, stocks, bonds, and gold benefit from decades of robust data. Bitcoin's shorter historical record introduces more noise and lower statistical confidence.

That is precisely why I included the question "How far has Bitcoin come?" With such a limited dataset, qualitative analysis must provide deeper insight into how Bitcoin may evolve as a new monetary standard, one resilient to fiscal dominance and financial repression. Even so, as with gold, it's worth examining bitcoin's relationship with the defining feature of fiscal dominance: money creation.

Bitcoin and Money Supply Growth

To measure that relationship, I calculate the correlation between bitcoin's price movements and money supply growth in the same way as for gold. In other words, I look at money supply growth over the past and coming twelve months to capture both lagging and leading effects. The results are displayed in the next chart.

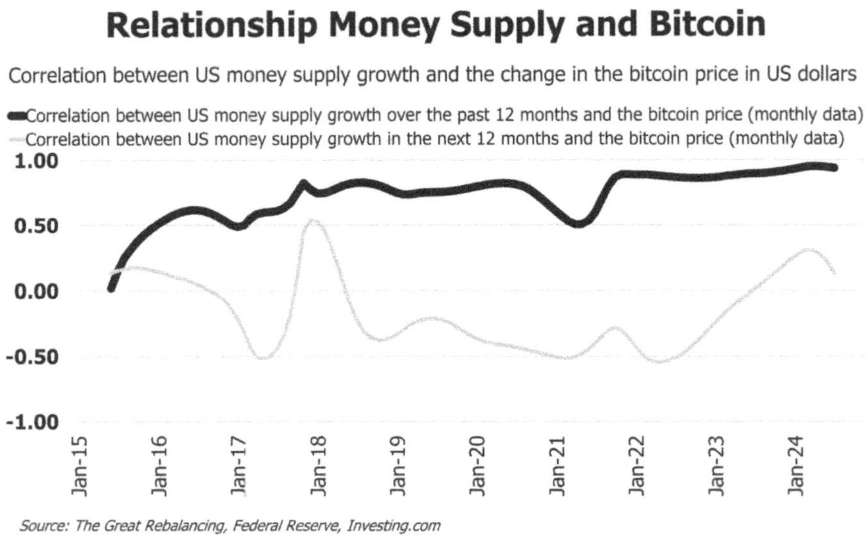

At first glance, the correlations appear somewhat surprising. Once again, there is a clear divergence between the two lines. Yet this time, it is the correlation between bitcoin's price and past money growth (black line) that stands out as particularly strong. That differs from gold, whose price tends to align more closely with future money supply growth. For bitcoin, there is hardly any relationship with future money growth. In fact, the relationship is slightly negative.

Given bitcoin's short data history, the likelihood of less robust or inconclusive outcomes is higher. Still, the difference between the two lines may be less puzzling than it seems. While bitcoin possesses many of the same qualities that make gold a viable store of value, factors such as adoption, regulation, speculation, and liquidity mean that its price remains highly sensitive to current developments. Investors, lacking long-term anchors, tend to react to the information directly in front of them, from whatever angle.

This suggests that bitcoin investors respond primarily to observable trends in money supply growth, rather than anticipating future monetary trends. Only when it becomes evident that the money supply is expanding do they take it as a signal to enter the market. When the headlines shift, for example to the approval of bitcoin ETFs, corporations adding bitcoin to their balance sheets, new regulation, or shifting market sentiment, those narratives take control of the price action.

This pattern aligns with findings from studies like Baur (2018) and Kristoufek (2020), which show that bitcoin's price is highly sensitive to episodes of monetary easing. Once those monetary effects fade, other forces take the wheel, resulting in a more reactive price dynamic.

This underscores my broader point: Bitcoin has not yet attained the historical stature that gold already commands. For centuries, gold has served as the default refuge in anticipation of future monetary disorder. It no longer depends on adoption, liquidity, or regulation to fulfill that role. That's why gold behaves far more consistently as a safe haven, especially when rising debt and central bank policy start to worry investors.

These differences in the factors driving gold and bitcoin prices have one important and highly attractive implication: Bitcoin and gold are not the same.

Speculation

Pointing to speculation as a driver of bitcoin's price is music to the ears of its staunchest critics. Even though many investments are to a degree speculative by nature, one of their main arguments is that bitcoin is nothing more than a speculative asset without utility or intrinsic value. They argue that bitcoin is nothing more than a speculative play devoid of utility or intrinsic value, and assume that when sentiment shifts, bitcoin will be the first to crash and will crash the hardest.

They often point to bitcoin's supposed correlation with US technology giants such as NVIDIA, Meta, and Tesla, companies that, along with the NASDAQ index they dominate, are frequently branded speculative themselves. To them, bitcoin is simply the NASDAQ on steroids.

That assumption, however, is simply wrong. The chart on the next page plots the correlation between weekly returns on bitcoin and the NASDAQ. Study it all you want, but the idea that bitcoin behaves like US tech stocks, popular among investors and on social media, simply does not hold. In fact, the correlation often hovers around zero, averaging just 0.07 since 2012. In other words, bitcoin and the NASDAQ largely move independently of each other. When the NASDAQ declines, bitcoin may just as easily rise, or fall.

Relationship NASDAQ and Bitcoin

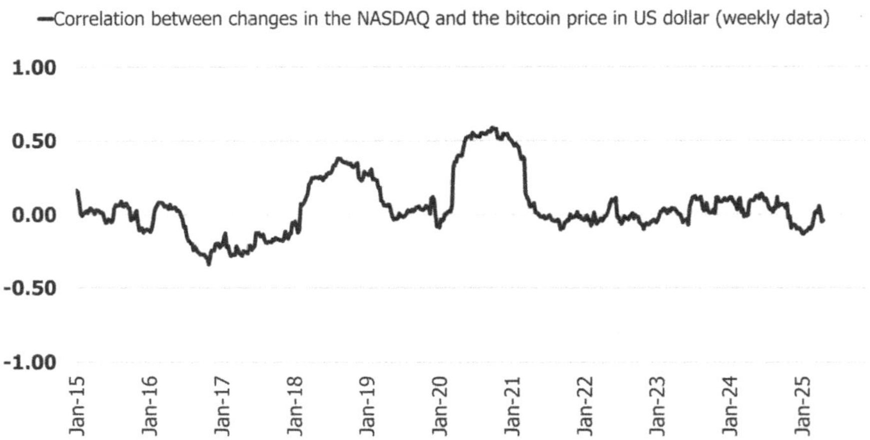

Source: The Great Rebalancing, Investing.com

The chart debunks a belief many investors and market commentators assume to be true. At the same time, it's a strong early signal that, beyond its coded scarcity and digital gold potential, bitcoin adds value to a well-diversified investment portfolio. Asset classes that move independently, with their own distinctive return patterns, are attractive because they provide valuable diversification benefits. They stabilize overall portfolio returns and reduce total portfolio risk.

Market Shocks

Another way to assess both bitcoin's speculative edge and its safe-haven potential is to examine how it behaves during episodes of financial market turmoil. In 2024, BlackRock, the world's largest asset manager and ETF powerhouse, published a study titled "Bitcoin: A Unique Diversifier." The paper analyzed the returns of US equities (via the S&P 500 index), gold, and bitcoin following six major financial and geopolitical shocks: the US-Iran escalation in early 2020, the COVID-19 outbreak, the US presidential elections of 2020, Russia's invasion of Ukraine in 2022, the US regional banking crisis of 2023, and the yen carry trade unwind of 2024.

Regarding that last event: Because Japanese interest rates have long been extremely low, a large group of global investors borrows money in Japanese yen and invests the proceeds elsewhere, often in the United States, chasing higher yields. Their goal is to pocket the yield "carry," the spread between Japan's rock-bottom interest rates and higher foreign yields.

This strategy works as long as the yen does not appreciate sharply. When it does, repaying those yen loans becomes far more expensive, forcing investors into losses. That is precisely what happened in August 2024. The Bank of Japan somewhat unexpectedly ended its ultra-loose monetary policies, causing the yen to soar in value. The swift yen appreciation forced investors to unwind their yen carry trades by selling assets to stem their losses.

Let's move back to the market shocks. BlackRock calculated the returns on US equities, gold, and bitcoin over the first ten and sixty days following each of those six major events. This offers insight into how these assets behave immediately after a shock and after two months of potential recovery. The result? When adding up the returns from all six events, bitcoin was by far the best-performing asset.

Since BlackRock's 2024 study, several new episodes of stress have occurred that deserve examination: for example, April 2, 2025, when President Donald Trump announced a sweeping package of reciprocal trade tariffs against numerous countries, symbolically dubbed "Liberation Day"; or June 13, 2025, the day Israel launched air strikes on Iran. In addition, there is one glaring omission in BlackRock's lineup: the British bond market meltdown of 2022.

It would, of course, be odd to omit the very event that served as the thriller-style introduction of this book. The Truss crisis of September

2022 remains a textbook case of what happens in a system burdened by high debt and fiscal dominance.

Let's briefly recap the key moments of this event. Proposed unfunded tax cuts blew up the UK budget deficit, sent gilt yields soaring, drove up inflation expectations, and drained liquidity from the bond market. Long-dated and inflation-linked gilts plunged by double digits within days. Pension funds faced acute stress, prompting the Bank of England to step in with massive bond purchases, despite rapidly rising inflation expectations. This was a classic case of fiscal dominance in action. And Prime Minister Liz Truss? She resigned after just 58 days in office, claiming the dubious record of the shortest premiership in British history.

This bleak scenario should not be ignored: The likelihood that bond markets will experience similar crises again is very high. With these additions, the list expands to nine events or shocks. They are summarized in the table below, showing ten- and sixty-day returns for US equities (S&P 500), gold, bitcoin, and US Treasuries. I include Treasuries because many investors still view them as safe havens during periods of stress, while I argue that they are increasingly the source of that stress. This allows us a sharp view of how different asset classes behave during market shocks, and how bitcoin performs during those events in particular.

Returns on stocks, gold, bitcoin, and bonds following major financial and geopolitical events

		S&P 500	Gold	Bitcoin	Bonds	S&P 500	Gold	Bitcoin	Bonds
Event	Date	Return after ten days				Return after sixty days			
Iran-US escalation	Jan 3, 2020	1.6%	-0.3%	11.8%	-0.3%	-7.2%	5.7%	20.2%	5.0%
COVID pandemic	Mar 10, 2020	-20.0%	-9.1%	-25.3%	-1.1%	1.7%	3.2%	20.6%	0.9%
US elections	Nov 3, 2020	6.4%	-1.0%	18.6%	0.0%	11.5%	-0.5%	130.7%	0.2%
Ukraine invasion	Feb 24, 2022	0.9%	3.5%	1.6%	1.2%	0.2%	-0.3%	4.6%	-4.9%
UK bond crisis	Sep 23, 2022	-4.6%	-0.6%	-0.1%	-0.7%	5.1%	4.0%	-18.8%	-0.6%
US banking crisis	Mar 9, 2023	-1.9%	9.7%	24.6%	3.5%	3.6%	11.2%	31.6%	3.9%
Yen carry trade	Aug 5, 2024	2.0%	0.2%	0.0%	-0.2%	6.6%	8.7%	2.8%	0.4%
Liberation Day	Apr 2, 2025	-5.4%	3.3%	-0.2%	-1.4%	4.2%	4.9%	22.6%	-0.6%
Israel-Iran strike	Jun 13, 2025	0.8%	-1.9%	-1.6%	0.5%	5.4%	-1.3%	12.1%	1.1%
Average		-2.2%	0.4%	3.3%	0.2%	3.5%	4.0%	25.2%	0.6%

Source: The Great Rebalancing, Investing.com

Let's first look at the short term, the returns over a period of just ten days after the start of each event. At the bottom of the table are the average returns across all nine episodes. Over that ten-day window, bitcoin produced the highest ten-day return, averaging 3.3 percent. In other words, in the immediate aftermath of market shocks, bitcoin outperformed all other asset classes in this analysis. Equities were the worst performers, with an average decline of 2.2 percent. These results highlight, again, that bitcoin is not some turbocharged version of equities moving in lockstep with them. On the contrary, when markets were under stress, bitcoin often moved in the opposite direction of equities. Those are diversification effects that strengthen any investment portfolio.

After ten days, bitcoin ranked last only once, during the COVID-19 outbreak. Across the remaining eight events, some other asset class always fared worse. Perhaps somewhat remarkably, bitcoin even outperformed gold, which in turn delivered a slightly better return on average than bonds.

What happens when we extend the window to sixty days? Bitcoin again emerged as the clear winner, with an average return of 25 percent. None of the other categories came anywhere near that level. In seven of the nine events, bitcoin posted the highest return, while ranking last only once. Notably, that lone miss came sixty days after the Truss government unveiled its budget, an episode BlackRock inexplicably left out. Gold followed at a respectable distance but nonetheless claimed second place. What's more, gold never registered deep losses after any event, a desirable trait during market turmoil.

Equities finished higher after sixty days in eight of the nine cases, confirming how quickly markets often rebound from shocks. Bringing up the rear were bonds, with a meager average sixty-day return of 0.6 percent. Treasuries finished in the red three times and were the worst performer in four out of the nine shocks, a pretty dismal record for an asset still marketed as a safe haven.

Based on these nine major market shocks, the only conclusion must be that bitcoin has weathered market turmoil impressively well. Granted, nine is a small sample, so the conclusion must remain cautious. Equally important is that, apart from the pandemic, there was no deep global crisis following the events, giving markets ample room to recover, which they did. Even so, critics cannot credibly maintain, based on the return data following market shocks, that bitcoin is merely a speculative asset that crumbles whenever sentiment sours.

The table highlights another crucial point. After many of these shocks, central banks swiftly abandoned their inflation targets to soothe markets and stabilize economies. The pandemic was the most prominent example, but similar reactions followed the collapse of several US regional banks, the unwinding of the yen carry trade, and the UK budget fiasco.

All three share the same roots: budget deficits, debt accumulation, and bond markets. Each time stress emerged from those factors, central banks had no choice but to intervene. By contrast, in geopolitical events such as Russia's invasion or the US elections, monetary intervention was far less pronounced.

When isolating the four events that did trigger central bank action, the results speak volumes: Bitcoin (+9 percent) and gold (+7 percent) returns tower above the rest. That outcome fits perfectly with the concept of gold and bitcoin as monetary anchors, providing protection against the increasingly extreme central bank policies required to keep a debt-driven financial system afloat.

How Far Has Bitcoin Come?

There is no escaping the limitations of bitcoin's short data history. Still, even within that limited time frame, clear evidence shows that bitcoin responds to periods of rapid money supply growth, the defining feature of fiscal dominance and financial repression. Moreover, the price of bitcoin did not collapse during episodes of market stress. It is therefore far too simplistic to dismiss bitcoin as nothing more than a speculative gamble.

Beyond that, numerous developments suggest that bitcoin, both as an investment and as a monetary system, is here to stay. It is steadily establishing itself as a store of digital value, powered by its intrinsic scarcity.

Below are several striking examples that demonstrate how far Bitcoin has come, and why it can no longer be ignored as a serious and legitimate asset class.

Adoption

When discussing bitcoin adoption, attention often centers on metrics such as the number of active users, transaction volumes, and digital wallet counts. These produce impressive charts showing, for example, that cryptocurrency adoption, not just bitcoin, has outpaced even the internet's early growth curve. These developments matter, a lot, as users are essential to run and strengthen the network. But these trends are also somewhat generic.

Gold, for instance, is fashioned into jewelry worn every day. Although holding wealth in that form can be a deliberate choice, as seen in India, such usage generally stands further removed from gold as a potentially attractive investment, sound money, and the foundation of the financial system.

With that in mind, it makes more sense to assess how bitcoin has entered the traditional financial system than to just tally its users. Gold enjoys a vast global infrastructure that allows investors to buy, trade, store, and even spend it efficiently. That same infrastructure ensures that, even though gold sits outside the fiat-based financial system, it can interact with it seamlessly, cheaply, and at scale.

Bitcoin ETFs

When it comes to bitcoin's integration into the current financial system, the approval of US spot bitcoin ETFs marked a true watershed moment on several fronts. In January 2024, after years of resistance led by SEC Chair Gary Gensler, the US Securities and Exchange Commission approved eleven US "spot" Bitcoin ETFs at once. The term "spot" refers to the fact that these Exchange-Traded Funds are allowed to invest directly in bitcoin, though initially through a somewhat complex structure (*not* through derivatives, as had previously been permitted).

The latter point yields an interesting observation. Until then, ETF providers could only offer bitcoin exposure through derivatives, which occupy the very bottom of Exter's inverted pyramid. The SEC justified its long resistance to spot ETFs by citing fears of price manipulation. Paradoxically, it's derivatives that are most often accused of enabling price manipulation.

The approved spot bitcoin ETFs became an instant success, smashing records at an astonishing pace. The two largest, BlackRock's IBIT and Fidelity's FBTC, crossed the symbolic $1 billion in assets under management (AUM) threshold within a week, a milestone reached by only a handful of ETFs in history. In the months that followed, inflows remained strong, even as investors withdrew large sums from the Grayscale Bitcoin Trust (GBTC). That closed-end fund, launched in 2013, had long traded at a discount to bitcoin's price due to its rigid structure, a constant frustration for investors. Following the SEC approval, GBTC converted into a spot ETF, ending its monopoly. Yet many investors still switched to cheaper alternatives.

By the end of 2024, less than a year after approval, total assets in US spot bitcoin ETFs, driven by net inflows and price appreciation, surpassed $100 billion. It marked the fastest rise ever recorded for a new ETF category. This is for an asset class valued at barely $2 trillion in total at the time. For comparison, total global equity market capitalization stood at $123 trillion at the end of 2024, a difference by a factor of sixty.

The success of these ETFs stems from two factors. First, they are allowed to buy "real" bitcoin. Just as with gold, paper bitcoin claims are not the real thing. You must own a slice of the finite supply. Second, familiar packaging plays a decisive role. Asset managers and financial advisors are accustomed to working with ETFs. These are familiar instruments, routinely and often automatically added to client portfolios. Since the approval of spot bitcoin ETFs in January 2024, that now applies to bitcoin as well.

The SEC's approval triggered a dramatic acceleration in bitcoin's evolution into a liquid, institutionally recognized, and globally accessible asset class.

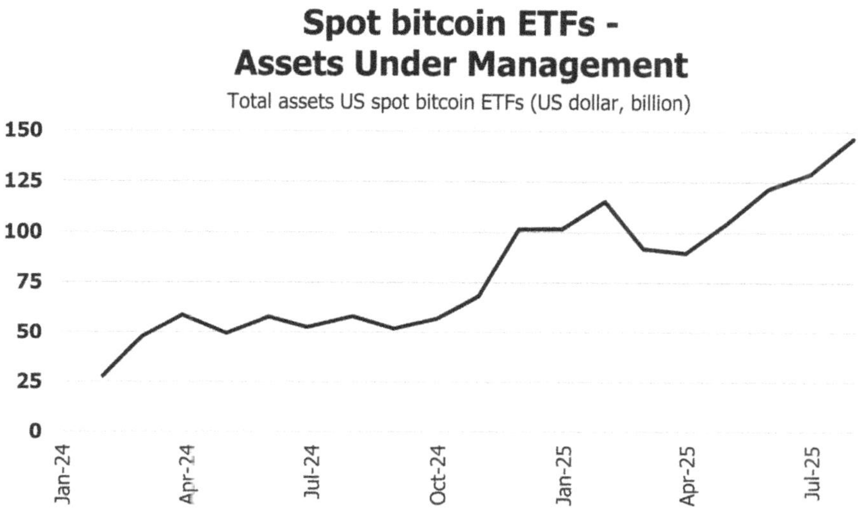

Source: The Great Rebalancing, Bloomberg

Custody

The approval of US spot bitcoin ETFs also served as a catalyst for another key development: institutional-grade custody. Since one of the most popular investment vehicles now provides direct access to a new asset class, demand for reliable, stable, and secure bitcoin storage has surged. Just as physical gold belongs safely locked and insured in a Swiss vault or elsewhere, investors want their bitcoin held in the safest possible way.

Features like cold storage (keeping bitcoin offline, disconnected from the network), multisignature wallets (requiring multiple keys to unlock funds), proof-of-reserves (third-party verification of custodian holdings), insurance against external attacks, and stringent regulatory oversight are becoming increasingly important.

While the deeper technical specifics lie beyond the scope of this book, and require considerable technological expertise, it is evident that secure custody is now a critical pillar of bitcoin's institutional adoption.

Major players such as Coinbase, Fidelity Digital Assets, and Anchorage Digital collectively safeguard billions of dollars in bitcoin. Custody is often offered as a stand-alone service, legally and operationally separated from trading activities. These firms increasingly comply with stricter regulations, provide robust insurance coverage, and, not least, have earned the trust of professional asset managers. By now, an estimated two million bitcoin, roughly ten percent of the total supply, are held by these leading custodians.

Settlement

The rapid improvement in custody standards will, in my view, profoundly shape bitcoin's role as digital gold. If bitcoin can be stored efficiently, cheaply, and with extreme security, it maximizes one of its most powerful advantages over gold: settlement time, the speed with which a transaction is finalized and ownership transferred.

This advantage is brilliantly articulated by Lyn Alden in her 2023 book *Broken Money*. In a monetary system where settlement and the transfer of actual value occur through gold, its physical nature acts as friction. Before we go further, consider how a gold settlement system differs from the current one, where fiat money settles virtually all transactions without intrinsic value, merely a promise of value based on trust.

Now imagine a world where every payment, no matter how small, requires the physical shipment of gold. Suppose, as a wine enthusiast, I order a case of fine wine directly from the Chilean winery Concha y Toro. If my order cost €100, then €100 worth of gold would need to make its way to Chile to settle the payment. Only then is the transaction settled with real value. That gold would be on the road for quite some time, as it's already a 17-hour flight from Amsterdam alone.

Such delays are obviously impractical for settling something as simple as a case of wine, not to mention the costs involved. But equally important, these delays also leave ample room for governments and, by extension, central and commercial banks, to steer, monitor, and even manipulate money flows through fiat currency.

Even without gold settlement, governments have long stamped their authority on the monetary system due to the physical and slow communication networks, like early telegraph lines, phone cables, and paper documentation. The slow (gold) settlements and physical limits of traditional systems allowed governments to control fiat flows through banks, legislation, and oversight.

But even in today's digital world, money flows remain heavily regulated under KYC (know your customer) and AML (anti-money laundering) frameworks, enabling governments to maintain control over monetary flows and transactions. If you think policymakers have loosened their grip or made regulation more efficient, think again. In my home country, the Netherlands, banks employ about 13,000 people solely for AML compliance. That's one in five bank employees, costing an astonishing €1.4 billion every year. Yet 2022 data reveal that only 0.003 percent of Dutch bank transactions were flagged or blocked as suspicious. This regulatory overreach is also why I have to ask clients of my investment fund to deposit their contributions several business days before month-end. There's always a chance the bank will still raise a question, even after full KYC is completed by the administrator.

Bitcoin breaks this pattern by settling transactions in a decentralized and rapid way, without the physical constraints of gold. It provides digital, low-cost, near-instant settlement, with no intermediaries involved: Transactions are confirmed within minutes, anywhere in the world, on weekends and bank holidays, and crucially, the underlying value transfers instantly. No bank or government needs to be involved. This gives individuals direct autonomy over both their financial transactions and their wealth.

Gold has long offered a form of financial independence, but bitcoin, with its digital, borderless design, elevates that autonomy to an entirely new level. This insight, so clearly articulated by Lyn Alden, is a powerful and still underestimated argument for why bitcoin deserves a place alongside gold at the top of Exter's inverted pyramid.

Scalability

Bitcoin allows people to make quick transactions to transfer (small) amounts of value back and forth, but what about scalability? You've likely heard that the Bitcoin blockchain can process only a limited number of transactions per second.

While that might sound like a serious limitation, several technical solutions help offset its impact, aided by the very technology on which Bitcoin is built. With a limited number of transactions that can be stored in the blocks on the blockchain, the network could choose to increase its capacity. However, this would require broad consensus, something that has proven difficult in the past. Launched in 2018, the Lightning Network offered an elegant solution: a protocol enabling instant, low-cost payments without recording every transaction directly on the blockchain. It operates as a second layer built on top of the original chain, allowing payments to occur off-chain while maintaining full settlement integrity.

Through the Lightning Network, users open payment channels between one another, enabling direct, peer-to-peer payments. Think, for example, of everyday micropayments like buying coffee on your way to the train, unlocking an online article, or leaving a digital tip. Only when the channel closes is the net balance of all transactions recorded on the chain. The opening and closing of the channel are the only transactions that occur on the Bitcoin blockchain. Though still young and with capacity fluctuating as channels open and close, the Lightning Network had surpassed $500 million in total capacity by January 2025, according to Fidelity Digital Assets.

Set aside the technological perspective for a moment, and the concept of Gresham's Law quickly comes into play. True to the principle that *bad money drives out good*, people are likely to hoard bitcoin rather than spend it. Gold, too, is rarely used these days as a medium of exchange within the fiat system, although it is still possible. Why spend sound money when you can part with worthless banknotes, or the ones and zeros in your digital account instead? This reduces, at least for now, the urgency for Bitcoin to handle vast numbers of transactions per second.

In rebalancing our debt-driven system, bitcoin's role as a store of value outweighs its function as a medium of exchange.

Corporations, Governments, and Pension Funds

The combination of resilience under stress, familiar investment vehicles such as ETFs, secure custody options, diversification benefits, and protection against rampant money supply growth has significantly accelerated institutional adoption of bitcoin in recent years.

River, a financial firm focused exclusively on bitcoin investment and custody, estimated in its 2025 report "What's Driving Bitcoin Adoption?" that by the end of 2024, roughly 40 percent of the $100 billion held in US spot bitcoin ETFs was owned by professional investors, including financial advisors, hedge funds, and asset managers. That last category also includes a few pension funds.

River also noted that between 2023 and 2024, the number of publicly listed companies holding bitcoin on their balance sheets surged by 139 percent, reaching nearly 80 firms. In 2025, the number increased to roughly 250. That still represents well below one percent of all listed companies worldwide.

More recently, a new trend has emerged: governments taking an active interest in bitcoin. As of this writing, just under twenty countries are known to hold bitcoin. The Central African Republic remains the only nation where it serves as full legal tender. Interestingly, El Salvador, under pressure from the IMF, partially rolled back its legal tender status in exchange for new loans. Elsewhere, bitcoin mining, trying to guess very large numbers to release new bitcoin, is actively promoted. Bhutan, for instance, harnesses its abundant hydropower to generate the electricity required to have a chance of winning the lottery.

Most government-owned bitcoin, however, comes from seizures tied to failed or shuttered crypto exchanges. The United States, the United Kingdom, and China are among the most prominent examples. In the latter country, bitcoin remains partially banned. Germany also previously held bitcoin, but due to a provision in its criminal code that requires seized assets that are highly volatile to be sold, those holdings were liquidated.

For years, only smaller nations engaged directly with bitcoin. That changed in March 2025, when the world's largest economy, the United States, under President Trump, announced a strategic bitcoin reserve. In practice, this means the federal government will retain the roughly 200,000 bitcoin already in its possession rather than liquidating them. Additional accumulation can occur, but only in budget-neutral ways. No taxpayer money may be used for direct bitcoin purchases.

The prevailing view is that Washington is in no rush to expand its strategic bitcoin reserve. The federal stance does leave room for individual US states to build reserves of their own. Around twenty states have explored this option, with several already passing legislation. Most of these laws mirror those of the federal strategic reserve. The state of Texas, however, is allowed to make direct bitcoin purchases, and actually did so in November 2026.

The strategic bitcoin reserve puts the United States at a full 180 degrees from most other Western nations, forcing them to rethink their stance on holding bitcoin on government balance sheets. It also reflects a deeper strategic calculus: Digital assets, or crypto, could serve as a new way to support demand for US Treasuries.

This strategy is most visible through so-called stablecoins, digital dollars backed by US Treasuries to verify their value. This suggests that Washington recognizes what I argued back in Chapter 11, that Modern Monetary Theory simply does not hold in practice. Faced with massive fiscal deficits and a fading dollar hegemony, the US must find every possible way to keep demand for its debt alive.

Make no mistake, that is a very different premise from viewing bitcoin as a new foundation of the financial system. Stablecoins, or digital dollars if you want, are nothing more than derivatives of fiat money. The value of stablecoins rests once again on the promise that US Treasuries will maintain purchasing power, a promise history shows cannot be kept. In essence, stablecoins represent a digital extension of the current monetary system, and ultimately a product of fiscal dominance. Washington knows this all too well. If those stablecoins were instead backed by gold, the story would be entirely different. But at that stage, you might as well skip a few phases and go straight to digital gold: bitcoin. Interestingly, in July 2025, the CEO of Tether, issuer of the world's largest stablecoin, USDT, revealed that the company owns gold securely stored in a vault in Switzerland, with gold making up about 5 percent of total reserves at the time.

Even so, the fact that major governments are now openly engaging with bitcoin marks a seismic shift. Not long ago, the idea that sovereign states would actively hold bitcoin, long dismissed as "a toy for nerds" or "fake money for criminals," was utterly unthinkable.

The Resistance of Central Banks

If governments give in, will central banks, willingly or not, follow suit? My view is that, at least in the near future, most central banks will fiercely resist bitcoin, because broadly speaking they cannot control it. More specifically, because they understand that bitcoin complicates their policies under fiscal dominance and, above all, financial repression. Bitcoin offers an escape hatch for capital that refuses to be forced into government bonds, and for wealth unwilling to sit idly by while inflation erodes its purchasing power.

In 2024, shortly after the launch of US spot bitcoin ETFs, two staff members of the European Central Bank made their stance unmistakably clear in a blog post on the ECB's website. They claimed that bitcoin is still used almost exclusively by criminals, that it is useless as money, and that it is unappealing as an investment. The latter, they argued, was because bitcoin generates no cash flows.

Another particularly absurd passage claims that gold's value derives solely from its "social benefits" as jewelry: two central bankers conveniently forgetting the purpose of the gold stored in their own institution's vaults.

After some more dramatic lines like "the currency of crime: financing evil," the authors conclude that bitcoin should either be tightly regulated or outright banned. Ironically, these are the same central bankers whose "job" is to protect the euro's value, by deliberately devaluing it 2 percent each year under their official inflation target.

I encourage you to read the ECB blog post "ETF approval for Bitcoin – the naked emperor's new clothes" for yourself on the ECB website.

The Counterattack

In my view, many central banks are quietly preparing a digital counteroffensive against bitcoin, cloaked in the rhetoric of "necessary financial innovation." In the end, effective monetary policy, including the artificial suppression of interest rates, depends on control. Central banks, together with their governments, already hold a monopoly on fiat money. But with the introduction of a central bank digital currency (CBDC), the control over money would become absolute.

A CBDC makes all money controllable, steerable, and, most importantly, programmable. In today's fiat system, individuals still retain a small degree of autonomy, for example by using cash. A CBDC would erase even that final layer of independence and privacy. A central bank could track every digital euro or dollar, block transactions, or even impose an expiration date.

During and after the pandemic, savers in several countries faced negative interest rates. You were, quite literally, penalized for keeping money in a savings account. In a system based solely on central bank digital currencies, central banks wouldn't need to impose negative rates indirectly, dependent on a transfer mechanism (think of banks and the interest rates on their reserves, for example). They could program your savings directly, justifying it as "a necessary step to contain yet another crisis."

Fail to spend, and your balance shrinks. Save "too much," "contribute too little to the economy," or "violate imposed rules," and you could be financially pressured, penalized, or outright excluded. If that sounds far-fetched, recall the Canadian truckers whose bank accounts were frozen, or Spain's maximum €150,000 fine for anyone who fails to provide sufficient proof of the origin of cash when withdrawing or depositing amounts above €3,000. And finally, also consider the official communications of central banks about CBDCs, which leave little to the imagination.

The example of Spain underscores the broader truth: Central banks and governments want to eliminate cash. Cash is hard to control; it slips through the financial surveillance that fiscal dominance and financial repression rely on. Programmable digital money allows governments and central banks to coordinate capital controls, trapping funds within their borders. Bitcoin, with its decentralized nature and position outside the traditional fiat system, is precisely the kind of instrument they cannot tolerate.

Equally important, a CBDC solves neither the structural shortage of economic growth nor the deeper problem of debt sustainability. A digital euro is worth exactly as much as a printed one: nothing. Financing chronic budget deficits still requires continuous monetary expansion. The erosion of purchasing power in savings and bonds will continue, and so too will the search for protection against inflation's corrosive effects. Central bank digital currencies represent the same system, the same dynamics, just repackaged in a digital shell of total control.

CBDCs are not neutral technological innovations. They are the forerunners of a new phase of financial repression. And for that very reason, they deserve far more critical scrutiny than they have received so far.

A Different Tone

Not all central bankers share the hostility of the authors of the ECB blog post. A notable exception is Aleš Michl, governor of the Czech

National Bank. In January 2025, he proposed a serious study of whether bitcoin should play a role in the country's foreign exchange reserves.

Michl stressed that this was not an ideological stance, but as a pragmatic step, to explore whether, despite its volatility, bitcoin could serve a long-term role in diversifying currency reserves. He also noted that central banks increasingly feel pressure to reassess the composition of those reserves, as traditional government bonds have become far less attractive.

Michl's position stands in stark contrast to that of most of his colleagues and peers. For now, it remains an exploratory phase, with the central bank board authorizing research into what a pilot bitcoin reserve portfolio might look like in practice.

Other central banks have been less explicit but maintain a certain degree of nuance. The Swiss National Bank has stated that it has "no fundamental objections" to including bitcoin in its reserves, provided the market matures in terms of liquidity, transparency, and volatility. The Norwegian central bank has repeatedly mentioned in its annual infrastructure reports that digital assets like bitcoin are being seriously studied as alternative stores of value, without being dismissed outright. A few years ago, the Reserve Bank of New Zealand ran stress-test scenarios placing bitcoin next to gold and government bonds to better understand its diversification properties.

But the real breakthrough for bitcoin as a central bank reserve asset will come only when policymakers, aware that extreme monetary policy is required to sustain the debt-driven system, recognize that bitcoin offers a possible way out when they stop seeing bitcoin purely as a threat and start viewing it as a scarce asset that, together with gold, can broaden the monetary base. Because in a financial system increasingly reliant on debt monetization through money supply growth, a broader value base enhances stability.

The big question is when that moment will arrive.

The Case for Bitcoin

To conclude, here is a concise summary of this extended chapter, and of the case for bitcoin. Bitcoin has demonstrated on multiple fronts that it can embody the role of digital gold. The combination of absolute scarcity, technological independence, and built-in trust forms a foundation unique in financial history. Where gold has proven itself as a store of value over thousands of years, bitcoin has shown in less than two decades that it is censorship-resistant, decentralized, and increasingly scalable thanks to innovations like the Lightning Network.

Trust in bitcoin, however, remains fluid and sentiment-driven, and the limited dataset makes it difficult to draw definitive conclusions about its relationship with variables such as money supply and inflation. At the same time, mounting evidence shows that bitcoin tends to protect investors most during phases of monetary expansion. Institutional acceptance, visible in the stellar rise of spot bitcoin ETFs, professional custody services, and early moves by pension funds and governments, confirms that bitcoin is no longer a passing experiment.

Still, bitcoin remains at the very start of its evolution as a possible new monetary standard. The direction, however, is unmistakable: An ever-growing number of institutions and people view bitcoin as an alternative to centralized control, a digital reserve that cannot be debased, and a potential hedge against fiscal dominance.

With bitcoin, the outlines of a new monetary era have come sharply into view. And that is exactly why it's becoming ever harder to ignore bitcoin as a serious component of a future-oriented investment portfolio.

CHAPTER 16

An Old Love

Introduction

Investors in physical gold and bitcoin often hold strong views about what's happening in the world around them. They tend to pay above-average attention to economic, social, and political developments and generally have less trust in policymakers, institutions such as central banks, and the financial system as a whole.

Given the preceding fifteen chapters, that attitude is anything but irrational. It is clear that we are living through a historical, social, political, and financial transformation. With this in mind, many gold and bitcoin investors turn their backs on the traditional financial world, convinced that it is destined to fail or collapse altogether.

But in doing so, they sell themselves short. As I argued in Chapter 14 on gold, a rebalancing of the financial system does not necessarily have to unfold through chaos or collapse. If the transition proceeds more gradually, one category within the traditional investment universe can still thrive and firmly deserves a place in every long-term investment portfolio.

Scarce Capital

In short, there are two types of capital: equity (stocks) and debt (bonds). When one of them floods the system, it inevitably affects the other. In a world awash with debt, meaning full of borrowed capital, equity capital becomes scarce, and therefore more valuable, provided, of course, that companies can deploy that equity capital into profitable activities. When they do, investing in equity becomes far more rewarding than in overabundant debt.

The gap in attractiveness between these two types of capital widens in an era of fiscal dominance, marked by low interest rates and higher, more erratic inflation. As shown in Chapter 13, bonds have delivered negative real returns since the start of this millennium. After more than twenty-five years of investing, meaning by taking risk, in global bonds, you would have lost roughly 10 percent of your purchasing power.

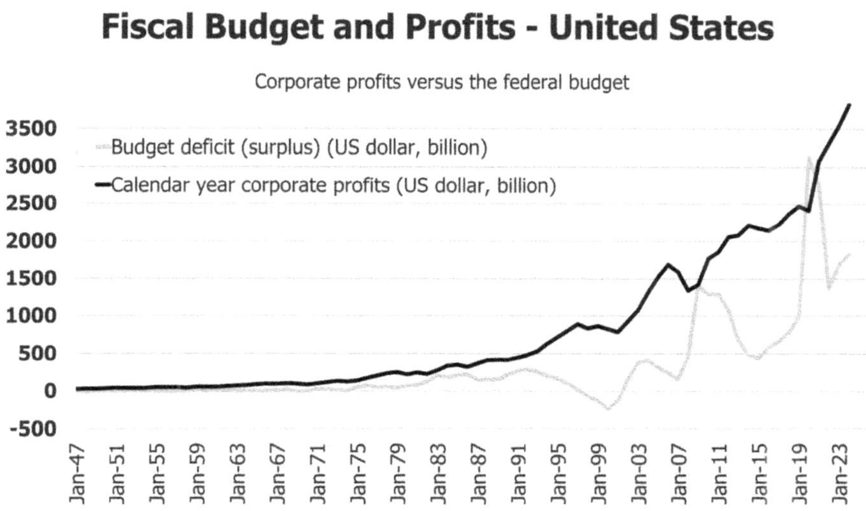

Source: The Great Rebalancing, fred.stlouisfed.org

So, what about equities? The chart above offers a telling clue: Even during periods of fiscal dominance and financial repression, companies have shown an impressive ability to generate solid returns on their equity. Chapter 10 already revealed that since 2008, the US budget deficit has outpaced growth in corporate and household lending nearly every year, a powerful signal of fiscal dominance. Government spending now outweighs corporate investment and household consumption, a hallmark of an economy that can barely sustain growth on its own.

The same comparison can be extended to US corporate profits. In the chart, the gray line shows once more the US federal budget in billions of dollars (again inverted, so a positive value in the chart represents a deficit). The black line in the chart tracks US corporate profits. Unlike lending to businesses and households, those profits have not been overwhelmed by public-sector deficits. Even when deficits went off the rails, such as during the pandemic, corporate profits held firm and even surged sharply higher (the black line shoots upward).

So even though government spending now dominates corporate and household lending, the profitability of corporate equity capital remains remarkably resilient. That is very encouraging news for equity investors who provide capital in exchange for a share of those profits, typically in the form of dividends, which remain a vital pillar of long-term equity returns.

The Holy Grail

In almost every so-called "diversified" investment portfolio sold to investors around the world, the allocation ultimately boils down to just two asset classes: equities and bonds. I will take an extended and wider view to show why this narrow idea of diversification is especially damaging. Investors who, whether through financial advisors, pension funds, private banks, or wealth managers, invest only in equities and bonds have missed out on substantial returns. More worryingly, they are very likely to do so again in the future.

My focus, unsurprisingly, will be on the traditional 60/40 portfolio, long hailed as the holy grail of investing. The logic behind the 60/40 portfolio is deceptively simple. Over the long run, equities deliver strong returns when companies grow their profits. And as the previous chart demonstrated, they do. Investors benefit from this growth through rising share prices and dividends.

The trade-off for realizing these strong returns is risk: Companies can go bankrupt during a recession, or because their business models fail. Since debt ranks above equity in most cases, shareholders run a real risk of losing their entire investment when a company fails. This higher risk translates into greater volatility: Stock prices fluctuate more sharply, especially when investors fear recession and question a firm's ability to stay profitable.

Bonds, so the thinking goes, are less risky. In corporate bonds, this is because bondholders are first in line to recover their money in the event of bankruptcy or liquidation, to the extent that funds remain. In the case of government bonds, it's because sovereign nations rarely default. We learned that sovereign nations controlling their own currency cannot technically go bankrupt simply because these governments can always print more money, with all the consequences that it entails. In theory, bond risk, or better, volatility, should therefore be lower than that of equities. But lower risk also brings lower returns: you are lending money instead of taking on more risk by providing companies with equity capital.

The core premise of the 60/40 portfolio is that combining two complementary asset classes creates a solid, well-performing portfolio. Equities deliver the higher return, while bonds deliver portfolio stability.

But that idea no longer holds. The traditional role of bonds as a risk stabilizer in an investment portfolio has become obsolete. Under fiscal dominance, interest rates are deliberately kept low while the likelihood of higher and more erratic inflation increases. That mix is highly toxic for bond returns.

And that's not all. The assumption that bonds are inherently low risk no longer stands up to scrutiny, especially not in a world where governments and central banks resort to extreme policy measures to sustain artificial growth.

The fact that interest rates are manipulated and inflation targets abandoned to keep the debt mountain under control does not mean that the underlying risks of that debt disappear. On the contrary, it increases the probability that this same mountain of debt will eventually strain, or even topple, the entire system.

An Honest Look at Returns

Why, then, do nearly all traditional asset managers continue to cling to the 60/40 portfolio? Professional investors typically justify their traditional preference for the combination of stocks and bonds by claiming that the two complement each other when comparing their "risk-return characteristics." Bonds offer lower returns but come with less risk. That pairs neatly with equities, which offer higher returns but also carry higher risk.

The relationship between risk and return can be expressed in a single number: the Sharpe Ratio, named after Nobel laureate William F. Sharpe. To calculate the Sharpe Ratio, you simply divide the return on an asset class (after subtracting the risk-free rate) by its volatility. The result serves as a kind of quality score. The higher the Sharpe Ratio, the more return you earn for every unit of risk you take. I will leave the risk-free rate aside here. When comparing stocks and bonds, it only clouds the picture (you subtract the rate from both equities and bonds) and, besides, because of fiscal dominance, I expect the risk-free rate, typically the yield on short-term government bonds, to hover close to zero in the future because of fiscal dominance.

Here's how it works: An investor earning a 5 percent return with 10 percent volatility has a Sharpe Ratio of 0.5 (five divided by ten). Another investor earning 8 percent with 20 percent volatility has a Sharpe Ratio of 0.4 (eight divided by twenty). The second investor realized a higher return, but also took on twice as much risk to do so. Once adjusted for that risk, which should always be the case, the first investor's return is of higher quality.

For decades, the story went that both equities and bonds each produced decent Sharpe Ratios and therefore combined well in a single portfolio. But that assumption is flat-out wrong. It (perhaps intentionally) overlooks a decisive element of return: inflation.

What's the point of a 10 percent return when inflation runs at 20 percent? It's worth as much as a 10 percent pay rise when prices in the shops climb 20 percent. So, not much at all. Even with seemingly strong performance (or a generous pay increase), your purchasing power still falls. That's why it is critical to include inflation when comparing Sharpe Ratios across asset classes. And it's absolutely paramount if you, like me, expect inflation to be higher and more erratic in the years ahead.

Yet Sharpe Ratios are almost never presented in *real* terms, adjusted for inflation. The table shown below does exactly that. To calculate the real Sharpe Ratios for equities and bonds, I once again use the basket of global government bonds introduced in Chapter 11, starting in September 2000. For equities, I use the MSCI World Index measured in euros over the same period, from September 2000 to September 2025. To be entirely clear, both equity and bond returns are adjusted for inflation using eurozone CPI data.

Real returns on global stocks and bonds (measured in euros)								
	Bonds	Stocks	Bonds	Stocks	Bonds	Stocks	Bonds	Stocks
	Since 2000		Last 20 years		Last 10 years		Since COVID	
Annualized return	-0.5%	3.2%	-0.5%	6.4%	-2.9%	7.7%	-6.3%	7.4%
Volatility	7.1%	14.2%	7.4%	13.4%	6.1%	14.1%	6.3%	15.6%
Sharpe Ratio	-0.07	0.22	-0.07	0.48	-0.48	0.55	-1.00	0.47

Source: The Great Rebalancing, Eurostat, Investing.com

First, the table confirms once more that over the past 25 years, global bonds have delivered outright negative real returns. On average, bond investors lost 0.5 percent of purchasing power per year, every year. That brings us to the striking reality: The Sharpe Ratio for bonds is negative. Besides confirming that bonds have been a loss-making investment in real terms, a negative ratio renders the metric itself meaningless as a measure of quality. Think about it: When returns are negative, greater volatility only makes the ratio less negative, giving a distorted impression of improvement.

Paradoxically, the Sharpe Ratio does not account for negative returns, and yet that is precisely what bond investors got over the last 25 years. A negative real Sharpe Ratio reveals two closely linked truths:

- You lost purchasing power by investing in that asset class.
- You were not compensated in any way for the risk you took.

That is a grim reality, far removed from the idea that investing helps you escape the erosive effects of inflation. Fortunately, the picture looks far brighter for equities. The data show that since 2000, equities have produced an average real annual return of 3.2 percent.

Investing in equities would have genuinely grown your purchasing power over the past 25 years.

When looking at shorter time frames, the performance gap between equities and bonds becomes downright extreme. Take the past decade, or even since the onset of the COVID crisis, including the sharp equity sell-offs at the start of the pandemic. During those periods, equities delivered real returns of 7.7 and 7.4 percent per year on average, respectively. Bonds, by contrast, produced real returns of minus 2.9 percent and minus 6.3 percent per year over those same periods.

Those numbers really hit home when you translate them into purchasing power. Suppose you invested €100,000 in global bonds at the start of 2020. By October 2025, the real value of that investment would have dropped to €69,000, a staggering 31 percent loss of purchasing power. The same investment in global equities would now be worth €151,000 in real terms, a difference of €82,000 (€151,000 minus €69,000).

During the inflation peak of 2022, media coverage focused on skyrocketing supermarket prices, but rarely on the unprecedented destruction of purchasing power in savings accounts, investment portfolios, and pension funds caused by that same inflation surge.

Also take a look at the row labeled "volatility" in the table. Government bonds are routinely marketed as "low risk." I cringe every time I see the term "risk-averse" splashed across the websites of asset managers. Because bonds are nowhere near as risk-free as they're made out to be. A volatility of 6-7 percent is not that low. In any case, it was high enough to deliver heavy negative returns and a major loss of purchasing power. And as we'll see later, the risk in bonds is climbing steadily. Even if you hold a bond to maturity and it repays its nominal value, inflation still destroys purchasing power along the way.

Stuck in the Past

The data raise an obvious question: How have traditional asset managers managed to get away with the Sharpe Ratio story for so long? On the one hand, because they have systematically left inflation out of the picture, leaving investors only partially informed (not every investor can just sit down and calculate real returns on their own). On the other hand, it's because the investment industry is stuck in deeply ingrained habits.

To understand how the habits took hold, we need to dig deeper into history. The next table again compares the inflation-adjusted Sharpe Ratios for equities and bonds, this time using US market data. The US offers a richer dataset, allowing for a far deeper and broader analysis. The comparison now begins in 1973, over fifty years ago. For further insight, I also calculate real returns, volatility, and Sharpe Ratios over the past forty, thirty, twenty, and ten years, as well as since the pandemic.

Real returns on US stocks and bonds (measured in US dollars)												
	Bonds	S&P 500	Bonds	S&P 500	Bonds	S&P 500	Bonds	S&P 500	Bonds	S&P 500	Bonds	S&P 500
	Since 1973		Last 40 years		Last 30 years		Last 20 years		Last 10 years		Since COVID	
Annualized return	2.2%	5.8%	2.5%	8.1%	1.4%	7.2%	0.3%	7.7%	-1.0%	5.4%	-3.7%	10.2%
Volatility	5.5%	15.6%	5.1%	15.4%	5.0%	15.4%	5.1%	15.3%	5.2%	15.6%	5.8%	17.0%
Sharpe Ratio	0.40	0.37	0.48	0.53	0.27	0.47	0.05	0.51	-0.18	0.35	-0.63	0.60

Source: The Great Rebalancing, Bureau of Labor Statistics, Investing.com

It now becomes clear where the industry's unwavering affection for the 60/40 portfolio really comes from. Go far enough back in time, and you will find periods where the Sharpe Ratios of equities and bonds were indeed similar. But the table shows you have to go back at least forty years to find that balance. Over that past forty-year stretch, the Sharpe Ratios for bonds and equities (0.48 and 0.53) were nearly identical.

For every shorter time frame, the real return on bonds falls and ultimately turns negative again. The real return on US Treasuries averaged 1.4 percent per year over the past thirty years, just 0.3 percent over the past twenty. And over the past ten years, the return averaged minus 1.0 percent per year. Is that surprising? Probably, if you've only got to listen to the stories told by traditional asset managers. But for investors who understand that the system stays afloat only at the discretion of low rates and high inflation, probably not.

Real equity returns, by contrast, have been consistently and significantly positive across all periods. Moreover, there's no sign of a downward trend. The conclusion practically writes itself: Based on real, inflation-adjusted returns, equities unquestionably deserve their place in a well-diversified portfolio.

To make the contrast between the two asset classes even starker, the chart below plots the real Sharpe Ratios of US equities and bonds over time. Here, the Sharpe Ratio is calculated as the relationship between the ten-year rolling average *real return* and the ten-year rolling *volatility*. As in earlier charts, "rolling" means the series shifts forward by one period (in this case, a month), after which the Sharpe Ratio is recalculated for each new ten-year window. The result is a compelling visual showing how the quality of returns in stocks and bonds has evolved through history.

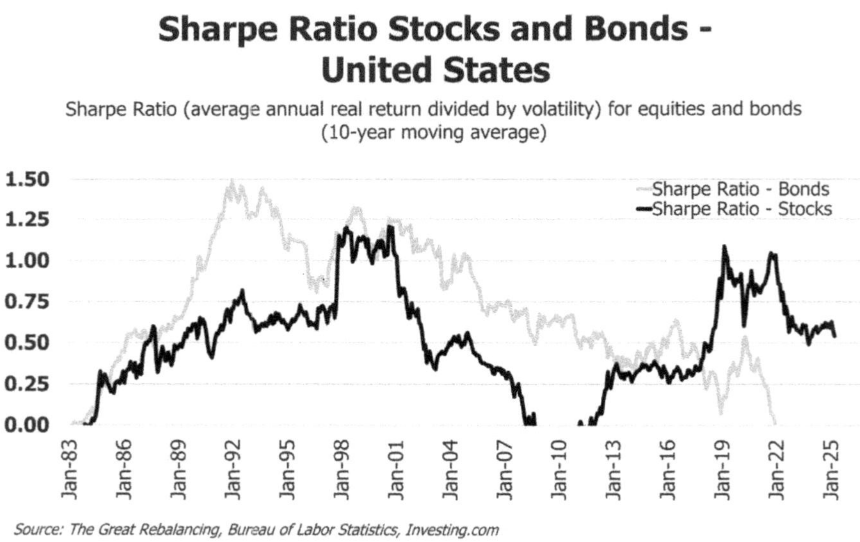

The results speak for themselves, and they are highly unfavorable for bonds. The chart above reveals that the Sharpe Ratio for bonds (gray line) has been declining almost continuously for the past thirty-five years. In the early 1990s, the ratio sat comfortably above 1.0, a level investors typically regard as strong. Since then, it has moved relentlessly downward. By late 2021, it plunged into negative territory and dropped off the chart entirely. The vertical axis is truncated at zero because negative Sharpe Ratios say little, only that an investment has lost purchasing power over the years.

For equities, the picture couldn't be more different. The equity Sharpe Ratio (black line) briefly dipped below zero during the global financial crisis of 2008, only to recover strongly thereafter. There is no structural downward trend for equities, unlike in the case of bonds. The dogma that both equities and bonds deserve a place in every investment portfolio because each offers a "respectable Sharpe Ratio" is, quite literally, yesterday's news. You have to go back four decades to find data supporting that claim.

One of the joys of writing a book is that by diving so deep, the pieces of the puzzle start to fit together better than you ever imagined. If fiscal dominance truly defines today's financial system, there must be a direct link between poor bond returns and the structural budget deficits of governments. The larger the deficit and the higher the public debt burden, the stronger the incentive to keep interest rates purposely low and drive inflation higher.

The chart on the next page compares the ten-year rolling average Sharpe Ratio of US bonds (gray line, left axis) with the ten-year rolling average US budget deficit as a share of GDP (black line, right axis). This time, the right axis is *not* inverted, meaning that a larger deficit drives the black line downward, while a smaller deficit sends it up.

Since the global financial crisis, when the effects of aging demographics accelerated and US debt accumulation kicked into high gear, a remarkably strong correlation has emerged between the Sharpe Ratio of bonds and the size of the federal deficit. Ever since Washington proved unable to run even a modest deficit, the rule has been simple: the bigger the deficit, the lower the bond Sharpe Ratio. Put more bluntly: the more debt out there, the worse that debt performs.

Sharpe Ratio Bonds and Fiscal Budget - United States

Sharpe Ratio (average annual real return divided by volatility) for bonds and the budget deficit as a percentage of GDP

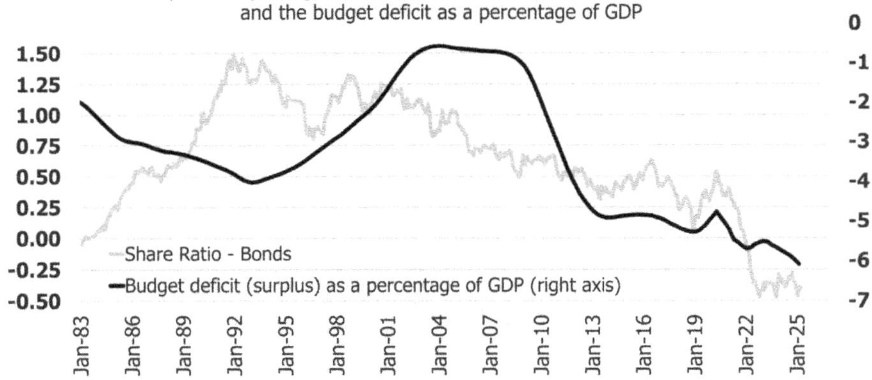

Source: The Great Rebalancing, Bureau of Labor Statistics, Investing.com

Equities as an Inflation Hedge

The data above already reveal why bonds drown under fiscal dominance while equities stay afloat. The difference is inflation. Bonds offer no protection against it, but equities do.

For bonds, the yield required by investors climbs when inflation expectations increase or when uncertainty about future inflation grows. That makes sense because higher inflation means the risk of losing purchasing power goes up. Unfortunately, in a regime where maintaining debt sustainability rules and interest rates are artificially suppressed, bondholders do not receive that additional yield. Quite the opposite: They face yields far too low to offset inflation.

An Elegant Theory

How does this work for equities? Irving Fisher, who we best know for his quantity theory of money, which links money supply growth to higher inflation, introduced another elegant theory in the early 1930s. Though originally focused on interest rates, it provides the foundation for a positive relationship between equity returns and inflation.

The Fisher effect holds that the nominal interest rate must equal the sum of the real interest rate and inflation.

The real interest rate determines how much purchasing power you gain. Suppose you aim to achieve a 2 percent real return by lending money to the government while expecting 3 percent inflation. To meet your target, the nominal interest rate must be 5 percent, 2 percent real rate plus 3 percent inflation. At a lower nominal rate, inflation prevents you from achieving your 2 percent purchasing power goal. Fisher argued that when inflation rises, nominal interest rates must adjust upward to keep the real rate unchanged. That's the essence of the Fisher effect.

Fisher extended the same logic to nominal equity returns, which must then be the sum of real equity returns and inflation. Nominal returns on stocks, he argued, should adjust fully to changes in the inflation rate so that their real value remains intact. In practice, this happens when companies raise prices in response to inflation, boosting their nominal cash flows. These higher cash flows translate into higher nominal profits and dividends that flow to shareholders.

Investors, in turn, adjust the nominal valuation of companies, causing stock prices, and thus nominal returns, to rise with inflation, thereby preserving the real value of equities.

Fisher's theory is both elegant and intuitive, though it rests on three key assumptions:

- Markets are efficient, meaning that changes in inflation are immediately reflected in stock prices.
- Companies can raise prices without significantly hurting margins or demand.
- Inflation does not materially harm economic growth.

While those are bold assumptions that invite nuance to the Fisher effect, there is ample empirical evidence that equities do, in fact, provide substantial protection against inflation.

Debates about equities as an inflation hedge often suffer from confusion over whether the focus is on short- or long-term protection.

In their 1993 study "Stock Returns and Inflation: A Long-Horizon Perspective," Jacob Boudoukh and Matthew Richardson show that equities provide significant long-term protection against monetary debasement. While the link between inflation and equity returns is mostly negative over one-year periods, over periods of five years or longer, the correlation turns decisively positive. Boudoukh and Richardson's argument is straightforward: Over the long term, companies can adjust their prices and therefore their profits to match inflation. This mechanism preserves real equity returns, just like the Fisher effect predicts.

Jeremy Siegel reached a similar conclusion in his celebrated 1994 book *Stocks for the Long Run.* He demonstrated that equities have consistently maintained, and even expanded, their real purchasing power despite heavy bouts of inflation. Long-term equity returns show that profitable business activity consistently outpaces inflation's damaging effects. Siegel goes a step further, calling equities "the perfect hedge against inflation."

As usual, most of these studies center on the United States, though Boudoukh and Richardson also include the United Kingdom. The landmark global dataset compiled by Dimson, Marsh, and Staunton in *Triumph of the Optimists – 101 Years of Global Investment Returns* (2002) contributes compelling broader evidence: Across countries and time, equities have acted as reliable inflation hedges UBS's annual *Global Investment Returns Yearbook*, which maintains and updates the Dimson, Marsh, and Staunton database, convincingly confirms that equities in most countries have grown their real value over the long run. Even during episodes of high inflation, equities proved capable of preventing a loss of purchasing power.

Formidable Opposition

Yet not everyone sides with Fisher and Siegel. One of the most influential counterarguments comes from Nobel laureate Eugene Fama, founder of the efficient market hypothesis. His core starting point is that the relationship between inflation and stock returns must be *negative*. Higher inflation actually means lower stock prices.

In his 1981 paper "Stock Returns, Real Activity, Inflation, and Money," Fama argued that the negative relationship is not caused by inflation itself but by the underlying real economy. His "proxy hypothesis" posits that high inflation coincides with weaker real GDP growth, which is what really drags down equity prices. High inflation prompts central banks to raise interest rates and slow economic activity. Since growth drives profits, and profits drive stock prices, stock prices fall when inflation rises, at least according to Fama.

Fama's approach differs fundamentally from Fisher's theory, which assumes that inflation affects (stock) prices but not the real economy. Profits rise automatically with prices without hurting production, consumption, or employment. Fama counters that inflation breeds economic uncertainty and tighter monetary policy, which ultimately depress stock prices.

Geske and Roll (1983) followed this line of reasoning in "The Fiscal and Monetary Linkage Between Stock Returns and Inflation." As their title suggests, they argue that inflation provokes government and central bank responses. As inflation rises, governments may cut spending and central banks will attempt to slow economic activity through interest rate hikes. More recently, Ang, Bekaert, and Wei (2012) reach a similar conclusion: Inflation surprises increase uncertainty about central bank policy. And investors very much dislike uncertainty, and that inversion translates into lower stock prices.

Though these are undeniably landmark studies dealing with the relationship between equity returns and inflation, their focus is almost exclusively on the role of the business cycle. These studies predominantly examine how inflation interacts with economic fluctuations and investor expectations about short-term growth. Viewed through that lens, the relationship appears negative. But when you look through the business cycle, the picture changes entirely: Over longer horizons, the relationship between inflation and equity returns becomes distinctively positive.

Beyond the short-versus-long-term distinction, there is a far more fundamental shift at play. Fama's theory makes sense within a traditional framework in which central banks operate independently, with the primary goal of fighting inflation through interest rate policy. But as I demonstrate throughout this book, this assumption no longer holds.

Central banks are not independent. In today's regime of fiscal dominance, monetary policy has been subordinated to the imperative of keeping government debt sustainable. Even when inflation rises, central banks suppress interest rates. The traditional feedback loop, where higher inflation prompts central banks to hike interest rates, has been broken.

This eliminates the core mechanism in Fama's framework and that of others, where higher inflation leads to tighter monetary policy, slower GDP growth, and, as a result, lower company earnings. Central banks no longer raise rates in step with inflation. Recall the European Central Bank. After the inflation wave of 2022, the ECB eventually lifted rates to only 4 percent, even as inflation peaked above 10 percent. When the ECB stopped hiking, inflation was still running above 4 percent. Within nine months after the final increase, it began cutting rates aggressively, and by mid-2025 the policy rate had already been halved to 2 percent.

The key point here is that under fiscal dominance, the link between equity returns and inflation tends to be positive, not negative. Not because Fama and his peers were necessarily wrong, but because the rules of the financial system itself have fundamentally changed. High inflation no longer triggers tighter monetary policy and slower economic growth. Instead, loose monetary conditions allow companies to raise prices freely. It is this exact pattern we witnessed after the pandemic, and it explains why the massive budget deficits failed to suppress corporate profits, as the first chart in this chapter illustrates. Governments and central banks engineered massive bursts of GDP growth, which, together with spiking inflation, supercharged corporate profits.

That is why, as the table above shows, global equities have delivered an impressive real return of 6.5 percent per year (in euros) since the COVID-19 pandemic, despite the highest inflation in four decades. In fact, it perfectly illustrates how fiscal dominance has rewritten the playbook: In this new era, inflation and equity performance march in the same direction.

In Search of Scarcity

Equities are increasingly outperforming bonds in a world shaped by fiscal dominance. The trends in real returns on equities and bonds, especially since the global financial crisis and the pandemic, make that abundantly clear. But does this hold true for all stocks?

The answer to that question is first "yes," and ultimately "no." Let me try to explain this. As the risk-return figures in this chapter show, equity capital, represented by listed stocks like those in the MSCI World Index, is superior to debt. Equity is a relatively scarce and valuable asset that is resistant to the key side effect of a debt-driven economy: inflation.

However, that definition needs important refinement. The first part should read: Equity capital *that is used to generate sustainable cash flows* is a relatively scarce and valuable asset. My analysis demonstrates that equities as a group have strongly outperformed bonds, but that doesn't mean every company can put its equity to work profitably. Not every firm is strong enough to remain profitable in a system characterized by slowing potential GDP growth or to pass on rising prices to its customers.

Only companies with exceptionally robust business models, strong pricing power, and solid balance sheets can sustain profitability, regardless of how the economic landscape changes. These are firms that combine the power of equity capital with the resilience needed to survive in a system no longer powered by productivity and growth, but by debt, fiscal largesse, and unconventional monetary policy.

This is where Fisher's and Fama's theories intersect. For Fisher, inflation boosts nominal returns through higher prices and profits; for Fama, inflation hurts the real economy, and only exceptional firms withstand the damage. You want to invest in this scarce group of companies that stand at the intersection of these fundamentally opposing theories. These are what investors tend to call quality stocks, but I prefer to think of them as "scarce stocks." After all, there aren't many of them.

Quality as Scarcity

In short, quality stocks are stocks of companies with superior business models and lasting, structural competitive advantages. Warren Buffett, considered by many investors the *GOAT* (greatest of all time), refers to such advantages as "moats." A moat, in medieval terms, is a defensive trench protecting a castle from attack. Just as moats protect castles from invaders, they protect companies from competitive attacks. Ideally, for as long as possible. Buffett's favorite companies not only possess strong competitive edges but are able to maintain and defend them for decades, even through periods of high inflation.

Sustainable competitive advantages, moats, stem from many sources: powerful brands, superior technology, patents, network effects, natural or regulatory barriers, economies of scale, or exclusive access to labor, raw materials, or resources. Apple and Coca-Cola exemplify brand strength. Their consumers happily pay more because their trust in these brands is almost unshakable. Companies like Meta, Microsoft, and Visa rely heavily on vast network effects, while NVIDIA and ASML thrive on technological superiority. Wholesale giant Costco benefits from economies of scale and operational efficiency, while Denmark's Novo Nordisk owes its edge to a strong portfolio of patents.

Although the sources of competitive advantage differ widely from one company to another, they tend to share common characteristics often identified in academic studies on the appeal of quality stocks. Below are the most important examples of these characteristics:

- Strong pricing power. Arguably, the most defining trait of quality companies. They can raise prices without meaningfully reducing demand and can actively defend profitability when inflation rises.
- High profit margins. Quality firms enjoy strong, durable margins, generating consistent earnings even in weak economic environments. An alternative measure is high *return on equity* (ROE), reflecting a company's ability to produce strong, lasting cash flows with its capital.
- Low leverage. Quality companies rely primarily on equity, not debt, to fund operations and produce stable earnings. This reduces the risk of default or refinancing stress during credit crises, a vital edge in today's debt-burdened world, where about three-quarters of all financial activity is simply refinancing old debt.
- Stable cash flows. Quality firms generate solid, predictable cash flows. While profitability often gets more attention, cash flow ultimately determines whether a business can fund future growth.

This list of quality factors is not exhaustive. In practice, many other attributes are cited when measuring company "quality." Two of the most common are strong management and customer loyalty. While both contribute to a company's overall quality, they are harder to quantify in academic research and to test empirically. Moreover, you could argue that strong management and loyal customers reveal themselves through the financial traits listed above: high margins, stable cash flows, and the ability to pass on higher prices without hurting demand. Taken together, these characteristics go a long way toward identifying truly scarce, high-quality businesses.

Quality as a Factor

Remarkably, the focus on quality stocks has only taken off in the past decade, both in academic circles and among professional investors. That's because "quality" has only since become a fully recognized investment factor. Unlike the classic equity factors momentum (added by Carhart, 1997 to the original Fama and French model), size, and value, long praised since the 1990s or even earlier for their superior risk-adjusted returns, the factor quality was acknowledged much later as an independent driver of stock performance.

Quality's real breakthrough came in 2015, when none other than Eugene Fama and Kenneth French expanded their legendary three-factor model. Fama and French stand, without question, among the most influential minds in modern finance. Their original 1993 framework explained equity returns through three drivers: overall market risk (whether markets rise or fall), company size (small versus large), and valuation (cheap versus expensive). It is probably the best-known equity model in the world and has dominated professional investment for decades. My own thesis at Erasmus University was grounded in the Fama and French three-factor model.

Yet, more than twenty years later, Fama and French concluded that their iconic model was no longer sufficient. They added two new factors: profitability (robust versus weak) and investment behavior (conservative versus aggressive). By doing so, they acknowledged that part of stock performance could not be explained by general market movements, size, or valuation alone. Factors tied to quality, profitability and capital efficiency (meaning the ability to grow earnings with relatively low investment), filled in the missing piece of the equity-return puzzle. Understanding the sources of returns has always been Fama and French's primary objective. Put simply, these factors helped explain why some stocks structurally outperform even when the classic variables fall short in explaining that performance.

As you would expect from Fama and French, their new five-factor model again sent shockwaves through finance. The results were strikingly clear: Companies with strong profitability and conservative investment policies consistently outperformed those with weaker profitability and aggressive investment expansion. Fama and French's extended model provided direct evidence that a company's quality is reflected in its market performance.

But that was not the only groundbreaking conclusion. Adding these new factors had a profound side effect: It knocked out the explanatory power of the value factor, long considered the cornerstone of Fama and French's original model. Value as a return factor no longer mattered. Whether a company was cheap or expensive no longer made a difference; what counted was profitability and the efficient use of capital to generate those profits.

Although this finding did not hold equally across all countries, the fact that quality displaced value in the world's most important equity market, the United States, came as a major shock to the professional investment community, especially to traditional value investors. Obviously, the findings of Fama and French reflected poorly on the vast array of "value funds" launched over the previous decades. In the years following 2015, investors pulled hundreds of billions of dollars from value funds. The industry called this a "renewed focus on factor investing," a polite way of saying that value investing had lost much of its appeal.

My own experience in traditional asset management supports that value investing quite often functions more as a marketing slogan than as a sound investment strategy. The idea of owning strong-performing yet "cheap" stocks undoubtedly sounds irresistible, but in reality, value stocks are nearly always cheap for a reason: They simply aren't very good.

Quality Is Scarce

Since the groundbreaking work of Fama and French in 2015, the *quality factor* has evolved at remarkable speed, from a relative latecomer to one of the most respected and powerful forces in factor investing. During my years as a portfolio manager at Robeco, one of the largest asset managers in the Netherlands, where factor investing has long been a strategic pillar, I saw this shift unfold firsthand.

From the moment quality appeared on the radar as a proven factor, I was convinced. Not just because the numbers prove high-quality companies consistently outperform, but above all because of what *quality* represents: exceptional businesses that are fundamentally healthy and deliver above-average results across the board. Quality is not about one-dimensional characteristics such as size or valuation but about companies that combine a rare mix of attributes to remain structurally profitable and create real long-term value. Unlike size or valuation, quality offers a much more complete assessment of the underlying strength of a company.

Because companies must jump through several hoops to earn the label "quality," they are better equipped to adapt to a changing economic regime. That brings us back to the central theme of fiscal dominance. The unique combination of characteristics that define quality companies enables them to thrive even amid slowing growth, extreme fiscal and monetary policy, and rising inflation risk. It goes without saying that there are not that many of these companies. In other words, quality firms are intrinsically scarce and cannot simply be created or engineered, which makes them an indispensable cornerstone of any future-proof investment portfolio.

How to Invest in Scarce Equities

The emergence of quality as an investment factor makes it possible to introduce an element of *scarcity* even within the traditional asset class of equities. Few companies can generate steady profits year after year, deploy capital conservatively yet effectively to produce cash flows, and pass the adverse effects of fiscal dominance, like inflation, on to their customers. These rare, exceptional companies are the ones worth investing in.

But how do you translate that idea into an effective and efficient investment strategy? In other words, how do you make sure your equity investments are genuinely high quality? And that these quality stocks are packaged within a transparent, cost-efficient structure that can be adjusted easily to manage portfolio risk?

That is less straightforward than it perhaps sounds, and in practice few investors succeed. For example, too often investing in quality stocks gets confused with stock picking. Stock picking is the selection of individual stocks with the aim of outperforming the broader market. That's usually where things go off track. Numerous studies show that both professional and retail investors struggle uncomfortably to beat the market consistently through stock picking. In fact, the opposite is true: On average, stock pickers lag the overall market, and often by a wide margin.

The numbers vary by study, but seen over longer periods, only a small fraction of active equity funds, most of them relying on stock picking, manage to outperform their benchmark. According to index provider S&P Global, best known for the S&P 500 index, only 15 percent of all active US equity funds outperformed their benchmark over the five years to the end of 2024. Stretch that horizon to ten years, and the figure drops to 10 percent. Finally, measured over fifteen years, only 7 percent of active equity funds manage to beat the market, an astonishingly low number. Just one in fourteen active US equity funds has managed to outperform the market over a long period of time.

One major reason active funds lag behind their benchmarks is the fees they charge for their services. Beyond all the research that goes into picking individual stocks, the costs of setting up and running a proper fund structure should not be underestimated. The sheer weight of regulation, from know your customer (KYC) rules to anti-money laundering (AML) requirements and the like, pushes costs through the roof. From experience, I can confirm that building a fully compliant professional fund structure is not only time-consuming but also unnecessarily expensive. Still, even when you look past these costs, active funds rarely succeed in outperforming the market consistently through stock selection.

Retail investors tend to fare even worse. Hundreds, if not thousands, of books have been written on this very topic, nearly all pointing to the same culprit: human psychology. The very instincts that once kept us alive on the savannah now sabotage our skills in the stock market. Think of unfounded overconfidence which makes us believe we can always beat the market. Or our refusal to cut losses and sell the losers, even when flashing red flags tell us a stock will not recover.

Other psychological pitfalls include anchoring (clinging to arbitrary price levels, usually the purchase price, as a meaningless reference point), herd behavior (blindly following others), and overtrading driven by our emotions. Daniel Kahneman captures this brilliantly in his masterpiece *Thinking, Fast and Slow* (2011), showing how our instinctive, emotional decision-making processes and primal reactions constantly interfere with rational investment choices. If you haven't read it, I strongly recommend you do; it will give a masterclass in understanding yourself as an investor. Kahneman's book is the main reason why I don't believe in traditional stock picking. It is extremely difficult to overcome your own instincts.

Lastly, it would be too simplistic to blame these human psychological biases solely on retail investors. The investment world is full of smaller asset managers run by a handful of older, gray-haired men trying to handpick "the next winner." These investors are no more immune to Kahneman's cognitive biases than anyone else.

I also wonder how they can credibly claim to have some informational edge that lets them beat the market. Most of what they read comes from public sources, newspapers, social media, and financial websites. Or they pay for lengthy research reports from major investment banks. But let's not forget: Those same banks, like Goldman Sachs or J.P. Morgan, had access to this information long before anyone else did. They are the ones sitting next to CEOs and CFOs of companies, advising them on financing structures or bond issues, and refinancing existing debt, with front-row access to the data.

Active Versus Passive

Don't worry, this is not another lecture insisting that everyone should invest passively. For one, it would imply that investors stop actively searching for information that shapes stock prices and valuations. Without active investors, not all relevant data would be reflected in stock prices, creating inefficiencies that active strategies could exploit. Second, the debate between *active* and *passive* investing is far too binary. Contrary to popular belief, you can invest actively using passive instruments such as Exchange-Traded Funds (ETFs) or similar vehicles that track segments of the market.

For instance, you can use ETFs to invest actively in scarce, high-quality stocks, without stock picking and immune to the many psychological pitfalls of discretionary investing. In short, this approach can be described as systematic investing in quality.

A prime example is the MSCI World Quality Index, which filters the broader MSCI World Index down to companies with "superior" quality traits: strong competitive strength, low debt levels, and high, stable profitability. Exactly the same factors identified by Fama and French, used to distinguish quality stocks, and shown to have a positive impact on returns.

Using MSCI indices as the foundation for quality investing keeps you within the same universe as the global benchmark, the MSCI World Index. It's by far the most popular benchmark for tracking the performance of global equity portfolios. It also allows consistent comparison across investment factors such as value, since MSCI has derived a World Value Index from the same parent index.

Contrary to what some stock pickers claim, choosing to invest solely in quality stocks via an ETF is without question an active decision. Based on MSCI's methodology, roughly 80 percent of the companies in the broader MSCI World Index are excluded. MSCI systematically ranks all constituents by those quality attributes that academic research shows to add value. Only the top 20 percent make it into the quality basket, without you having to pick a single stock yourself. The goal is to capture the quality factor as broadly and as diversified as possible. In doing so, the scarcity and superior returns of these companies are directly reflected in an investment portfolio of scarce assets.

The next chart compares the performance of three MSCI indices: quality stocks, value stocks, and the broad MSCI World Index. If you had invested $100,000 in global quality stocks in 1981, the launch year of the MSCI Quality Index, it would have grown to $17 million by October 2025. The same $100,000 investment in value stocks would have turned into about $5.7 million, while the broad index would have delivered around $6.5 million. Quality stocks have crushed the overall market, whereas value stocks have lagged behind the broader index over the past forty years. This aligns perfectly with Fama and French's finding that the value factor no longer adds excess return to US equities.

Performance of Stocks

Nominal value of $100,000 invested in quality stocks, value stocks, and the MSCI World Index

Source: The Great Rebalancing, Bloomberg

It is a spectacular chart, but to assess the true appeal of quality stocks, one must look again beyond nominal returns, which must be adjusted for inflation and risk.

The next table presents these results. To capture a longer time span, I take the view of a US investor allocating to either the broad MSCI World Index or the MSCI World Quality Index (containing only the top-tier quality firms). Real returns are calculated using US inflation data. For completeness, I also include US Treasury bonds. As already shown, bond performance has deteriorated steadily as fiscal dominance deepened. The table spans up to forty years of market history.

Real returns on global stocks, quality stocks, and bonds (measured in US dollars)															
	Bonds	Stocks	Quality	Bonds	Stocks	Quality	Bonds	Stocks	Quality	Bonds	Stocks	Quality	Bonds	Stocks	Quality
	Last 40 years			Last 30 years			Last 20 years			Last 10 years			Since COVID		
Annualized return	2.5%	6.6%	9.4%	1.4%	5.2%	8.0%	0.3%	5.9%	8.2%	-1.0%	4.4%	5.3%	-3.7%	8.2%	9.2%
Volatility	5.1%	15.3%	14.6%	5.0%	15.2%	14.6%	5.1%	15.6%	14.5%	5.2%	15.0%	15.2%	5.8%	16.1%	16.9%
Sharpe Ratio	0.48	0.43	0.64	0.27	0.35	0.55	0.05	0.38	0.56	-0.18	0.29	0.35	-0.63	0.51	0.55

Source: The Great Rebalancing, Bureau of Labor Statistics, Investing.com

The numbers speak loud and clear. Across every time frame, from forty years to the post-pandemic period, the average annual real return on quality stocks exceeded that of the broad MSCI World Index. Apart from the brief post-pandemic window, the risk (measured as volatility) of quality stocks was lower. In all periods, the Sharpe Ratio (here return divided by volatility) of quality stocks was higher than that of the market as a whole.

These are compelling figures supporting a powerful philosophy: In a world of slower economic growth and higher inflation, quality stocks rise to the top.

The Best of Both Worlds

This chapter demonstrates that attractive scarce assets are not confined to the so-called "alternative" investment universe of gold and bitcoin. Within traditional equities, too, there exists a segment defined by scarcity: quality stocks.

Companies with structural competitive advantages or moats, high profitability, low debt ratios, and stable cash flows are rare. Decades of research, most notably by the celebrated duo Fama and French, show that these traits translate into higher returns and superior Sharpe Ratios.

Making quality stocks even more compelling is their ability to pass rising inflation on to customers, thereby shielding investors from the relentless erosion of purchasing power.

With quality equities as one of the pillars of a portfolio built on scarce assets, alongside physical gold and bitcoin, you take another decisive step toward protecting your wealth against financial repression and fiscal dominance.

And it raises another interesting question: *"Are there more scarce assets worth owning?"*

CHAPTER 17

More Scarcity?

Introduction

A few years ago, I considered writing my first book entirely about scarce investments. Those ambitions were interrupted by the launch of the Blokland Smart Multi-Asset Fund, which, as you may know, invests exclusively in scarce assets. In hindsight, that delay turned out to be a blessing for this book. I'm convinced that the experience of running the fund, and the extensive analysis and reading that come with it, makes this book a much sharper guide to constructing a truly future-proof investment portfolio.

And if my early assumption, that you could fill an entire book with scarce assets, teaches anything, it's that the search for additional scarce investments could easily stretch into a book of its own.

Still, I will keep this chapter focused on the essentials. That way, I keep all options open for a second book, but more importantly because many other scarce assets do not yet meet all the criteria required to earn a place in the future-proof portfolio.

Key Characteristics

Not every scarce asset automatically qualifies as part of a fiscal-dominance-proof investment portfolio. Scarcity is a necessary but not sufficient condition for an asset to qualify as a suitable investment. Another indispensable requirement is utility. Scarce assets must serve a function, fulfill a purpose, and contribute to lasting value creation, that is, to the preservation of purchasing power.

To illustrate this, consider art. It is undeniably scarce and certainly not "useless," but its utility is fundamentally different from that of monetary assets. Art delivers aesthetic and emotional value, and many people are willing to pay for that experience. Yet this kind of utility is consumptive, subjective, and personal. It does not translate easily into broad, scalable, or liquid investment demand.

That is precisely why art, despite its cultural value, does not function well as a monetary store of value for most investors. Its utility is real, but not of the type required to anchor a portfolio in a regime of fiscal dominance.

This chapter explores the additional characteristics that scarce, useful assets must possess to make them attractive investment alternatives. For bitcoin, physical gold, and high-quality stocks, these traits are evident, assuming the previous chapters have done their job. For other scarce assets like art, vintage cars, real estate, or commodities, the case is far more nuanced.

To qualify as a compelling and investable scarce asset, an asset must score well on the following five key dimensions:

- Liquidity

Liquidity, in the broadest sense, measures how easily you can buy or sell an asset at any given time, close to its (observed) market price, at reasonable costs. Think again of art, rare wines, or vintage cars. You can't exactly trade those assets for cash at the click of a button. Liquidity is also linked to the existence of universally tradable structures that make buying, owning, and selling an investment straightforward. Just ask yourself how many accessible, liquid, and cost-efficient investment funds or ETFs allow you to invest easily and efficiently in classic cars, art, or wine?

- Divisibility

This is what characterizes many scarce assets such as art and luxury goods. They cannot be divided without destroying their value. Take, for example, Jane Birkin's original Hermès Birkin bag, sold at Sotheby's in July 2025 for €8.6 million after just ten minutes of bidding. Investing in such a scarce asset requires substantial wealth; you can't buy just a piece of that bag. This also makes it impossible to manage its weight within a well-diversified portfolio of scarce assets. There is only one original Birkin, and even if there were two, you would still need millions more to own it. The same lack of flexibility is reflected in overall portfolio risk: With these assets, it's all or nothing, leaving little room for portfolio management.

- Subjectivity

For several scarce assets, this is their Achilles's heel. How do you decide, or have someone else decide for you, whether a painting by Van Gogh or Picasso is the better investment? Or whether you should buy a Château Pétrus or Château Lafite Rothschild vintage. And from which year? Even if you are lucky enough to know the answers to these questions, value still depends heavily on taste, popularity, and fashion. What is deemed valuable today may have lost that value a decade from now. This lack of homogeneity and universal value makes art, wine, and classic cars notoriously difficult, and undeniably subjective, as investments.

- Monetary Store of Value

Fiat money has no intrinsic value; since abandoning the gold standard, its value rests entirely on trust. As government and central bank policies erode that trust, it makes sense to hold part of your wealth in assets universally accepted as stores of value, assets that hold their worth when trust fades. An investment or asset that has proven its ability to preserve value precisely when inflation rises.

From this perspective, physical gold and, increasingly, bitcoin are the most interesting candidates, as they represent the monetary bedrock of the financial system (or, in the case of bitcoin, is beginning to). Both come without counterparty risk, a unique feature in an environment where capital is coerced into financing public debt.

The same applies less to quality stocks, though some central banks do hold them on their balance sheets. Art, commodities, land, luxury goods, real estate, and vintage cars have little or no historical role as money or as anchors of the financial system.

- Costs

Costs (insuring, storing, trading) demand a place on the list. High costs, combined with weak investor psychology, are a major reason most investors underperform the market. For many alternative scarce assets, the costs of owning, maintaining, trading, and insuring them are high, if not painfully high.

Scoring Scarcity

The table on the next page scores the best-known scarce assets across the five characteristics just discussed. The list of assets is not exhaustive, nor is the list of key characteristics. This table illustrates my (subjective) assessment of how these assets measure up as fully qualified scarce investments.

I want to stress here that I find every one of these scarce assets inherently interesting, and in any case, more appealing than cash sitting in a bank account or bonds that steadily lose purchasing power in a traditional investment portfolio. Their scarcity and utility, by definition, make them more attractive than fiat money or debt. That said, some still have ground to cover before they can fit into a cost-efficient, liquid, and well-balanced portfolio.

Key characteristics of scarce assets					
Scarce assets	Liquidity	Divisibility	Subjectivity	Store of value	Costs
Bitcoin	High	High	Low	Average	Low
Gold	High	High	Low	High	Low
Quality stocks	High	High	Low	Low	Low
Commodities	High	High	Low	Low	Average
Classic cars	Low	Low	High	Low	High
Art	Low	Low	High	Low	High
Land	Low	Average	Average	Low	Average
Luxury goods	Low	Low	High	Low	High
Real estate	Average	Average	Average	Low	High
Whisky and wine	Low	Low	High	Low	High

Source: The Great Rebalancing

It goes without saying that this table is a stylized, simplified snapshot of reality. You can't just add up the scores and call it science. But if you were to assign two points for the best score on each characteristic (which can be "high" or "low"), one for average, and zero for the worst score, bitcoin, gold, and quality equities would come out on top.

In practice, though, the arithmetic doesn't quite hold up. Take art again as an example. Not only is it extremely illiquid, but top pieces can take months or even years to sell at Sotheby's or Christie's, and its trading costs are astronomical. So high that this characteristic alone makes art a poor fit for any efficient, broadly accessible investment portfolio. Sotheby's, for instance, charges a *buyer's premium* of 27 percent (as of 2025) on hammer prices up to one million US dollars at its New York auctions, dropping to "only" 15 percent for pieces above eight million. And that still ignores the issue of subjectivity. After all, which eight-million-dollar painting would you pick? My answer, out of personal preference and lack of expertise, would always be a work by René Magritte.

Commodities: Not Intrinsically Scarce

Let's briefly turn to two other asset classes often seen as scarce: commodities and real estate. As the table revealed, commodities hold up fairly well across the five characteristics discussed earlier. By commodities, I refer to a broad basket that includes oil, gas, industrial metals like copper, precious metals, agricultural products such as wheat and corn, and sometimes even livestock. Commodities are frequently touted as an attractive addition to an investment portfolio.

That may be true, but not because of their scarcity. Most commodities are, in fact, anything but intrinsically scarce. They exist in large quantities underground, can be replaced or substituted, reproduced, or all of the above. While the amount of proven oil reserves may be declining, vast amounts of global investment in alternative energy sources are simultaneously intended to replace oil altogether.

In 1931, Harold Hotelling set out his now-famous *Hotelling's rule* stating that the price of a nonrenewable natural resource should rise over time, unless technological innovation or substitution prevents it. In the case of oil, the latter clearly applies.

Copper may face temporary scarcity due to the rise of electric vehicles, but for other applications, it is increasingly replaced by aluminum or plastics. Corn and wheat are replanted each year, with weather and seasons largely determining supply. Technology, too, plays an important role here. Crop yields per square meter have been rising steadily for decades. The dire prediction made by Thomas Malthus that food production would fail to keep up with population growth is now more than two centuries old. Since then, the global population has increased more than eightfold, yet there is no structural global food shortage.

If the goal is to invest exclusively in proven scarce assets, commodities, apart from gold, and perhaps silver, should be ruled out.

It is worth adding that investing in commodities almost always happens through derivatives such as futures and forward contracts. These are paper claims on underlying goods, and it's not guaranteed you could ever take physical delivery. It's no coincidence that these commodity derivatives sit at the very bottom of Exter's inverted pyramid.

Real Estate: A Pure Investment?

Real estate is scarce, but with an asterisk. Property in prime locations such as Manhattan, New York, London's Mayfair, or central Amsterdam is undeniably scarce, as is housing in major Asian megacities like Hong Kong and Tokyo. But that does not make real estate a universally scarce asset.

In most places, real estate can be expanded, at least on paper. Moreover, real estate value depends on numerous, often subjective factors that can shift significantly over time. Think of location preferences (living in versus outside the city), regional dynamics (economic growth, net migration, labor markets), and political decisions (rent controls, taxes, zoning laws). In *Capital in the Twenty-First Century*, Thomas Piketty argues that real estate prices are primarily driven by inequality and demand, not intrinsic scarcity, except, of course, at those few top-tier locations.

Another material point: For most "investors," real estate isn't really an investment at all. It's a home, a roof over one's head. In that sense, property is also a consumption good. When you invest in property, you're not just buying bricks and mortar, you're buying utility, sentiment, policy risk, and a kind of scarcity that's far from stable.

For most households, their primary residence makes up the bulk of their total wealth. Because the goal for most people is to live in it, not invest in it, that's hardly a deliberate choice. Since you can't buy a slice of a house and still live in it, most households are forced to borrow heavily to buy one. As a result, this compulsory "investment" ends up dictating how household wealth develops over time.

With that in mind, it rarely makes sense for households to own even more property on top of their primary home from a diversification perspective. To illustrate: If you own a house worth €600,000 with €200,000 in home equity (price appreciation) and invest an additional €100,000 in quality stocks, gold, and bitcoin, you are already heavily overexposed to real estate. A 5 percent increase in the home's value adds €30,000 in housing wealth. For the other investments to generate the same €30,000 gain, they together would have to rise by 30 percent in value. Not impossible, but still a pretty demanding scenario.

Moreover, while real estate often isn't a pure investment, governments increasingly treat it as one for tax purposes. Real estate is uniquely vulnerable to financial repression: You simply cannot move a house abroad to escape taxation. This inconvenient attribute is precisely why governments are targeting property ever more aggressively to fund persistent budget deficits. In addition to taxing the property itself, a rising number of governments are eyeing unrealized capital gains as a tempting future revenue source.

Combined with its limited divisibility, low liquidity, and high subjectivity (a house in the Netherlands, a winter stay in the Algarve, or an apartment in Dubai), these are compelling reasons why the Blokland Smart Multi-Asset Fund does not invest in real estate.

Tokenization

Before turning to the final part of this book, where I will show that it's by no means too late to invest in scarce assets, I want to briefly highlight one significant development. Tokenization is a technology-driven trend with the potential to dramatically lower one of the biggest barriers to investing in scarce assets: divisibility.

Tokenization converts scarce assets into digital tokens, recorded on a blockchain. These tokens represent ownership rights in a scarce good, say, a Van Gogh painting, but in purely digital form. While the physical painting cannot be cut into pieces (unless you are willing to destroy its value), the ownership can be divided digitally using tokens. Hence the name tokenization.

Tokenization doesn't just allow ownership of, in this case, a Van Gogh painting, to be digitally divided; it makes those fractions tradable. With tokens, you can digitally "slice" a physical object, so its fractions can be bought and sold. As with bitcoin, the blockchain ensures that these digital ownership rights remain tamper-proof and secure, and that token transactions are transparent and irreversible.

Tokenization tackles one of the fundamental issues of scarce physical assets: limited divisibility. Think again of a bottle of Château Pétrus, a classic Ferrari, or a René Magritte painting, which I would love to hang on my wall.

Developments in tokenization, and the broader "democratization" of illiquid investment markets, are moving fast. According to McKinsey (2024), the total market value of tokenized assets could soar from a few tens of millions today to $2 trillion by 2030. That's still less than bitcoin's market capitalization at the time of writing, but it represents explosive growth, nonetheless.

Platforms like Masterworks and Artory already allow investors to buy into masterpieces with relatively small sums. In August 2025, Masterworks had raised around $1 billion from investors and sold close to $80 million worth of art for its clients. Vinovest, dVINlabs, and Cask Capital let you buy fractional stakes in fine wine or whisky, while Rally provides access to collectibles such as vintage cars, baseball cards, and comic books. Even real estate (via RealT and Propchain) and farmland (via AcreTrader) can now be accessed digitally through tokenization.

Still, the tokenization market remains young, small, and largely experimental, very much in its infancy. Most of these platforms have yet to prove themselves. Moreover, tokenization currently solves only one problem: divisibility. As Don Tapscott noted in *Blockchain Revolution* (2016), subjectivity remains an issue. The value of a digital token in a painting, a bottle of wine, or a piece of land still depends on taste, location, and fashion. Tokens broaden market access but do not fundamentally change the nature of the underlying asset.

That said, I expect tokenization to grow exponentially in the coming years. Not just because it opens up the universe of proven scarce assets to a wider audience, but also because, over time, it could enhance liquidity, tradability, and perhaps even transparency. This, in turn, leads to lower costs. In doing so, tokenization meaningfully raises the odds that a genuinely new scarce investment may one day be added to the investment universe, another scarce asset that meets all the right conditions to earn a place in a broader portfolio, such as my investment fund.

For now, however, among the assets that score highest on divisibility, subjectivity, liquidity, and true monetary store-of-value status, physical gold and bitcoin remain the most suitable scarce investments.

Part V

The Great Rebalancing

CHAPTER 18

60/40 Revised

Introduction

An investment fund that combines only scarce assets, but from both the traditional investment universe (quality equities) and the "alternative" universe (bitcoin and physical gold), is almost unheard of. When I launched my fund, I searched hard for competitors, only to find you could count them on one hand. Even then, they are more like "friendly rivals" than true competitors, as their approach is similar in spirit but not in substance. What unites us is the shared ambition to offer investors a portfolio that is genuinely better and far more resilient than the traditional one.

What is also striking, though no longer surprising, is that traditional asset and wealth managers defy their own principles when constructing client portfolios. Categories outside the standard universe of stocks and bonds are systematically avoided, entirely at odds with their own theoretical models.

If these asset managers actually followed their own frameworks, client portfolios would look far different from today.

This is only one of several observations confirming that we are still in the early stages of what I believe to be a long-term structural adjustment in the average investment portfolio. In this fifth and final part of the book, I focus on a series of trends and forces that together lead to what I call The Great Rebalancing. A prolonged and uneven journey during which more and more investors will decide to move away from assets that fail to protect them against the effects of fiscal dominance.

Mega Investors

When I studied the portfolio allocations of numerous pension funds, sovereign wealth funds, family offices, endowments, and other large institutional investors, one thing stood out. These investors preach diversification across a broad set of asset classes, but the numbers reveal the opposite: They talk a great deal more than they act.

The world's "mega investors" remain strikingly loyal to the traditional 60/40 principle, translating into vast allocations to bonds. They keep doing so despite the fact that bonds have performed abysmally in recent years, and despite the near certainty that they will fail to keep up with inflation in the years ahead.

Japan's Government Pension Investment Fund (GPIF), one of the largest sovereign wealth funds in the world, follows a strict 50/50 allocation rule. The fund invests 50 percent in equities (half of that domestic, and half international) and 50 percent in bonds (again half domestic, and half international). Therefore, this giant pension fund actually invests more in bonds than the 60/40 rule prescribes. That may hardly sound surprising in a country with one of the world's oldest populations. Conventional wisdom still insists that as investors age, their portfolios should tilt further toward bonds.

Norway's Government Pension Fund Global allocates 30 percent of its portfolio to bonds, less than the traditional 60/40 split, but still a hefty allocation. The bulk of those bond holdings is parked in government debt. The Dutch civil servants' pension fund, ABP, follows the 60/40 rule almost exactly, though you must dig through countless pages of sustainability investment practices in its annual report to find the actual numbers. Other mega investors tend to be much more transparent. South Korea's National Pension Service, for example, allocates roughly 35 percent of its portfolio to bonds, including 26.5 percent in domestic debt.

According to the "Global Pension Assets Study 2024" by the Thinking Ahead Institute, pension funds in the seven largest pension markets, called the "P7" (Australia, Canada, Japan, the

Netherlands, Switzerland, the United Kingdom, and the United States) invest an average of 36 percent of their assets in bonds. For simplicity, I round that up to the "sacred" 40 percent.

This is merely a glimpse into the allocation of the world's biggest investors. Most of them are pension funds whose primary task is to pay out future benefits. Pension liabilities are highly interest-rate sensitive, which is the key reason these funds hold bonds. By holding fixed income, they can offset the interest-rate sensitivity of their liabilities with similar sensitivity on the asset side of the balance sheet in a practice known as "matching."

Yet that doesn't change the fact that during the accumulation phase, the period when the value of pension investments must increase, bonds offer little use. The odds of losing purchasing power are uncomfortably high. Pension funds may hedge interest-rate risk, but doing so often sacrifices the real value of assets during the build-up phase. This trade-off, which is in many cases decided by regulators rather than participants, rarely makes headlines.

That is remarkable, given how profoundly asset allocation choices during the accumulation phase determine long-term outcomes. Suppose a pension fund holds a portfolio of scarce assets that earns 8 percent per year. After thirty years, a €100 contribution would grow to more than €1,000. With an annual return of just 4 percent, that same €100 would grow to only €324. That's a threefold gap.

Of course, not every pension contribution compounds for the full thirty years, since new payments are added monthly. Even so, the math is clear: If the return differential is large enough, it pays not to hedge interest-rate risk, to hedge it only partially or later in the accumulation phase. You build so much more wealth during the accumulation phase that even a late spike in interest rates, making pensions more expensive, still leaves you ahead.

These return gaps during accumulation matter even more in aging societies, where pension systems increasingly push investment risk onto individuals. Workers who save individually for retirement, outside the safety of collective guaranteed pension pools, undermine their future purchasing power by investing heavily in bonds. The same is true, if not more so, for supplementary pension plans, which are becoming both more popular and more necessary to plug the growing gaps in retirement income. The ever-present risk of inflation and relentless demographic pressure make it remarkable, to put it mildly, that pension funds are allowed (and willing) not to pursue maximum real returns, especially when that decision is made without the consent of the participants who are obliged to contribute to these funds.

Returning to the main topic, mega investors and scarce assets, the fact that the largest investors allocate vast sums to bonds doesn't automatically mean there's no room for scarce assets such as gold and bitcoin. Sadly, that space is purely theoretical. None of the major investors mentioned above, nor most other major sovereign wealth funds like the China Investment Corporation, Kuwait Investment Authority, Saudi Arabia's Public Investment Fund, Singapore's GIC, or the Hong Kong Monetary Authority Investment Portfolio, include gold or bitcoin in their strategic asset allocation. The one exception being the Abu Dhabi Investment Council, which tripled its bitcoin ETF position in November 2025.

Most invest slightly less in government bonds, typically between 20 and 30 percent, but even that modest reduction from the traditional 40 percent does not flow into gold or bitcoin. The vast majority of mega investors simply do not invest in scarcity.

The Yale Model

What about two other types of large investors that are less constrained by government policy or pension obligations? Endowments, which manage gifts to universities and other institutions, and family offices, which oversee the fortunes of wealthy families, are often described as more forward-thinking. Moreover, their investment objectives tend to focus more on preserving wealth than on achieving specific returns to meet (pension) liabilities. Anyone focused on preserving wealth inevitably thinks about inflation, which naturally leads to scarce assets.

Again, unfortunately, endowments and family offices also invest little to nothing in gold or bitcoin. The chart below shows the average portfolio composition of global family offices at the end of 2024, as reported by UBS. According to their "Global Family Office Report," family offices allocate just 2 percent of their assets to gold and other precious metals. And even that modest 2 percent is likely the result of performance rather than active choice: The prior year, the weight was just 1 percent. Since gold performed exceptionally well in 2024, the sharp rise in the price of gold is likely the real reason its portfolio weight increased to 2 percent, not because family offices actually decided to buy more gold.

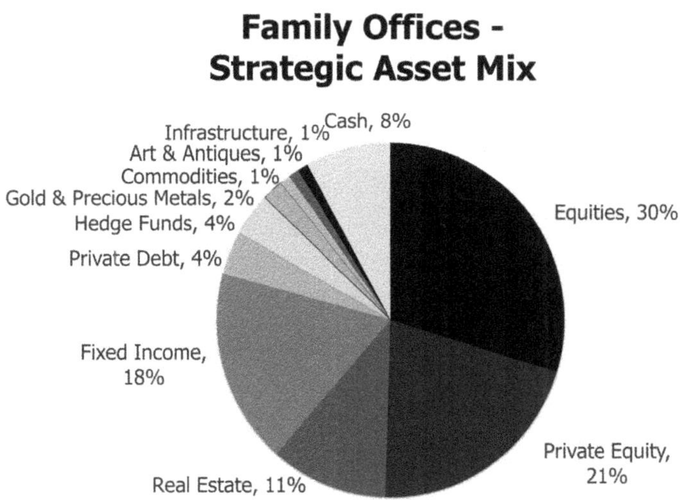

Source: The Great Rebalancing, UBS

Art and antiques, tangible assets that wealthy families can easily invest in without needing tokens or blockchains, still only represent 1 percent of family office portfolios. And unsurprisingly, the allocation to bitcoin is again zero. In the entire UBS report, the word "bitcoin" doesn't appear even once. Looking again at the average family office portfolio, I get the impression that many of them still mirror the allocation style of large university endowments.

When former Yale student and derivatives trader David Swensen took over management of Yale University's endowment in the 1980s, he broke radically with the traditional 60/40 portfolio. Convinced that markets were growing ever more efficient, Swensen saw little future in portfolios built solely on listed stocks and bonds. Instead, he embraced illiquid alternatives such as private equity, hedge funds, venture capital, and real estate. Swensen was a genuine investment pioneer, but one who notably refused to invest in gold, arguing that it provided too little "illiquidity premium."

Swensen's philosophy aligned perfectly with the nature of a university endowment: an infinite investment horizon, no payout obligations, and the time and flexibility to build long-term relationships with top-tier fund managers. That last element proved to be a masterstroke. Over half of Yale's market-beating returns came from its partnerships with truly exceptional fund managers.

This last point also explains why the Yale Model is so difficult to copy. Other large US endowments tried to emulate it, but most did not succeed. Family offices, too, looked to Yale for inspiration. They eagerly piled into alternatives like real estate, hedge funds, and especially private equity. Private equity alone makes up over 20 percent of the average family office portfolio. Yet most of these family offices have been far less successful than Swensen's Yale. And there's a telling reason why.

The Marketing Machine

When David Swensen started exploring alternative investments in the mid-1980s, he was among the first to venture beyond the traditional asset mix. Family offices and other professional investors followed much later, almost all at once and on a massive scale. The result was an unprecedented flood of money poured into unlisted companies in record time. Indisputably, for some companies, this influx of fresh money was a blessing, fueling a series of profitable private equity investments. But that is really different from assuming that the number of great private firms automatically doubles when the flow of private-equity capital does. More money doesn't necessarily mean more opportunity.

As private equity's popularity surged, and with it the often exorbitant fees, new PE firms mushroomed everywhere. If nothing else, humans are opportunists. Now, with so much fresh capital that must be deployed within tight deadlines to produce returns, investors are increasingly forced to allocate to second-tier companies, or worse. The sheer weight of fresh capital chasing attractive deals makes it inevitable that underperforming private firms find their way into those portfolios too.

Private equity is not only a case of too much money chasing too few great companies: It has become a marketing juggernaut, a finely tuned machine built to sell a narrative. It's no longer about Swensen's illiquidity premium, which only delivers excess returns when invested in genuinely promising, high-performing companies. Today, the allure of private equity revolves mainly around the illusion of low volatility and limited correlation with other asset classes.

On paper, private equity ticks all the boxes required to justify its place in a diversified portfolio, like those of endowments and family offices.

But those appealing characteristics are little more than a clever accounting deception. Unlike publicly traded stocks, private companies aren't priced every day. Their valuations are updated infrequently and irregularly: sometimes quarterly, sometimes only once a year. As a result, during any given reporting period, only part of the portfolio receives a new valuation. The rest remains booked at the outdated price. That static portion of the portfolio doesn't fluctuate, even though its underlying economic value most likely did. Consequently, officially reported returns for private equity portfolios look far smoother and steadier than they really are.

In finance, this phenomenon is called "return smoothing," the synthetic flattening of price movements caused by infrequent valuations. The predictable outcome is that reported volatility, the measure of return variability, appears artificially low. And because private equity valuations move only partially, if at all, while the prices of listed equities and gold, for example, move daily, the correlations with other asset classes become distorted. Suppose stock markets drop by 2 percent while private equity remains flat on paper, even though its economic value also fell by 2 percent. It creates the hallucination of diversification when, in truth, there is none.

It seems pretty obvious that such valuation methods lead to artificially low volatility and muted correlations. Yet this is rarely openly disclosed. Let's just say it doesn't fit well within the marketing narrative. Yet, in practice, it's quite simple to "desmooth" private-equity returns. With a touch of statistical know-how, you can correct reported returns for the lack of valuation frequency and reveal the actual underlying volatility.

Venn, a portfolio-analysis platform developed by Two Sigma, regularly publishes studies on the effects of return smoothing. In one of its largest studies from 2024, Venn adjusted 25 years of private-equity returns, with major impact. The volatility of a well-known private equity index jumped from 9.2 percent to 16.7 percent, an increase of more than 80 percent. The smoothing of valuations had understated risk by nearly half. The *true* volatility of private equity, Venn concluded, was almost identical to that of listed equities, exactly what you'd expect from two assets that both carry the name "equity."

The distortion is even more pronounced in real estate, where valuations are just as infrequent, sometimes even more so. According to Venn's data, when the returns of the leading NCREIF Property Index were adjusted, volatility more than doubled. For both private equity and real estate, the true correlation with public equities turns out to be far higher than the official numbers suggest. In reality, they move in lockstep with public markets far more often than the glossy reports admit. As a result, those "amazing" diversification effects, so widely promoted by private-equity funds, collapse under honest scrutiny.

Cliff Asness, founder of the quantitative powerhouse investment firm AQR, goes a step further. He accuses the private-equity industry of "volatility laundering," deliberately ironing out volatility to make the asset class look safer than it truly is. According to AQR, the true volatility of private equity lies between 20 percent and 25 percent, even higher than that of listed equities.

As with all marketing campaigns, the effect eventually wears off. Returns on private equity have faded, and regulators, among others, are increasingly questioning the valuation methodologies used behind the scenes. In April 2025, Yale University's endowment announced plans to unload up to $6 billion in private equity, citing disappointing performance. That's about 15 percent of Yale's entire endowment. At that point, private equity was underperforming listed equities across every time frame from one to ten years. Some investors who entered the asset class as early as 2016 still hadn't seen their money back.

Harvard has also begun scaling back its private-equity holdings. Family offices and other professional investors were missing out on returns because their capital was sitting idle, unable to be deployed toward suitable opportunities. In 2025, Oxford professor Ludovic Phalippou, a long-time critic of private equity, revisited his earlier research, arriving at the same conclusion as he did before. When calculated fairly and consistently, US private-equity performance is no better than that of the S&P 500 index.

Now that private equity's flaws come to light and the myth of low risk and high return unravels, I expect that part of the capital currently trapped in private equity will begin to migrate toward *scarce assets*. Not least because none of these mega investors discussed so far hold structural positions in gold, let alone bitcoin. Once investors finally grasp that these assets do provide genuine diversification, another major rebalancing of investment portfolios becomes inevitable. The observation that, just weeks after Harvard announced plans to reduce its private equity holdings, news emerged that the university had invested more than $100 million in a bitcoin ETF fits perfectly with my expectations.

Exceptions That Prove the Rule

So, are there truly no large investors allocating to gold or bitcoin? There are, though the list is short. In Switzerland, several pension funds hold a small share of their assets, typically a few percentage points, in gold. In Germany, gold is popular among *multi-asset funds* (funds investing across several asset classes), unlike most of their global peers. The shadow of Weimar's hyperinflation still looms large in the German investment mindset; German investors carry a deep-rooted fear of inflation and do more than most to guard against it, making gold the default portfolio choice.

In India, regulation mandates that multi-asset funds spread across three buckets: equities, bonds, and commodities. The latter, partly due to cultural factors and preferences, is often expressed through gold.

Only a small group of US financial advisors recommends gold to their clients. According to an annual Bank of America survey, around 20 percent of advisors suggest an allocation of between 1 percent and 5 percent. Yet nearly 80 percent of US advisors still keep gold out of their clients' portfolios entirely. Remarkably, despite gold's sharp rally in recent years, the share of advisors recommending not owning any gold is actually growing. Financial advisors often chase the market, but gold remains an exception. The share of advisors recommending more than 5 percent gold is effectively zero.

In 2025, three US pension funds grabbed the headlines by briefly investing a tiny portion of their portfolios in bitcoin. The State of Wisconsin Investment Board (SWIB), which manages roughly $160 billion and is widely regarded for its disciplined governance and investment rigor, was the most prominent. Nevertheless, SWIB sold its bitcoin position just a few months later.

The Mubadala Investment Company, a sovereign wealth fund from the United Arab Emirates, has held about 0.1 percent of its portfolio in bitcoin ETFs since 2024. A sub-fund of Stanford University's endowment invested 7 percent of its total assets in bitcoin that same year. Notably, that sub-fund is managed by Stanford students themselves. Their decision to allocate 7 percent to bitcoin reflects a radically different view of what a diversified portfolio should look like compared to the managers of Stanford's main endowment. Keep that in mind. The generational divide in investing, and its impact, will take center stage later in this book.

Bhutan's national investment fund has chosen a very different path. Leveraging its abundant hydropower resources, Bhutan has built a significant bitcoin position through mining, participating in the lotteries guessing large numbers, to release new coins (see Chapter 15). This green approach to mining aligns seamlessly with Bhutan's unique national growth metric, *Gross National Happiness*. Bhutan channels its bitcoin proceeds into public services like healthcare, supporting both social welfare and environmental ambitions.

Then there are the bitcoin treasury companies. These are companies that hold bitcoin as a strategic reserve on their balance sheets, outside the traditional financial system, to diversify fiat holdings and as a hedge against inflation and fiscal dominance. These firms aim to grow their bitcoin holdings over time, meaning that they actually think and value in bitcoin, not in euros or dollars. The most prominent example is Strategy (formerly MicroStrategy), the company led by Michael Saylor, the pioneer of this balance sheet strategy.

According to BitcoinTreasuries.net, by October 2025, roughly 200 listed companies held bitcoin on their balance sheets, still far below 1.0 percent of all public firms worldwide. MicroStrategy alone accounts for more than 600,000 bitcoin, by far the largest bitcoin holding of any publicly traded company.

In summary, the overwhelming majority of professional investors worldwide still have no exposure to scarce assets, and certainly not to physical gold or bitcoin. That's not a bad starting point if you, like me, believe that interest in scarcity will grow exponentially in the years and decades ahead. That conviction only strengthens when you realize that the absence of scarce assets directly contradicts the very frameworks professional investors use to construct their strategic portfolios.

The Trinity of Good Investing

Most professional asset managers remain intensely loyal to the sacred 60/40 mix, pouring massive amounts of wealth into bonds that systematically destroy purchasing power. Or they're overloaded with private equity, whose supposedly superior qualities have been overhyped, and more importantly, convincingly debunked.

Scarce assets barely register in the world of professional investors. That is puzzling when you consider the models almost all of these firms use to determine the long-term strategic asset mix for their clients' portfolios. These models almost exclusively gaze in the rearview mirror and focus on what I call the "trinity of good investing": return, volatility (risk), and diversification.

So, why do professional investors rely solely on historical data when constructing their strategic asset mix? Partly because of the way their organizations are structured, and partly out of fear of reputational damage if their forward-looking forecast turns out wrong. On that last point, no one wants to be the first major investor to buy bitcoin at exactly the wrong time.

At large asset managers, it's invariably the statistics departments, the "number crunchers," as they're sometimes half-jokingly called, that decide the strategic allocation. These are econometricians, often lacking deeper economic or financial understanding, attempting to capture reality by aggregating, analyzing, and modeling as much historical data as possible.

There is virtually no room for forward-looking judgment; historical data, however limited or misleading, must do all the work. Conveniently, this allows asset managers, fearful of reputational damage, to hide behind the past. When their strategic investment portfolios underperform, they can always claim that markets simply behaved differently this time.

An Alternative 60/40

However, even if I accepted the obsession of traditional asset managers with historical data, I still can't make sense of the strategic allocations most asset managers come up with. The table below compares the real return, volatility, and Sharpe Ratio (here, return divided by volatility) of the traditional 60/40 portfolio, 60 percent equities and 40 percent bonds ("60/40 B" in the table), with an alternative version where bonds are swapped entirely for gold. Meaning, a portfolio made up of 60 percent equities and 40 percent gold ("60/40 G" in the table).

The analysis mirrors the one in Chapter 16: All returns are adjusted for inflation. Only inflation-adjusted returns reveal whether you have truly gained in real terms. Using US data from 1973 (the euro dataset is shorter but shows similar results), I also examine ten-year intervals and the period since the COVID crisis.

Real returns on the traditional (stocks-bonds) and alternative (stocks-gold) 60/40 portfolio (measured in US dollars)												
	60/40 **B**	60/40 **G**	60/40 **B**	60/40 **G**	60/40 **B**	60/40 **G**	60/40 **B**	60/40 **G**	60/40 **B**	60/40 **G**	60/40 **B**	60/40 **G**
	Since 1973		Last 40 years		Last 30 years		Last 20 years		Last 10 years		Since COVID	
Annualized return	4.7%	5.8%	6.2%	6.9%	5.2%	7.0%	5.0%	8.6%	3.0%	5.4%	4.8%	11.9%
Volatility	9.9%	12.1%	9.5%	10.9%	9.4%	11.5%	9.3%	11.9%	10.0%	11.5%	11.9%	13.4%
Sharpe Ratio	0.47	0.48	0.65	0.63	0.55	0.61	0.54	0.72	0.30	0.47	0.40	0.89

Source: The Great Rebalancing, Bureau of Labor Statistics, Investing.com

The key results:

- Across every time horizon, the 60/40 portfolio with 40 percent gold outperformed the traditional 60/40 portfolio with bonds.
- Volatility was slightly higher in five out of the six time windows, but the difference was modest. On average, the 60/40 portfolio with 40 percent gold was 1.8 percentage points more volatile than the traditional 60/40 mix. With an average volatility of 10 percent for the traditional 60/40 portfolio, this translates into a volatility of 11.8 percent. Recall the earlier example of "desmoothing" private-equity returns, where volatility jumped from 9.2 percent to 16.7 percent.
- Over the past 30 years, and across all shorter horizons, the Sharpe Ratio of the 60/40 portfolio with gold was higher than that of the traditional 60/40. Since 1973 and over the past 40 years, the gap in

Sharpe Ratios has been limited. If the statisticians of institutional investors had to judge blindly, they would almost certainly pick the 60/40 portfolio with 40 percent gold as the winner.

From their own trinity of return, volatility, and diversification, professional investors have no choice but to conclude, based on the data above, that gold deserves a place in their strategic portfolios. Even if they only focused on the longest available dataset, going back to 1973, it is baffling that two assets with nearly identical performance metrics, offering diversification benefits, are not both included.

Mathematically, there's no way to justify excluding gold from the strategic mix. Plug these numbers into a standard optimization model and the resulting gold allocation ranges from about 10 percent to well over 30 percent. Incrementum, an investment firm focused largely on scarce assets, calculated in its 2024 report, "The Optimal Gold Allocation," that gold's ideal weighting lies between 14 percent and 20 percent, based on the classic trinity of investing.

A Shift in Volatility

Most investors and statisticians treat volatility as fixed: a number that barely moves through time. Statistically, that's not entirely wrong because historically, volatility has behaved much steadier than returns. But trusting that assumption blindly is dangerous.

A central conclusion of this book is that governments and their central banks must pursue increasingly extreme policies to keep their debt loads sustainable. Bond-buying programs designed to suppress interest rates have become a permanent feature of those policies. By controlling interest rates, central banks directly manipulate bond prices and distort market dynamics in the process. These same policies fuel inflation, which puts upward pressure on interest rates as bondholders demand compensation for the rising risk of inflation.

To keep interest expenses, on top of all the other mandatory government expenditures, from spiraling out of control, central banks intervene by pushing rates down against market forces. Think of it as holding a ball underwater. You must push constantly to keep it there, and the moment you let go, the ball shoots back up. To submerge it again, you have to push it down again, using more force.

The bond market behaves much the same way. Rates must stay low, but as soon as central banks tighten policy even slightly, they spike up, propelled by market forces. And so the cycle repeats: It takes ever more extreme monetary muscle to shove rates back down. Unsurprisingly, this power struggle plays out through higher volatility in the bond market. Add that, even with low rates, underlying concerns about debt sustainability are not erased by artificially suppressed interest rates, and you get an effective mix pushing up bond risk.

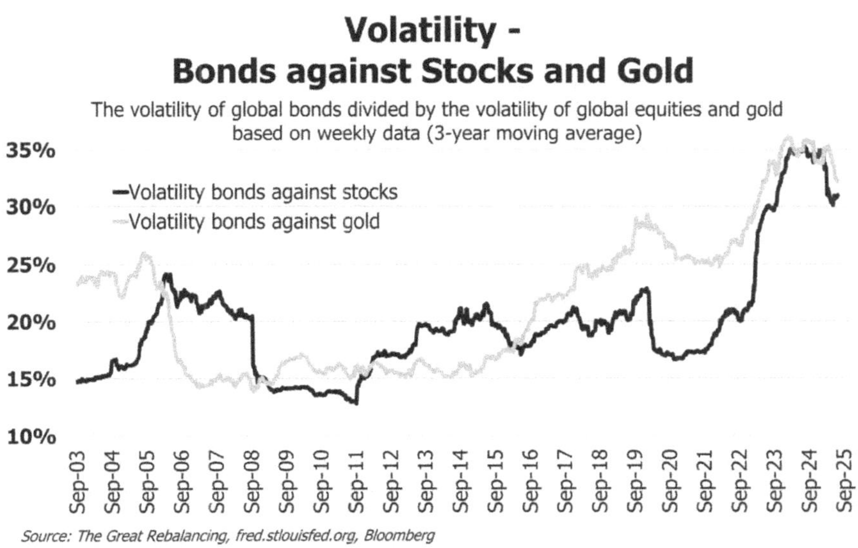

You can see this dynamic vividly in the chart above. The black line tracks the ratio of bond volatility to equity volatility, meaning bond volatility divided by equity volatility. The higher the number, the more volatile bonds are compared to equities. Suppose bond volatility is 3 percent and equity volatility measures 15 percent, that gives a risk ratio of 0.2 (3/15). If bond volatility climbs from 3 percent to 5 percent while equity volatility stays flat, the ratio jumps to 0.33 (5/15). The volatility ratio may feel abstract at first, but it captures perfectly how diversifying across asset classes manages overall portfolio risk. It is the relative risk between asset classes that decides how effectively they combine in a single portfolio.

The black line reveals that bonds have grown markedly more volatile relative to equities in recent years, and far riskier than in the past. Besides, the increase in the volatility ratio reflects a genuine rise in bond volatility. While this episode of elevated bond volatility may still be short, it's reasonable to assume it will persist, keeping the "holding the ball underwater" metaphor in mind. When central banks and markets pull in opposite directions and erratic inflation emerges as central banks abandon their targets, volatility becomes inevitable.

The same chart also shows the ratio between bond and gold volatility (gray line). The picture is similar: Bond volatility has risen sharply compared with gold, and this trend has been building for years. For the past decade, bonds have grown consistently riskier against gold. This observation fits perfectly with the earlier picture of fiscal dominance, where bond returns grow less attractive and more uncertain, while scarce assets like physical gold offer refuge.

That gray line, the ratio between bond and gold volatility, mirrors Exter's inverted pyramid, a visual echo of shifting risk within the financial system. Growing anxiety over debt sustainability and periodic stress in bond markets (think back to the UK in 2022) trigger capital flows to move upstream from bonds toward gold at the top of the pyramid. Most investors focus solely on nominal returns, yet it's the shifting risk dynamics that truly show how rising debt is reshaping the financial system.

For the architects of professional portfolios (the number crunchers), this means only one thing: Bonds are losing their primary role as a reducer of overall portfolio risk. Their ability to act as a risk buffer, the cornerstone of the traditional 60/40 portfolio, has deteriorated dramatically.

This surge in relative bond volatility also creates a dangerous paradox. Because bonds are still less volatile than equities in absolute terms, traditional asset managers must add even more bonds to keep the overall portfolio volatility steady. After all, these managers have boxed themselves into only two asset classes, stocks and bonds. To keep, for example, a 10 percent volatility target steady means that these asset managers now need 50 percent, instead of 40 percent, in bonds, with the devastating result that client portfolios become even more exposed to low rates and high inflation. Exactly what investors don't need.

The Diversification Trap

Traditional investors cling to another convenient excuse to keep gold (and bitcoin) out of their portfolios: diversification. When bonds perform well during equity downturns, they act as powerful diversifiers, cushioning portfolio losses and reducing volatility. Even if bond returns are modest, their negative correlation with equities makes a valuable addition to a multi-asset portfolio, so the story goes.

To evaluate how well bonds diversify, we again need to look at correlation, the statistical relationship between the returns of different asset classes. Asset managers focus primarily on identifying assets with negative correlation. If the correlation between stocks and bonds were at the minimum of -1, their prices would always move in opposite directions. When equities fall, bonds rise, and vice versa. Negative correlation, in other words, creates powerful diversification within a portfolio.

Here is where many investors go wrong. Most of them were raised and trained during a forty-year period, 1980 to 2020, during which interest rates and inflation moved almost exclusively downward. Throughout much of that era, stock and bond returns were negatively correlated. And because most academic studies draw from that same window, generations of investors have come to believe that this negative relationship is universal and permanent. Except, it isn't.

This narrow frame of reference created a dangerous illusion: Stocks and bonds always move in opposite directions, and combining them automatically ensures robust diversification.

The powerful chart below, drawn from the remarkable long-term study by my former colleagues at Robeco (Molenaar, Sénéchal, Swinkels, and Wang, 2024), shatters that assumption. Rather than analyzing the past forty years, they extended the data all the way back to 1804 for the United Kingdom and from 1874 for the United States. Over more than two centuries of data, they found something I guess most investors do not expect: The long-held belief that combining stocks and bonds is a smart diversification strategy completely breaks down.

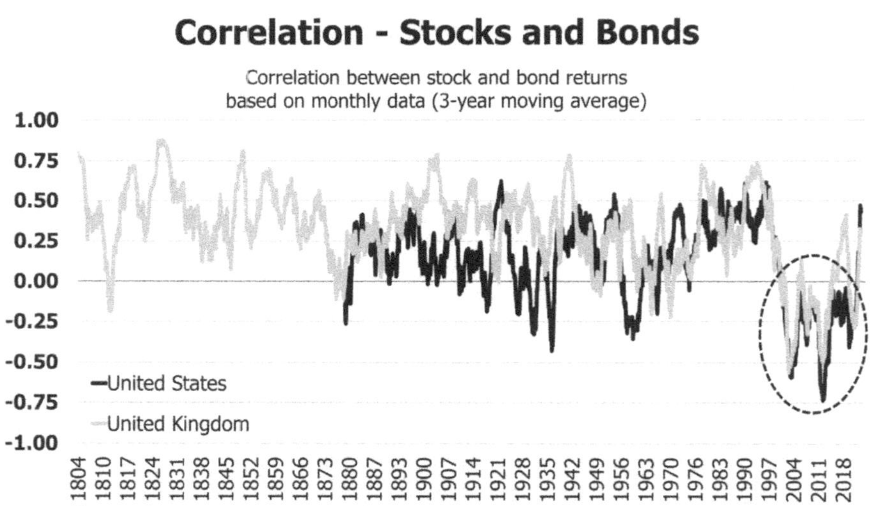

Source: The Great Rebalancing, Robeco, Molenaar, Senechal, Swinkels and Wang (2024) Empirical Evidence on the Stock-Bond Correlation, Financial Analysts Journal

Historically, the correlation between stocks and bonds has not been negative at all. In other words, for most of financial history, stocks and bonds have tended to move in the same direction, not opposite ones. The period from the late 1990s to 2020 is the major exception. That unique window, marked by structurally falling interest rates and lower inflation, produced a sustained negative correlation between the two asset classes, meaning stocks and bonds worked beautifully together in a portfolio.

I began investing in the late 1990s, and it took me a good 15 years before I seriously questioned whether stocks and bonds always diversified each other. Every time I looked at my Bloomberg terminal, when stock prices rose, bond prices fell, and the other way around. Only later in my career, as I studied the long-term history of inflation, did I start to wonder what really drives the stock-bond relationship.

Turning back to the chart for a moment, the correlation between equities and bonds has turned positive again recently. And it's likely to stay that way, as a direct result of fiscal dominance. When central banks force interest rates lower, bond prices stay artificially high. But that same policy also inflates the money supply, raising inflation risks. As a result, the prices of scarce assets that protect against inflation, such as quality equities, rise as well. Bonds, faced with structurally low yields, however, offer little protection against that rising inflation. Scarce assets, by contrast, do.

To summarize: Today, bonds bring weaker diversification, higher correlation with stocks, and, as an unwelcome bonus, unattractive real returns.

Diversification That Works

If there's one lesson I've learned in my years as an investor, it's that diversification matters most when markets fall apart. When equity markets plunge 20 percent or more, emotion overtakes rationality almost instantly. Anger, fear, and impulsive behavior emerge almost instantly. Losses do strange things to the human mind, a dynamic powerfully described by Daniel Kahneman (2011).

My experience is that the true value of diversification reveals itself when sentiment turns deeply negative. The focus understandably falls on equities, as they tend to drop sharply from time to time. Spurred on by a flood of grim headlines across financial and social media, panic takes hold, and investors make costly mistakes. How reassuring it is when an asset class exists that doesn't collapse when equities sink.

The chart below reveals exactly that asset class. It shows the global equity returns during their twenty worst-performing months between 2008 and October 2025, including the global financial crisis. Each black bar represents equity market performance in one of those months, with losses ranging from roughly 5 percent to more than 10 percent. For those same twenty months, I calculated the returns on gold, shown as the gray bars.

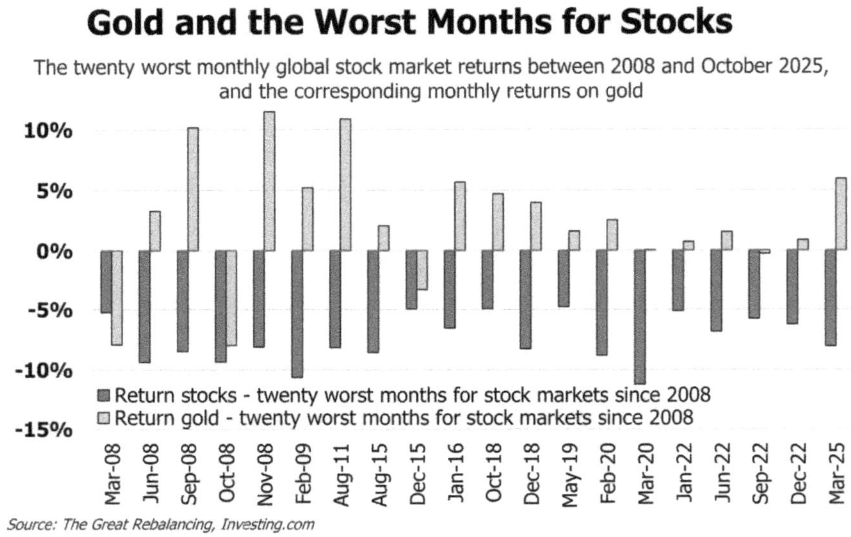

During the twenty worst months for equities, the average monthly loss equaled 7.5 percent. Painful for any investor, but if you had held gold alongside equities, you could have significantly reduced that pain. Gold delivered an average positive return of nearly 3 percent over those twenty months. In sixteen of those twenty months, or 80 percent of the time, gold posted positive returns while equities fell. And in all but one of the twenty months (March 2008), gold reduced losses compared with investing in equities alone.

The conclusion is clear: When markets turn ugly, gold delivers real damage control. The degree of protection you get depends, of course, on how much gold you hold in your portfolio. But as the chart clearly suggests, be sure not to own too little of it.

Wondering how bonds fared as diversifiers in those dark months for equities? Unfortunately, not particularly well. During the worst months for equities, bonds fell too. The loss was small, just 0.03 percent on average, but it speaks volumes. Returns were negative in nine out of the twenty months, nearly half the time. I would not call that great diversification. And since diversification counts most when losses mount, gold outshines bonds by a wide margin. Investors looking to limit downside risks from equities, and that's probably nearly all of them, would be better served by holding gold, ideally *instead of* bonds.

One final point: When we look across all months since 1975, not just the worst months since 2008, the correlation between gold and equities is exactly zero. That is true diversification.

All Roads Lead to Scarcity

In my presentations, I often emphasize that whether you start from the logic of *fiscal dominance* or from traditional asset-allocation models based on historical data, you inevitably end up in the same place.

If traditional investors honestly accounted for negative real bond returns, rising volatility, and two centuries of positive stock-bond correlation, not in a million years would they land on an optimal bond allocation of 40 percent. The numbers for gold are simply too compelling to ignore. In fact, if you fix the weight of equities at 60 percent, as in the traditional 60/40 portfolio, my optimization model allocates nearly all of the remaining 40 percent to gold.

I haven't covered bitcoin here explicitly, mainly because of its shorter data history. That limited history is the go-to excuse for traditional managers to exclude it from their models and investment universe. But if the quant departments at pension funds, endowments, family offices, and asset managers ran their models over shorter horizons and added bitcoin, the case for bonds would all but vanish.

Bitcoin is extremely volatile, but because its returns have been even more extreme, its Sharpe Ratio over the past decade actually tops that of equities. Bonds, as we know, delivered a negative Sharpe Ratio because of their negative real returns. In the relatively short period covering bitcoin return data, bonds would have been excluded entirely from the strategic asset mix. Bitcoin, however, would have earned its spot.

Using hard data on returns and risk, the fact that gold and bitcoin remain absent from nearly all institutional investment portfolios is outright irrational. What stands in the way is the fee-driven business model of these asset managers. Their shareholders have no interest in questioning the management fees earned on bond funds, even when those funds deliver negative real returns and a loss of purchasing power to clients. Still, the pressure from the results of traditional portfolio models on statistics departments must be immense by now.

I strongly believe that we are on the verge of a major shift in the strategic composition of traditional investment portfolios, driven by overwhelming historical evidence that scarce assets can no longer be ignored.

The message from both history and the future is unmistakable: The Great Rebalancing is imminent. It is inevitable.

And there is more.

CHAPTER 19

A New Standard

Introduction

This book demonstrates that the challenges facing today's financial system are substantial, and so is the likelihood that something will go seriously wrong. I also do not deny that at times it makes sense to start over entirely rather than to keep patching up a fragile structure that's already wobbling. Yet, as outlined in the introduction to Chapter 16, that doesn't necessarily have to be the case for the current system.

There is a way to make it more resilient without requiring a full-scale implosion first. That way involves establishing a new monetary standard, one not based solely on trust: a system in which broadly accepted stores of value, anchored in scarcity, take center stage. Fortunately, history provides plenty of leading examples, some of which I already covered, that show exactly how such a standard works.

Trading Trust

Since the final abandonment of the gold standard in 1971, the financial system has rested on a single foundation: *trust*. Trust in governments, institutions, and central banks. Trust that euros, dollars, and yen can be exchanged for goods and services almost anywhere in the world. Trust that those same currencies will be worth roughly the same tomorrow as they are today. And trust that banks, businesses, and people in general will continue to accept them.

That trust, however, is challenged from multiple directions. When ever more money is created without any intrinsic value behind it, uncomfortable questions stop being optional. And when that surge of money collides with rising inflation, asking questions is no longer enough. It becomes imperative to act immediately to safeguard your money and wealth from inflation's relentless erosion of purchasing power.

Another example of pressure on trust as the foundation of the financial system comes from countries eager to end the dollar hegemony, but, at the same time, lack a viable currency to take its place as the global reserve. Think back to the "small group" of nations (China, India, Russia, and Turkey) dismissively labeled as such by the Federal Reserve. In reality, this dilemma applies to all currencies, including the euro. For a country wanting to move away from the dollar, it needs to find an alternative beyond its own currency.

Next, countries with "small" currencies that aim to keep their exchange rates stable need large foreign exchange reserves to do so. They are repeatedly forced to intervene in currency markets to defend stability, making effective diversification of their reserves indispensable. Finally, nations facing a heightened risk of having their fiat reserves frozen or confiscated due to political conflict have little choice but to seek safety in assets outside the fiat system.

I'm referring here to what countries can do when trust in the financial system, and therefore in money itself, starts to fade. However, in practice these issues are often delegated to the central banks of these countries. Through their reserve policies, central banks can rebuild or strengthen trust by holding more reserves in scarce assets, assets that people inherently trust because they possess intrinsic value. By doing so, central banks can trade trust in institutions, including themselves, for trust built on real value.

Whether central banks seek to expand their monetary base (as in highly indebted economies such as the United States or Japan), distance themselves from dollar dominance (China and India), must maintain large and diversified reserves (Switzerland), or shield themselves from having their international assets frozen (Russia), in all cases, gold and bitcoin offer an attractive solution. At least for now, central banks remain focused primarily on gold because of its long, proven history as a monetary anchor.

Under fiscal dominance, there's an even stronger reason for central banks to hold more gold. Governments, perpetually chasing GDP growth through deficit spending, have an unrelenting tendency to create more money. When governments control money, its supply will never cease to grow, specifically now that the primary source of economic growth, labor, is largely exhausted.

History shows an overwhelmingly clear pattern: Once the limits of intrinsic economic growth are reached, governments and central and commercial banks inevitably invent "creative" mechanisms to expand the money supply artificially. This is inflation in its purest form, neatly reflecting its original definition: the swelling of the money supply that debases the intrinsic value of that same money.

We've already encountered several telling historical examples, such as the debasement of the Roman denarius and the English pound under Henry VIII and the hyperinflationary collapse of Germany's Weimar Republic.

Other episodes include the Mississippi Company, founded by John Law in early eighteenth-century France, which issued vast amounts of paper money backed by the promise of boundless riches in the

"New World" (Louisiana). Around the same time in Britain, the South Sea Company converted government debt into shares, feeding a speculative bubble around a barely existing trading monopoly. And, of course, my "own" Dutch East India Company (VOC), founded in 1602, which encouraged mammoth speculation on future spice profits through share and debt issues, helping ignite the infamous, and perhaps somewhat embellished or even fantastical, Tulip Mania. Let's not forget this unfolded against the backdrop of extraordinary Dutch financial innovation: the first modern stock exchange, the Amsterdam Wisselbank, and a wave of early-1600s experimentation that turned the Low Countries into the world's financial laboratory.

These episodes share the same pattern: a combination of financial innovation followed by painful proof that excessive money creation without value makes a monetary reset inescapable.

More Gold in Reserve

Over the past decade, gold reserves as a share of total central bank foreign exchange holdings have steadily increased worldwide. In 2015, gold made up less than 10 percent of global central bank reserves. By 2024, that share had more than doubled to 21 percent.

To illustrate this reversal in central bank behavior, I draw on data from Jan Nieuwenhuijs, gold analyst at *Money Metals*, an online precious-metals platform. While official figures from institutions such as the World Bank reveal the same upward trend, they only include officially reported gold holdings. China, in particular, which has been a huge buyer of gold in recent years, often conducted these purchases through unofficial channels. The Nieuwenhuijs data include these hidden purchases, providing a more accurate estimate of how much gold central banks really own.

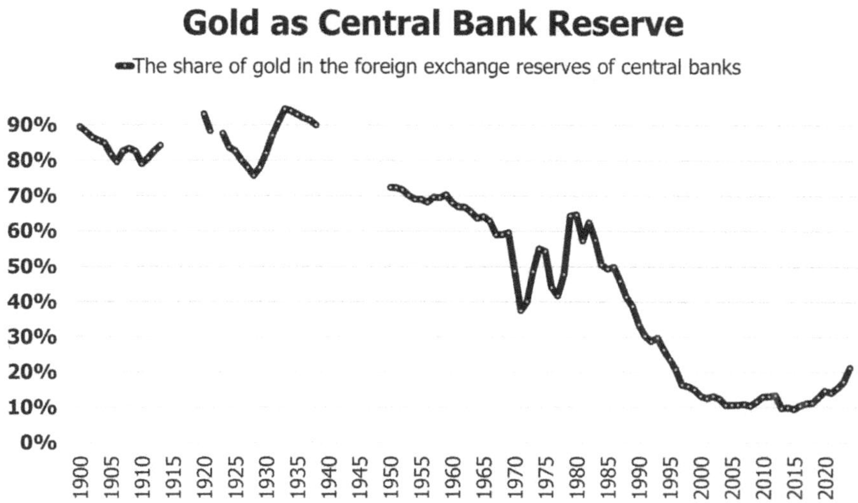

Source: The Great Rebalancing, Jan Nieuwenhuijs, Money Metals

The rising trend in central bank gold reserves over the past decade is not the only important message revealed by the chart above. Before President Nixon abolished the gold standard in 1971, gold accounted for roughly 60 percent of the average central bank reserve. Before World War II, gold accounted for as much as 80 to 90 percent. From the early 1980s onward, the share of gold in central bank reserves declined rapidly. As the system came to rely on trust and on the dollar, issued in massive quantities to meet global demand, central bank balance sheets and reserves evolved accordingly. Gold was replaced by US dollars and US Treasuries tied to it, which became the core component of global reserves.

If today's debt-driven, trust-dependent financial system, defined by rampant debt growth and money creation, were to move toward a renewed, implicit gold standard, the current 20 percent reserve allocation would without doubt be insufficient given the historical levels of gold backing. But how much would be enough?

Posing the question is far easier than answering it since there are countless ways to approach it. If you believe that the US dollar will remain the global reserve currency for decades to come, and that governments, despite their exploding mandatory expenditures, manage to rein in fiscal deficits, a rise in gold's share toward 25 to 30 percent might suffice. In any case, a higher gold allocation is required regardless, given the torrent of recent evidence showing governments increasingly struggling with their finances. Currently, trust is in too short supply.

But if, on the other hand, budget deficits remain structurally large, central banks effectively abandon their inflation targets, the ballooning debt volcano sparks ever more uncertainty and sharper market reactions, and rising geopolitical tension undermines the dollar's hegemony, then even the 60 percent level from before 1971 is very likely insufficient. A noteworthy detail: In an inflation study published in July 2025, Deutsche Bank found that since 1971, not one of the 152 countries it analyzed has managed to keep inflation at or below 2 percent.

The Shortfall of Emerging Economies

It is important to distinguish between advanced and emerging economies when it comes to central bank gold reserves. The share of gold in the reserves of the first group is significantly higher than that of the second. This is especially true for several Western European countries, including Germany, France, Italy, and the Netherlands, though not the United Kingdom (more on that below), and for the United States (albeit indirectly through gold certificates, as the government owns the gold), where gold often represents 60 to 80 percent of total central bank reserves.

The picture looks very different in emerging markets. In China, gold represents barely 10 percent of total reserves, despite the colossal buying spree of recent years. According to the World Gold Council, China bought 225 tons of gold in 2023 (a ton equals 1,000 kilograms), the largest amount since records of central bank purchase data began in 1977. In 2024, China again ranked among the world's top five central bank gold buyers.

Again, these figures refer only to official purchases. As Nieuwenhuijs's data show, China's true gold accumulation likely far exceeds the official numbers. Even so, China's gold reserves still pale in comparison to those of the United States and many European countries. The same is true for other major emerging economies such as Brazil (4 percent gold reserves), Mexico (5 percent), Indonesia (4 percent), and South Korea (2 percent). Even in India, known for its deep cultural affinity with gold, the metal makes up only 13 percent of its central bank reserves.

A few emerging economies stand out with much higher gold reserves, most notably Poland, Russia, and Turkey. That's no coincidence. Each of these countries faces one or more of the trust challenges described earlier.

Poland, a country with a fraught wartime history, sits uncomfortably close to Russia as a neighbor of Ukraine. During World War II, gold played a pivotal role in Poland's survival. After the 1939 German invasion, the Bank of Poland evacuated its gold reserves abroad. Those reserves financed the Polish government in exile and supported resistance operations. Today, Poland presents itself as a pillar of stability within the European Union, with gold serving as a symbol of monetary sovereignty, financial strength, and trust.

In recent years, Adam Glapiński, president of the National Bank of Poland, has repeatedly emphasized gold's role in safeguarding the country's independence and security. Reading between the lines, it's not that hard to detect a conscious effort to reduce reliance on the US dollar. By diversifying its reserves and lifting gold's share to at least 20 percent, Poland aims to achieve greater monetary autonomy.

In Turkey, gold holds an exceptionally prominent place in the nation's central bank reserves. Turkey has long struggled with runaway inflation, averaging above 50 percent since 2022, and a relentless weakening of the Turkish lira. And I'm not talking about some five or ten percent drop. Since the global financial crisis of 2008, the lira has lost 96 percent of its value against the euro and 97 percent against the US dollar.

Turkey's geopolitical position, bordering Iraq, Iran, and Syria, adds another dimension to safeguarding its (financial) sovereignty. In 2024, Turkey ranked second only to Poland among the world's largest central bank gold buyers. In 2021, President Erdoğan called on Turks to hand over their gold jewelry in exchange for lira, to prop up the battered-down currency. Similar to Gresham's Law, where good money is hoarded while bad money is spent, Erdoğan's plea predictably fell on deaf ears.

Finally, Russia is the prime example that reserves held in fiat currencies are not inherently safe. After the Russian invasion of Ukraine in 2022, the G7 nations and their allies froze roughly $300 billion in Russian central bank assets, mostly held in foreign currencies. Physical gold, securely stored outside the fiat system, cannot be frozen, assuming it is held within a country's own borders.

While most countries probably (and thankfully) have no intention of invading their neighbors, the seizure of Russia's central bank reserves served as a harsh wake-up call. If reserve diversification is the ultimate goal, as it should be, then nations must think hard about the nature of these reserves. Gold quickly emerges as an attractive alternative, thanks to its long history as a stable, tangible store of value outside the current fiat system. Of course, that only holds if a country maintains access to its physical gold. Seen in this light, it cannot be a coincidence that several nations, including Austria, Germany, Hungary, India, the Netherlands, Poland, and Turkey, have repatriated part of their gold holdings in recent years, while others are considering doing the same.

The Optimal Reserve

The *Liberty Street Economics* blog of the Federal Reserve Bank of New York, discussed in Chapter 14, already revealed how Western policymakers consistently underestimate, or outright deny, the desire of emerging economies to detach themselves from the dollar. The blog writers dismissed this as the ambition of a "small" group of countries, which, incidentally, represents "only" 25 percent of the world economy.

From here, the question of how much gold emerging economies would need to address their various trust issues quickly comes to mind. Like before, the answer to this question is hard to pin down. What is abundantly clear, however, is that gold reserves of 10 percent or less, as is common in emerging economies today, are nowhere near sufficient.

A few years ago, the Bank for International Settlements (BIS) published an eye-catching study examining what constitutes a justifiable gold allocation within central bank reserves. Its conclusion? For reserves held mainly in "stable" currencies and short-term government bonds, an allocation of 0–5 percent gold would suffice.

That the study produced a relatively low reserve percentage should not surprise you. The BIS sits firmly at the heart of the fiat-money system. Beyond operating like a think tank, the BIS is one of the main architects of the modern global financial system. For instance, through the Basel Committee, the BIS dictates which assets count, and under what conditions, as mandatory liquidity buffers for banks. These assets are labelled high-quality liquid assets, or HQLA. To qualify as HQLA, assets must meet strict BIS criteria for liquidity, credit quality, and volatility.

You can probably guess what comes next: Gold does not make the HQLA list of top-tier bank buffers. Knowing this, it should be unsurprising that the BIS assigns gold only a marginal role in central bank reserves. Equally unsurprising, US Treasuries and fiat reserves reign supreme as the BIS's preferred HQLA.

If that sounds like a paradox, it's because it really is one. Gold helps central banks mitigate the erosion of trust in the financial system, yet the BIS discourages its use by assigning gold a low-quality score in bank buffers. The BIS has intentionally written the rules in such a way that banks must hold fiat currencies and government bonds to meet their buffer requirements. Yet another reminder that financial repression, the not-so-silent twin of fiscal dominance, shouldn't be underestimated. In the BIS setup, central banks, including the central bank of central banks, team up with governments to keep public debt funded. On a country level, the same pattern emerges with regulators compelling financial institutions to hold government debt on their balance sheets.

But even under its strict buffer rules, the BIS must twist itself into knots to defend such a low gold allocation. This is the point where the BIS study gets really interesting. For example, the BIS explicitly notes that gold deserves a much larger weight in reserves when the duration of a central bank's balance sheet increases. Duration refers to the average maturity of all bonds held on the balance sheet, and it matters greatly. If a central bank buys mostly short-term bonds, the duration of the balance sheet drops. And when a central bank purchases long-term bonds (for example, with twenty- or thirty-year maturities), the duration of the central bank balance sheet increases.

The longer the duration, the more sensitive the balance sheet becomes to changes in interest rates. The prices of long-maturity or high-duration bonds fluctuate far more in value when rates move than short-term bonds do. As duration rises and interest-rate risk sensitivity increases, more gold is needed on the balance sheet to offset that interest rate risk. The BIS analysis shows how pronounced this effect can be: At a balance sheet duration of ten years, central banks would need gold reserves of at least 10 percent but up to as much as 30 percent.

Here's the striking part: Between 2006 and 2025, the Federal Reserve's balance sheet duration doubled from four to eight years, a trend mirrored by many other major central banks. Equally important, under fiscal dominance, the rise in central bank balance sheet duration makes perfect sense and will be structural. Central banks are mandated to buy ever more government bonds to preserve debt sustainability, including long-maturity bonds which push up central bank balance sheet duration.

Moreover, because central banks can directly control short-term interest rates through monetary policy, they face growing pressure to buy longer-term bonds instead. As we know, the money creation related to central bank bond buying fuels inflation, prompting markets to push up longer-term interest rates. Through standard monetary policy, central banks have less control over those longer-term rates. Without extraordinary intervention, long-term yields would surge, like the ball that is released from underwater, driving up government interest expenses and threatening debt sustainability. This is the exact reason why the Bank of Japan anchored its yield curve control policy around the 10-year rate. By doing so, it effectively controlled the 20- and even 30-year rates as well.

For the Federal Reserve, as issues of the world's reserve currency, the doubling of duration to eight years is perhaps not an immediate concern. But for China, facing both rapid aging and explosive debt growth, and for other emerging economies, the same dynamics apply. As balance sheet duration increases, so does the need for gold as a stabilizing buffer against interest rate swings. With gold's reserve shares barely above 10 percent in China and lower elsewhere, these reserves are, even by BIS standards, deeply inadequate.

Emerging economies face another challenge. The BIS paper further notes that central banks operating in volatile currencies, such as the Brazilian real or the Indian rupee, require even more gold on their balance sheet. For those central banks, the recommended gold allocation can climb as high as 50 percent. The BIS draws the same conclusion for other emerging markets such as Mexico (peso) and Indonesia (rupiah): Significantly higher gold reserves are needed to manage balance sheet risks. Perhaps somewhat surprisingly, the BIS points out that even a country like Australia, with 12 percent of its reserves in gold, faces the same currency volatility challenge. This perfectly reinforces my point: Every country faces variations of the same underlying fiat-currency problems, with the United States, the issuer of the global reserve currency, the only partial exception, for now.

A final word on the BIS, the very institution that helped design the current financial system. Even though its set of rules compels central and commercial banks to hold government debt like US Treasuries, it firmly acknowledges gold's special role in times of crisis and stress. Obviously, the BIS will never publicly declare that the global system is under strain, but were it to conduct a study focused explicitly on potential times of crises and stress, it would have to conclude that 0–5 percent of gold reserves is undeniably insufficient.

And the final line of the report says it all: "There is more to gold than risk and return."

Central banks, especially those in emerging economies, face shared and recurring challenges: small, volatile currencies, high inflation, economic instability, and geopolitical tensions. Many of these economies long to reduce their dependence on the US dollar, yet still hold less than 5 percent of their reserves in gold, a level that the BIS itself suggests is far too low.

As a result, central banks in emerging markets still have a long way to go in gold accumulation before reaching their strategic goals. And that makes them largely indifferent to gold's price. Unlike most private gold investors, they care little, if at all, about the price they pay. Their common overarching goal is stability, diversification, and ultimately a deliberate step away from the dollar.

Brown's Bottom

While the BIS might argue that central banks in the United States and Europe hold too much gold, the likelihood of them selling part of their reserves is virtually zero. On the contrary, the central banks of the world's biggest gold holders increasingly emphasize gold's strategic importance. The more gold there is, the more stable the (fiat money) system, and the stronger the trust it inspires.

In May 2025, the European Central Bank (ECB) published an analysis in its *Financial Stability Review* explicitly describing gold as a safe-haven asset with no counterparty risk, and as an effective hedge against geopolitical tensions, sanctions, and currency risks. These facts, because that's what they are, underscore just how biased the ECB's earlier blog post on bitcoin, discussed in Chapter 15, really was. In that piece, the authors claimed with a straight face that gold's value stems merely from its "social benefits" as jewelry.

What the ECB won't say outright, yet quietly admits between the lines (as do other central banks), is that gold helps sustain the debt-driven economic system and even restores some balance to it. It goes without saying that central banks are far too "independent" to ever say that out loud. Nevertheless, central banks, particularly those in highly indebted countries, must feel pretty grateful for gold's steady rise in value. That includes the Federal Reserve, which carries the US government's gold holdings (or, more precisely, the gold certificates representing those claims as the gold is owned by the government) on its books at a fraction of their market value. In theory, the Fed could revalue that gold and use the accounting gain to cancel part of the US government debt it holds on its balance sheet, essentially offsetting government liabilities with reappraised assets.

Either way, don't expect another "Gordon Brown moment." Between 1999 and 2002, the then British Chancellor of the Exchequer, Gordon Brown, sold 395 tons of gold, about 60 percent of Britain's reserves, at an average price of $276 per troy ounce (31.1 grams). The sale generated $3.5 billion at the time. Officially, the sale was meant to "diversify" Britain's reserves, but in reality, it aimed to ease growing concerns over fiscal policy. The sale is now infamously known as "Brown's Bottom," a textbook example of catastrophically bad timing and limited monetary foresight. At today's gold price of roughly $4,000 per troy ounce, that policy blunder carries a price tag of nearly $50 billion.

Digital Gold for Central Banks?

A recurring theme in many books about money, such as *Money* by David McWilliams, is that economies and financial systems eventually hit growth barriers when they run short of underlying value. That's precisely the point at which governments and policymakers, under the banner of "financial innovation," open the toolbox of monetary tricks to stretch the money supply as far as possible, right until trust in the entire system starts to crack, and sometimes breaks altogether.

It's worth revisiting this dynamic because it determines whether a fragile financial system survives or collapses when trust erodes. It also directly ties into Exter's inverted pyramid. Sooner or later, the monetary bag of tricks runs empty, and the top of the inverted pyramid becomes too narrow to sustain additional growth. This describes perfectly where today's financial system stands.

Government deficits and debt have reached such extreme levels, and potential GDP growth has declined so much, that the current gold reserves of central banks are no longer sufficient to underpin trust in our money. The foundation of the financial system can no longer hold without reinforcement.

Bitcoin, characterized by programmed scarcity and a unique mechanism for storing value (blockchain), could serve as a complement to that foundation. Where Exter's pyramid rests on gold as its monetary base, bitcoin could deepen that base in a fully digital economy. Not instead of gold, as many Bitcoin maximalists expect (or hope), but alongside it. Bitcoin is not a substitute for gold but rather adds what is missing from today's financial system: digital scarcity that is decentralized, independent, and fully transparent.

That sounds promising on paper. In practice, however, there is little sign that bitcoin is getting accepted as a legitimate component of central bank reserves. Central banks remain trapped in a system of fiat currencies and sovereign debt, constrained on one side by fiscal policy and declining independence, and on the other by the rulebooks of institutions like the BIS. Given how recently central banks have (re) discovered gold, and how low gold's share in reserves still is, bitcoin may have to wait its turn before seeing any meaningful adoption.

Though the same argument may apply to gold, central bankers perceive bitcoin far more as a threat that undermines their policies. In response, they are developing their own digital, programmable money, known as central bank digital currencies (CBDCs). For now, that is a far cry from integrating bitcoin to reinforce the foundations of the fiat system.

However, if bitcoin ultimately fulfills its promise and gains global acceptance as a uniquely scarce, indestructible digital form of value, it could, paradoxically, help central banks restore trust in the system they currently defend.

The Dollar-Gold Rebalancing

Let's return to the central theme: constructing a future-proof investment portfolio built around scarce assets. While central banks may take years to adapt their policies, you can already position yourself for the structural changes required to keep the debt-driven system afloat.

If the arguments throughout this book have landed as intended, that should sound compelling. Yet many investors, after years of soaring prices, now suffer from vertigo. It's one of the many unhelpful quirks of human psychology. The question many investors ask themselves these days is whether they are already too late. Which is why I will close this chapter with what I believe is convincing evidence that The Great Rebalancing has only just begun.

A key example of that evidence lies in the tight relationship between the US dollar's share of global foreign exchange reserves and the price of gold. In the next chart, the gold price (in US dollars) is shown on the left axis (gray line), plotted on a logarithmic scale, where values increase exponentially. On a logarithmic scale, moving from 100 to 1,000 equals the move from 1,000 to 10,000. This way, wide price swings in gold, here from $400 to almost $4,000, appear less extreme, making it easier to reveal the underlying trend.

On the right axis (black line) is the US dollar's share of global central bank reserves, measured in percentage points. Note that the right axis is inverted, meaning that when the line rises, the dollar's share in reserves actually declines.

When you plot the gold price and the dollar's share of central bank reserves in this way, a remarkably strong relationship emerges. Since 2000, the two lines have moved almost perfectly in sync. When the US dollar's share of global central bank reserves declines (the black line on the right axis moves up), the gold price (the gray line on the left axis) goes higher, and vice versa.

Looking at this chart immediately allows a few puzzle pieces to fall into place. Over the past 25 years, the dollar's share of central bank reserves has steadily fallen from 72 percent to 58 percent, a trend that aligns perfectly with the growing desire of an increasing number of countries to loosen their dependence on the dollar. As shown earlier, these same countries have been buying gold en masse to achieve that goal. The shift from dollars to gold by central banks lifts gold prices, a move both geopolitically and empirically consistent with the data. The higher gold price, in turn, restores greater balance to the system (think back to Exter's pyramid).

I have left out the scatter plot this time, but that should not detract from the fact that the relationship is statistically very significant: Changes in the dollar's share in central bank reserves explain roughly 80 percent of the changes in the gold price (R-squared = 0.8).

That's without question strong enough to use the relationship as a basis for estimating where gold is heading.

Before I move on, I have learned from experience to be careful with price predictions. In April 2024, during a Holland Gold podcast, I "predicted" that gold could double in price within five years. At the time, the price was about $2,300. While the yellow metal is well ahead of schedule, people rarely miss a chance to remind you of that prediction, especially when prices dip.

Despite this disclaimer, investing is ultimately about having the bravery to look ahead and act on it. So here I will attempt an estimate of the future gold price using a reasonable projection of the dollar's future share in global central bank reserves. First, a quick recap of the key facts. Recent years have brought the highest inflation since the early 1980s, the war in Ukraine, President Trump's tariff wars, rising geopolitical tensions, the rise of a multipolar world with the US and China as rival poles, growing efforts to escape dollar dominance, and, above all, relentless debt accumulation combined with heavy money creation.

Based on these developments, I expect the share of gold in global central bank reserves to rise from 21 percent today to at least 40 percent. Nearly a doubling, but also well short of the levels that prevailed before the gold standard was abandoned. The major Western economies will continue to rely on gold as a foundation for financial stability and debt sustainability and are unlikely to reduce their holdings. Emerging economies, covering China, eager to escape the dollar's grip, and with fragile, volatile currencies, will have little choice but to build much larger gold positions. At the same time, the BIS scenarios, featuring rising central bank balance sheet duration, higher interest-rate sensitivity, elevated currency volatility, and financial stress, all point to larger gold holdings and lower dollar reserves.

Let me take that 40 percent gold share in reserves as the starting point for a simple thought experiment. For gold's share of reserves to roughly double from current levels (21 percent), fiat currencies together would need to lose nearly 20 percentage points of their weight in central bank reserves. Assuming the reduction occurs proportionally, with the dollar currently accounting for 58 percent of reserves, the dollar would absorb 58 percent of that decline. Thus, the dollar's share in global reserves would fall by nearly 12 percentage points (58% × 20%) to 46 percent (58% – 12%).

Using the projected dollar share in the regression formula behind the chart above puts the price of gold at around $5,500 per troy ounce. If breaking dollar dominance becomes the central theme and the dollar's share falls not by 12 but by 20 percentage points (equal to the full rise in gold's share in this example), the gold price should approach $7,500 per troy ounce.

Let me be clear: The odds of this forecast landing exactly right are close to zero. Despite its strength, the relationship does not capture every factor influencing gold prices, and other developments, such as structurally higher inflation, will impact the outcome.

What is fairly certain, in my view, is that as long as the share of gold in central bank reserves rises, so, too, will the price of gold. And the odds of that scenario unfolding are exceptionally high.

A Great Rebalancing of Value

To conclude, I want to illustrate the dynamic between (the value of) scarce assets and debt from another angle, this time including bitcoin. It's one of my favorite ways to make The Great Rebalancing tangible and to show just how far we still have to go.

The chart on the next page compares the total market value, in US dollars, of the four assets at the core of my rebalancing theory: bitcoin, gold, money, and debt. Bitcoin and physical gold appear on the left, while the total global money supply and total global debt are shown on the right. The contrast is striking. In a single image, you can see the monumental imbalance between the intrinsic value underpinning the financial system (gold and ultimately bitcoin) and the monetary toolbox used to buy more economic growth (fiat money and debt).

Bitcoin currently has a market value of roughly $2 trillion, and gold about $30 trillion. Huge numbers, yet almost trivial compared to the total amounts of money and debt in the world. As of October 2025, the world holds $114 trillion in money and a staggering $338 trillion in debt.

You can interpret these values as follows: For every dollar of fiat money in circulation, there is about 26 cents worth of gold (30/114). In other words, gold covers barely a quarter of the world's money supply. For every dollar of global debt, less than 9 percent (30/338) is backed by the value of gold. Note that my numbers include all above-ground gold, of which central banks own only 17 percent. Adjusting for that, the effective gold coverage of global money shrinks more than fivefold, to about 5 percent for money and just 1.8 percent for global debt.

For bitcoin, the ratios are another fifteen times smaller. Against every dollar of fiat money, there are less than 2 cents of bitcoin value (2/114). Against global debt, the number turns microscopic: just 0.6 cents of bitcoin for every dollar of debt worldwide.

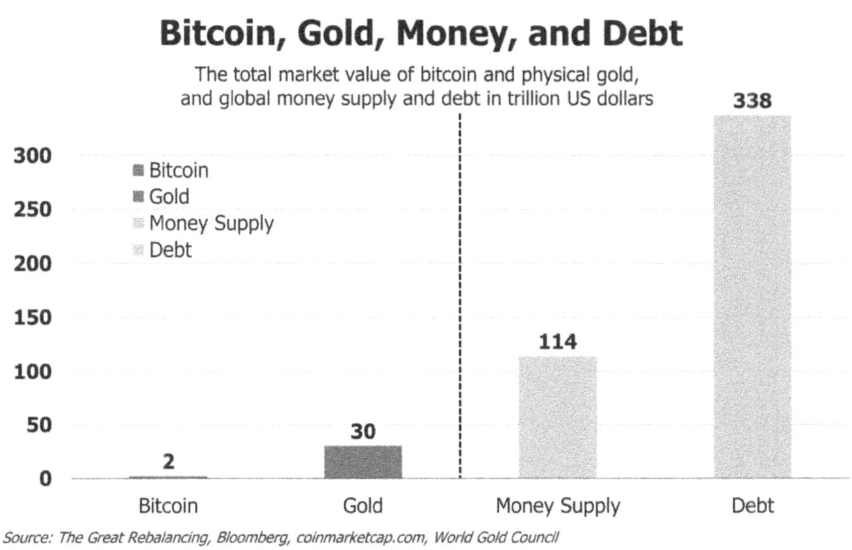

A crucial yet often overlooked point about this chart is that these numbers are not static, quite the opposite. This insight is key for understanding the potential value boom in gold and bitcoin: Our unrelenting desire for growth translates into an ever-expanding amount of money and debt. To make things worse, fiscal dominance acts as a strong catalyst, meaning that figures on the right side of the chart (money and debt) not only rise, but they do so at an accelerating pace.

The conclusion is simple but huge: To restore balance in our debt-driven financial system, the market values of bitcoin and gold can't just increase sharply; they must rise exponentially.

It's not that hard to incorporate this relentless growth on the right-hand side into my projections. Over the past twenty years, the global money supply has grown by about 7 percent per year, while total debt has increased by roughly 5 percent per year. To be clear, these are long-term averages. Since the global financial crisis, and especially since the pandemic, growth in both money and debt has been significantly faster. To smooth out short-term distortions and to take a cautious approach in deriving future values, I base my calculations on these twenty-year growth averages.

At those growth rates, the world's money supply will hit $160 trillion within five years, while global debt will spike to an eye-watering $431 trillion. Now, what do these astonishing numbers imply for the potential value of gold under the assumptions of The Great Rebalancing? Let's start with a modest scenario, where gold coverage of the money supply rises from 26 percent to 39 percent, and of global debt from 9 percent to 13.5 percent (both a 50 percent increase). That would translate into a total market value for gold between $58 and $62 trillion (13.5% × 431 and 39% × 160), roughly a doubling from today's level.

Again, this is a conservative assumption, considering the gold reserves held by central banks in the past. If, as in earlier eras, half of the money supply were backed by gold, the implied market value would approach $80 trillion (50 percent × 160), compared to $30 trillion today. That would mean a gold price north of $10,000 per troy ounce.

For bitcoin, the numbers are even more extreme. The current ratio of bitcoin's market value to gold's is roughly one to fifteen. Suppose bitcoin joins gold as a monetary foundation of the system at one-fifth of gold's value. In that case, with gold covering 39 percent of the money supply, bitcoin's share would be almost 8 percent. That implies a market value for bitcoin of nearly $13 trillion, more than six times its current value.

Of course, these estimates come with a very high degree of uncertainty. You should not treat them as point estimates for the future price of gold or bitcoin. Besides, to turn these price projections into returns, you must also estimate how long it will take for bitcoin and gold to reach those assumed coverage percentages. I typically work with a five-year horizon, though recent years hint that it could unfold more quickly.

A gold market value of $60 trillion and bitcoin at almost $13 trillion would correspond to average annual returns in dollars of roughly 15 percent and 45 percent, respectively. That is likely less dramatic than many might imagine and underscores the massive impact of compounding returns.

I want to stress here once more that these are price increases and returns displayed in nominal dollars. As highlighted repeatedly in this book, positive nominal returns are entirely different from a rise in purchasing power. Adjusting for inflation would add a layer of complexity, not least because these wide estimates already come with a high level of uncertainty. Still, the distinction between nominal returns and purchasing power should not be underestimated or ignored.

The Catalyst Against Imbalance

The extreme imbalance that has emerged between the core value stored in the current financial system and the sheer "value" of worthless money and the unparalleled pile of debt creates enormous upside potential for scarce assets.

And it is The Great Rebalancing within the current financial system that acts as the catalyst for the unprecedented increase in relative value. Endowments, family offices, pension funds, sovereign wealth funds, and traditional asset managers will be forced by hard data, reality, and their clients to rethink their portfolios. In addition, there are investors like myself who refuse to wait for traditional institutions to move, and design and launch new investment solutions themselves. Solutions that do make room for scarce assets to shield against inflation and the destruction of purchasing power.

The Great Rebalancing is further amplified by private investors who prefer to stay in control and who recognize the wisdom of holding part of their wealth outside the traditional system to avoid getting trapped in financial repression. And by central banks that own too few scarce assets to participate in the new implicit gold-bitcoin standard. They sit on fiat currencies nobody really wants, push to accelerate their move away from the US dollar, and try to protect themselves against steadily rising geopolitical tensions. All this unfolds against the backdrop of infinite money creation and perpetual debt accumulation.

You are not too late. Quite the opposite. You are perfectly on time to be part of The Great Rebalancing. All the more so once you understand there is another, final, overarching reason driving the rebalancing.

That reason is the powerful conclusion of this book.

CHAPTER 20

The Great Wealth Transfer

Even if you suffer from a touch of vertigo, consider the following developments:

- The exhaustion of the labor force as the original source of economic growth
- Long-term trends in budget deficits, tax burdens, and mandatory government spending tied to aging populations
- The need for a regime of fiscal dominance with structurally low interest rates and persistently high inflation, potentially reinforced by capital controls
- The near-universal use of the outdated 60/40 philosophy in global investment portfolios, with virtually no allocation to scarce assets
- The growing push to diversify central bank reserves and weaken the dollar's long-standing hegemony
- The transition toward a multipolar world marked by persistently elevated geopolitical tensions
- And the huge imbalance between intrinsic value on one side and fiat money and debt on the other

Together, these are compelling reasons to assume that the process of The Great Rebalancing is only just beginning. In this final chapter, I add one more force to the equation: ourselves. When we change, our investments change with us. And that inevitably shapes our portfolios of the future, especially when it coincides with the largest transfer of wealth in history.

The Great Wealth Transfer

In the decades ahead, Baby boomers will ignite the largest transfer of wealth in human history, with far-reaching implications for how we construct our investment portfolios. Born between 1946 and 1964, Baby boomers are the richest generation the world has ever seen. Boosted by long stretches of economic prosperity, soaring property values, broad access to financial markets, decades of falling interest rates, and potent equity markets, Baby boomers have amassed extraordinary wealth. In the United States, this generation owns more than half of all household wealth, despite representing only about 20 percent of the population. And while data for other regions are less comprehensive, the picture is similar: Baby boomers across the globe hold a disproportionately large share of total wealth.

The youngest Baby boomers are in their early sixties, and the oldest are near eighty. This phase of life ushers in a historic shift in wealth: the Great Wealth Transfer. Cerulli Associates, a research firm focused on asset managers, estimates that between now and 2048, an astronomical $124 trillion will transfer from Baby boomers (and a small portion of the Silent Generation before them, born between 1928 and 1945) to younger generations.

To put that number into perspective: All publicly traded equities worldwide are worth about $135 trillion, according to Bloomberg. As noted in the previous chapter, the total market value of bitcoin and physical gold stands at $2 trillion and $30 trillion, respectively. By comparison, the upcoming wealth transfer is colossal.

The next chart shows how the wealth transfer is distributed among younger generations: Generation X (born between 1965 and 1980), Millennials (born between 1981 and 1996), and Generation Z (born between 1997 and 2012). Roughly half of the $124 trillion in total transfer flows to the youngest cohorts, Millennials and Gen Z.

UBS reports somewhat lower numbers but offers a global breakdown. Over the next twenty years, more than $50 trillion will change hands in the Americas, $21 trillion in Europe, the Middle East, and Africa, and $11 trillion across the Asia-Pacific region.

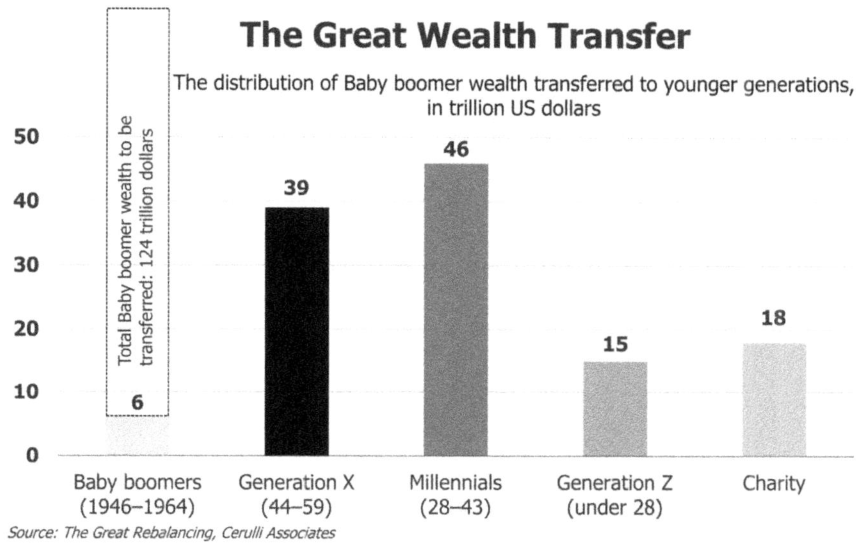

Such seismic shifts in wealth across generations are in any case worth scrutinizing and evaluating for their likely consequences. But the reason I explore this topic explicitly at the end of my book is that the Great Wealth Transfer aligns perfectly with The Great Rebalancing. The reinforcing power of these two major long-term trends suggests that the portfolios of the future will likely change far more dramatically than most people imagine.

In short, newly acquired capital among younger generations meets a bold and emerging investment philosophy. Judging by the outdated structure of their portfolios, traditional wealth managers are paying little attention to and are largely unprepared for this pivotal encounter between new capital and a new investment standard.

The Great Wealth Transfer is far from evenly distributed, also within generations. In reality, only about one in five Americans will receive an inheritance, and for most of them, the amount will be modest.

Because the wealthiest 10 percent of households in the US (and Europe) own roughly two-thirds of total assets, the bulk of transferred wealth will flow to a relatively small elite. Notably, that elite group consists largely of women. According to Bank of America, about 70 percent of the coming wealth transfer will go to women, daughters, granddaughters, spouses, and other female relatives.

Younger, Wealthier Women

The concentration of wealth transfers within affluent families, particularly toward younger female family members, will heavily reshape the way future portfolios are constructed. Wealthy Millennials and Generation X members are, on average, far more likely to invest than their less-affluent peers, for the simple reason that they own spare capital to deploy.

Moreover, younger generations invest significantly more in alternative asset classes than their parents and grandparents. While the skewed distribution of wealth and inheritances is never ideal from a social perspective, the transfers themselves drive a gradual yet far-reaching shift in both investment philosophy and portfolio composition.

That shift is further accentuated as women also tend to have different financial priorities from men, placing particular emphasis on long-term security. Women often cite insufficient pension income and future healthcare costs as key threats to their financial security as they get older. They are also more likely to define specific goals aimed at preserving their current standard of living.

Reading between the lines quickly reveals that for women investors, inflation is the principal enemy that can derail those goals. Many investors still mistakenly regard government bonds as "safe," often because of incomplete or misleading information. It seems plausible that younger female investors will become less enthusiastic about bonds once they fully grasp the risks to their long-term goal of wealth preservation when returns fail to keep pace with inflation. Loss of purchasing power poses an even greater risk to women than to men.

That desire for long-term financial security makes gold, and increasingly bitcoin, appealing for younger women. The Royal Mint, the UK's official coinage institution, reported that the share of women investing in gold and silver had climbed to 26 percent in 2024 from only 8 percent in 2018. This suggests that the recent surge in inflation, fueled by extreme fiscal and monetary policies, has prompted these women to act and reallocate, or more precisely, safeguard, part of their wealth.

Even so, actual investments in gold and other alternatives remain limited for both men and women. The previous chapter showed that this is largely because these options are simply not included in the portfolio mixes of traditional asset managers, family offices, and pension funds. Those institutions cling to conventional stock-and-bond portfolios for as long as they can, even as these portfolios no longer match the evolving preferences of younger generations of investors.

This seemingly deliberate lack of flexibility and choice is evident in how the industry approaches female investors. Consultancy firm McKinsey identifies three structural shortcomings of traditional asset management that prevent young women from building their "optimal" portfolio: a lack of diversity within advisor teams (only one in five advisors is female), a reflexive focus on male clients as the primary decision-makers, and insufficient engagement with younger women.

When women do decide to seek financial advice, they often do so after the age of 45. Many Millennial and Gen Z women leave their wealth untouched. McKinsey & Company estimates that of the $20 trillion in additional assets women will inherit by 2030, roughly half will remain unmanaged. I fear this means their wealth will sit in low-interest savings accounts, where its purchasing power will be gradually eaten away by inflation. That is nothing short of ironic, given that women worry more than men (rightfully so) about maintaining their future living standards and being able to pay the bills later in life.

You would expect that, given the enormous sums involved in the wealth transfer, traditional wealth managers would try harder to meet the needs of increasingly affluent women. The clearest of those needs centers around designing alternative investment mixes that are better aligned with the priorities of younger generations.

Radically Different

Younger generations view investing in ways that are radically different from their parents and grandparents. According to a 2024 study among wealthy Americans by Bank of America Private Bank, a striking 72 percent of younger investors aged 21 to 43 (Millennials and Generation Z) believe it is impossible to achieve above-average returns with a portfolio consisting solely of stocks and bonds. Nearly three-quarters reject the traditional 60/40 portfolio, an astonishingly high share. Among investors aged 44 and older, that number drops to just 28 percent. That is significantly lower than among younger generations, confirming that it is primarily the younger generations who want to construct their portfolios in fundamentally different ways. For instance, younger investors see far greater opportunity in crypto and digital assets, private equity, and, interestingly, their own businesses or brands. To emphasize the contrast with older generations: The first and last sit near the bottom of the list of promising investments for investors aged 44 and over.

It is somewhat unfortunate that most studies on digital assets, especially those from traditional wealth managers, fail to distinguish between bitcoin and crypto. By lumping them together, these studies create an awkward comparison, much like comparing gold with commodities.

If that distinction were made, it would offer greater insight into how younger investors perceive these two fundamentally different asset classes. It is also another confirmation that the traditional investment industry does not fully grasp these differences, conveniently labeling everything as "crypto" or, worse, "cryptocurrencies." Whenever I'm asked about crypto, I first have to point out the differences with Bitcoin.

Younger investors also view tangible assets, including gold, as more attractive investment options than their older counterparts do. Nevertheless, they do not appear at the top of the list. Perhaps this is because the definition applied by the Bank of America (tangible assets) was very broad. Gold is hardly comparable to a classic Ferrari or a painting, yet the Bank of America study places them in the same group. Chapter 17 already showed that many of these tangible investments come with characteristics that make them insufficient as liquid investment alternatives. But perhaps tangible assets and gold rank lower just because they are not digital enough.

Curiously, younger wealthy Americans view domestic equities as far less appealing than their older peers do. That may reflect the relentless marketing machine of private equity, or it may be because a large share of their wealth is already tied to their own business. Still, these findings contrast with the rankings of the most traded stocks on digital trading platforms, which are mostly used by younger investors and where US technology stocks consistently dominate trading activity. Real estate, meanwhile, is the only asset class that is favored among all generations.

Beyond the divergent view young investors have of what makes an attractive investment portfolio, the Bank of America study highlights another critical point: a strong sense of urgency. An overwhelming 93 percent of wealthy investors under 43 surveyed said they plan to expand their exposure to alternative assets within five years. Given that alternatives currently account for just 17 percent of their portfolios, there is ample room to do so.

The gap between how young investors want their portfolios to look and how they actually invest remains huge.

Similar trends are emerging elsewhere, though with regional nuances. Crypto is especially popular among young Asian investors, while gold is less fashionable. In Germany, a notable exception when it comes to gold investing, younger generations show interest in both crypto and gold, but also favor traditional equities, often through ETFs. That last observation very likely reflects Germany's lack of a true investment culture, resulting in relatively low equity allocations.

In China, gold also ranks prominently among assets that (younger) investors like to add to their portfolios. Years of declining property prices, weak consumer confidence, and a softer currency have all contributed to gold's appeal. While asset class preferences between countries and regions can be substantial, the overarching pattern is hard to miss: a decisive shift away from traditional assets toward alternatives such as bitcoin (often part of crypto), gold, private equity, and real estate.

To conclude: The Great Wealth Transfer and The Great Rebalancing, both driven and accelerated by younger generations, are not one-way streets. Quite a few participants in my investment fund are families: mothers and fathers investing together with sons and daughters, with the younger generation actively helping their parents rebalance their portfolios in advance. The awareness that a well-diversified portfolio no longer consists solely of stocks and bonds is spreading across generations.

Preaching to their own Choir

Unsurprisingly, even in the midst of the Great Wealth Transfer, traditional asset managers continue to steer their (new) clients toward the classic equity-and-bond model. In exploring the numbers and trends behind the Great Wealth Transfer, I came across countless blogs, interviews, publications, and video clips from private bankers and financial advisors insisting that young investors should load up on bonds as they age.

I can only hope that everything I have written so far makes clear how misguided that reasoning really is. If my book demonstrates anything, it's that bonds are overwhelmingly likely to destroy real wealth, not grow it. Why would any investor, young or old, embrace that? Under the banner of "financial education," investors are being shepherded toward allocations that serve the business models of wealth managers far better than the interests of their clients.

The good news is that younger generations are relying less and less on those traditional firms for their information. Yet a massive knowledge void remains around what risk and return really look like in a rapidly changing financial system. And how fiscal dominance, a debt-driven growth model, and fading trust in central banks and fiat money turn saving and traditional bond investing into losing strategies.

Fortunately, given their growing experience, investment insights, and personal preferences, it is fair to assume that the trillions in wealth flowing to younger generations over the next two decades will radically transform the design of the standard model portfolio. Within a few decades, Generation Z may well become the richest generation in history, a generation that will likely look back on forty years in which old-fashioned bonds produced no real returns while their focus steadily shifted toward alternative investments. If things go their way, they can put that incoming wealth to work right away, not least because the slightly older Millennials will be running the investment show by then.

Working with Tomorrow's Leaders

What stands out is that studies on the Great Wealth Transfer focus almost solely on the volume of wealth involved and the generational differences in investment preferences.

What should not be overlooked is that The Great Rebalancing, despite the rigid attitude toward change, will also come from within the traditional investment industry itself. Millennials and Gen X are not just clients with radically different portfolio preferences: These generations also produce the new leaders, new policymakers, new CEOs of traditional wealth-management firms, regulators, central banks, and so on.

These new leaders are far less anchored to 60/40 thinking than their predecessors. They understand that the financial system they grew up in is fundamentally different from that of their predecessors. They know from experience that returns no longer automatically arise from simply diversifying across equities and bonds, but demand new choices in a financial system driven by debt sustainability and fiscal dominance. Moreover, they have no sentimental attachment to bonds, nor to a central bank that responds to every crisis by buying massive amounts of bonds and printing money.

As Millennials and Gen Z take their places as leaders and decision-makers of asset managers, family offices, pension funds, and, not to forget, central banks and governments, they will help disrupt the investment landscape. They have the responsibility not to distract investors with outdated truths but to explain honestly and transparently how returns are generated in a debt-driven world and construct their clients' portfolios accordingly.

Even though I am neither a Millennial nor part of Generation Z (I am too old), I look forward to working with these new leaders to help transform and reshape the investment industry and to make The Great Rebalancing accessible to all.

With this book, I hope to contribute to that inspiring and ambitious mission.

Afterword

This Is Only the Beginning

We are at the opening chapter of a crucial and sweeping transition. The economic growth model that carried us for centuries can no longer be taken for granted. This conclusion collides head-on with our unrelenting desire to keep expanding. Debt is a powerful yet addictive lever we must now pull to manufacture growth in swiftly aging economies. To keep the machine running, policy must increasingly bend to the primacy of debt sustainability. If debt sustainability is not enforced, the system would crumble almost instantly. That is the foundation and the necessity of fiscal dominance: a regime where structurally low rates and higher inflation support the debt machine, but only at the expense of the purchasing power and wealth of savers and bondholders.

This book delivers that uncompromising message in a direct, clear, and above all, factual way. Without exclusively doom and gloom, or apocalyptic fantasies. Just analysis, data, and a long roster of real-world episodes from the world's largest economies, each one pointing to the same conclusion: The 60/40 era is over. As Millennials already expect, you are unlikely to preserve your purchasing power with a bond-heavy portfolio.

For many policymakers, economists, journalists, and academics, cataloging problems has become a sport, their core business at times. Dramatic stories on everything that is wrong will get you the headlines, but offering solutions creates value. My book builds a strong case for investing in scarcity. Allocate to assets that cannot be issued without limit or that cannot be endlessly created with the stroke of a button. Assets that do not rely solely on trust, but on real value.

Bitcoin, physical gold, and quality equities are three uniquely scarce assets that have proven their ability to protect wealth and that work remarkably well together in a portfolio. Line up their characteristics and it almost feels designed, which makes it all the more astonishing and frustrating that traditional managers refuse to embed them meaningfully in client portfolios. For an industry that claims to put the client first, the cognitive dissonance is hard to ignore. The stories I have heard over the years from experts, advisors, and fund managers doing everything they can to avoid confronting the hard truth their own models spit out are often excruciating. Yet even those stories cannot hide the fact that The Great Rebalancing has begun and will not reverse.

What if I'm wrong?

I ask myself that often. What if, for reasons I cannot yet see, debt stops compounding? What if Brynjolfsson is right, and we are heading for a massive productivity revolution driven by artificial intelligence? What if society chooses, collectively, to stop chasing growth? And what if the scenario of David Rogers Webb's *The Great Taking* comes to pass, with a tiny elite seizing everything?

That last dystopian vision may seem far-fetched, yet plenty of people believe in it. I do not, simply because the narrative doesn't add up. If a tiny group of "super-powerful" were to take everything, people would simply cease to participate. Society as a structure collapses, productivity falls to zero, leaving zero profits to confiscate. If there was ever a perfect moment for this elite to let the system fail, it was the global financial crisis. The opposite happened, however; governments and central banks moved heaven and earth to keep the system alive.

As for the other questions: I simply do not see, given the evidence in this book, how aging demographics, the explosive rise in mandated government spending, and the structural downshift in potential GDP growth can be neutralized at scale. Sure, these trends could evolve more positively (or far more negatively) than current data imply, but the direction is nonetheless irreversible. And after a decade of extraordinary monetary experiments, negative interest rates, bruising inflation, and a massive loss of purchasing power, I struggle to imagine investors turning their backs on The Great Rebalancing.

Time to Act

This book was written to create urgency, to push you to the point where you think, "I need to do something." And you do, but with the encouraging message that you are anything but late. Recall the chart showing that the combined market value of physical gold and bitcoin is dwarfed by the total amount of global money and debt, both of which will keep rising. Recall, too, that traditional investors' portfolio mixes resemble absolutely nothing of this reality.

My book helps you respond to that. To take concrete action. Not with cheerful predictions, but with a solid framework. Not with certainty (the world is inherently uncertain), but with direction. In my introduction, I noted that the label "investment book" is too narrow. Treat it as a field manual, a source of inspiration, or a practical self-help guide for your capital. The label is irrelevant: What matters is that it moves you to act. As long as it helps you protect your wealth.

Looking ahead

Looking ahead, I see a financial system and an investment universe where scarce assets are the rule and no longer the exception. Thanks to the twin engines of The Great Rebalancing and the Great Wealth Transfer, investment portfolios will finally be truly diversified. Gold and bitcoin won't be fringe holdings; they will become an integral part of any respectable investment mix, adopted not out of ideology, but because of the numbers, advancing insight, and common sense.

I expect that gold and bitcoin will not only rise in value relative to fiat currencies but will also add stability to a financial system that will still be saturated with debt. In such an environment, quality companies can continue to thrive.

And perhaps, just perhaps, we will also become a bit more decentralized and less polarized as a society. As Harari wrote in

Sapiens, humans excel at building networks even without central leadership, a boss, or a CEO. The Great Rebalancing could lead to a more robust, more resilient, and, yes, fairer system.

Acknowledgments

A book is not a solo effort. If I were to list everyone who, in one way or another, helped or inspired me while writing this book, the list would run for dozens more pages. Even so, I want to extend my heartfelt thanks to all of them for their advice, help, information, knowledge, willingness to listen, cooperation, and support. Writing a book is far more than just an intellectual exercise. It is an intense experience, at times a draining process, an endless search, a continuous test, and above all a very long journey. In my case, that last part is also literally true: I decided to rent a house in Portugal for a few months, where I could retreat from time to time to write. Anyone who first starts an investment fund and then decides to "just" write a book on top of it can only pull that off with an environment that accepts and supports that choice. So, to my wife, Natasja: thank you for making this possible.

I'm tremendously proud of this book. Not only because of its content (the feedback from early readers suggests the book resonates quite nicely), but also because of the path it took to get here. That journey has given me a great deal of energy. And yes, the perfectionist in me already sees places to sharpen and extend it, or perhaps even write a sequel. But that is something for another time.

Finally, I want to thank you, the reader. For being willing to take in this story, and for staying with it all the way to the end. If this book moves you even one percent, in your investments, your understanding of the economy and financial markets, or the way you look at the world, then my mission is accomplished.

Questions or thoughts? Or curious about my investment fund? Email me at jeroen@bloklandfund.com or visit https://bloklandfund.com/.

Thank you.

Bibliography

Acemoglu, D., and P. Restrepo. "Secular Stagnation? The Effect of Aging on Economic Growth in the Age of Automation." *American Economic Review* 107, no. 5 (2017): 174–79. https://doi.org/10.1257/aer.p20171101

Ackerman, A. "U.S. Preparing to Relax Big-Bank Capital Rules." *The Washington Post*, May 15, 2025. https://www.washingtonpost.com/business/2025/05/15/bankcapital-fed-trump/

Alden, L. *Broken Money: Why Our Financial System Is Failing Us and How We Can Make It Better*. Timestamp Press, 2023.

Alderman, L. "France Proposes Cutting Two Public Holidays to Avert Budget Crisis." *The New York Times*, July 15, 2025. https://www.nytimes.com/2025/07/15/business/france-debt-deficit-spending-taxes.html

America Private Bank, Bank. "The Generational Divide: New Insights into the Mindsets of Younger Investors." 2024. https://www.privatebank.bankofamerica.com/articles/generational-divide-wealth-study.html

Ammous, S. *The Bitcoin Standard: The Decentralized Alternative to Central Banking*. Wiley, 2018.

André, C., P. Gal, and M. Schief. "Enhancing Productivity and Growth in an Ageing Society: Key Mechanisms and Policy Options." *OECD Economics Department Working Papers* (Paris), no. 1807 (2024). https://doi.org/10.1787/605b0787-en

Ang, A., G. Bekaert, and M. Wei. "Do macro variables, asset markets, or surveys forecast inflation better?" *Journal of Monetary Economics*

54,no.4(2005):1163–212.https://doi.org/10.1016/j.jmoneco.2006.04.006

Asness, C. "Volatility Laundering." Blog Post by C. Asness. 2023. https://www.aqr.com/Insights/%20Perspectives/Volatility-Laundering

Back, A. "[ANNOUNCE] Hash Cash Postage Implementation [E-Mail to Cypherpunks Mailinglijst." March 28, 1997. http://www.hashcash.org/papers/announce.txt

Banerjee, A., J. Sevillano, and M. Higginson. "From Ripples to Waves: The Transformational Power of Tokenizing Assets." *McKinsey & Company*, June 20, 2024. https://www.mckinsey.com/industries/financial-services/our-insights/fromripples-to-waves-the-transformational-power-of-tokenizing-assets

Barro, R.J. "On the Determination of the Public Debt." *Journal of Political Economy* 87, no. 5 (1979): 940–71. http://www.jstor.org/stable/1833077.

Baur, D.G., K. Hong, and A.D. Lee. "Bitcoin: Medium of Exchange or Speculative Assets?" *Journal of International Financial Markets, Institutions and Money* 54 (2018): 177–89. https://doi.org/10.1016/j.intfin.2017.12.004

Bindseil, U., and J. Schaaf. "ETF Approval for Bitcoin – The Naked Emperor's New Clothes." *European Central Bank*, 2024. https://www.ecb.europa.eu/press/blog/date/2024/html/ecb.blog20240222~0929f86e23.en.html

Biswas, P., and A. Bhandari. "Harvard University Exploring $1 Billion of Private Equity Stakes Sale, Source Says." *Reuters*, April 24, 2025. https://www.reuters.com/world/us/harvard-university-exploring-1-billion-private-equity-stakes-sale-bloomberg-news-2025-04-24/

BlackRock. "Bitcoin: A unique diversifier." 2024. https://www.blackrock.com/us/financial-professionals/literature/whitepaper/bitcoin-a-unique-diversifier.pdf.

Bolhuis, M.A., J. Koosakul, and N. Shenai. "Fiscal R-Star: Fiscal-Monetary Tensions and Implications for Policy." 2024. https://www.imf.org/en/Publications/WP/Issues/2024/08/09/Fiscal-R-Star-Fiscal-Monetary-Tensions-and-Implicationsfor-Policy-552877

Bordo, M.D., and A.J. Schwartz. "Monetary Policy Regimes and Economic Performance: The Historical Record (NBER Working Paper No. 6201." *National Bureau of Economic Research*, ahead of print, 1997. https://doi.org/10.3386/w6201

Boudoukh, J., and M. Richardson. "Stock Returns and Inflation: A Long-Horizon Perspective." *The American Economic Review* 83, no. 5 (1993): 1346–55. https://www.jstor.org/stable/2117566

Brynjolfsson, E., D. Rock, and C. Syverson. "Artificial Intelligence and the Modern Productivity Paradox: A Clash of Expectations and Statistics." National Bureau Of." *Economic Research Working Paper*, no. 24001 (2017). https://www.nber.org/system/files/working_papers/w24001/w24001.pdf

Brynjolfsson, E., E. Dinlersoz, L.S. Foster, et al. "AI Adoption in America: Who, What, and Where." NBER Working Paper No. 31788. *National Bureau of Economic Research*, 2023. https://www.nber.org/papers/w31788

Cavallo, E.A., G. Sánchez, and P. Valenzuela. "Gone with the Wind: Demographic Transitions and Domestic Saving." IBD Working Paper 688. 2016. https://doi.org/10.18235/0011730

Cecco, L. "Canadian Police Secure Downtown Ottawa as Truckers' Protest Ends – Including Powers to Freeze Bank Accounts." *The Guardian*, February 20, 2022. https://www.theguardian.com/world/2022/feb/20/canadian-policeottawa-truckers-protest.

Cerulli Associates. "Cerulli anticipates $124 trillion in wealth will transfer through 2048." 2023. https://www.cerulli.com/press-releases/cerulli-anticipates-124-trillion-in-wealth-will-transfer-through-2048

CFA Institute. *New CFA Institute Survey Highlights Investment Industry's Concerns over Soaring U.S. Government Debt.* 2024. https://www.cfainstitute.org/about/press-room/2024/survey-highlights-government-debt

Chaum, D. "Blind Signatures for Untraceable Payments." *Advances in Cryptology: Proceedings of Crypto '82*, Springer, 1983, 199–203. https://link.springer.com/chapter/10.1007/978-1-4757-0602-4_18

Chrisafis, A. "Why France's Austerity Budget Is Causing a Political Storm." *The Guardian*, November 28, 2024. https://www.theguardian.com/business/2024/nov/28/why-france-austerity-budget-political-storm

Cochrane, J.H. *The Fiscal Theory of the Price Level.* Princeton University Press, 2023.

Committee for a Responsible Federal Budget. "The Long-Term Budget Outlook: 2025 to 2055." 2025. https://www.cbo.gov/publication/61187

Cowen, T. *The Great Stagnation: How America Ate All the Low-Hanging Fruit of Modern History, Got Sick, and Will (Eventually) Feel Better.* Dutton, 2011.

Czech National Bank. "Governor Michl's Thoughts on Bitcoin – a Test Portfolio in CNB's Foreign Exchange Reserves." January 29, 2025. https://www.cnb.cz/en/public/

Dai, W., and H. Finney. "Reusable Proofs of Work (RPOW." 1998. https://nakamotoinstitute.org/b-money/

De Nederlandsche Bank. "The ECB's Monetary Policy." https://www.dnb.nl/en/the-euro-and-europe/the-ecb-s-monetary-policy/.

Denison, E.F. *The Sources of Economic Growth in the United States and the Alternatives before Us.* Committee for Economic Development, 1962.

Dimson, E., P. Marsh, and M. Staunton. *Triumph of the Optimists: 101 Years of Global Investment Returns*. Princeton University Press, 2002.

Dimson, E., P. Marsh, and M. Staunton. *UBS Global Investment Returns Yearbook 2025*. Summary. UBS Global Research, 2025. https://www.ubs.com/global/en/investment-bank/insights-and-data/2025/global-investment-returns-yearbook-2025.html

Domar, E.D. "The Burden of the Debt and the National Income." *The American Economic Review* 34, no. 4 (1944): 798–827. https://www.jstor.org/stable/1807397

Dotsey, M., S. Fujita, and L. Rudanko. "Where Is Everybody? The Shrinking Labor Force Participation Rate." *Economic Insights* 2, no. 4 (2017): 17–24. https://www.philadelphiafed.org/-/media/frbp/assets/economy/articles/economic-insights/2017/q4/eiq4_where-is-everybody.pdf

Dougherty, S., P. Biase, and Lorenzoni L. "Funding the Future: The Impact of Population Ageing on Revenues across Levels of Government." *OECD Working Papers on Fiscal Federalism* (Paris), no. 39 (2022). https://www.oecd.org/content/dam/oecd/en/publications/reports/2022/08/funding-the-future_3fcedfd6/2b0f063e-en.pdf

Douglass, P., L.S. Goldberg, and O.Z. Hannaoui. "Taking Stock: Dollar Assets, Gold, and Official Foreign Exchange Reserves." *Liberty Street Economics*, 2024. https://libertystreeteconomics.newyorkfed.org/2024/05/taking-stock-dollar-assets-gold-and-official-foreignexchange-reserves/

Enache, C. "Corporate Tax Rates around the World, 2024." *Tax Foundation*, December 17, 2024. https://taxfoundation.org/data/all/global/corporate-tax-rates-bycountry-2024/.

European Central Bank. "Fiscal Policy, Public Investment and Debt Sustainability in the Euro Area." *ECB Economic Bulletin*, 2024. https://www.ecb.europa.eu/press/economic-bulletin/articles/2024/html/ecb.

European Central Bank. "Is Monetary Policy Dominated by Fiscal Policy? (Speech by Isabel Schnabel, Member of the Executive Board, at a Conference Organised by Stiftung Geld Und Währung on 25 Years of the Euro – Perspectives for Monetary and Fiscal Policy in an Unstable World." Frankfurt, June 7, 2024. https://www.ecb.europa.eu/press/key/date/2024/html/ecb.sp240607~c6ae070dc0.en.html

European Central Bank. "Verbatim of the Remarks Made by Mario Draghi." *President of the European Central Bank, at the Global Investment Conference in London*, July 26, 2012. https://www.ecb.europa.eu/press/key/date/2012/html/.

European Commission. "Climate Mainstreaming." June 7, 2023. https://commission.europa.eu/strategy-and-policy/eu-budget/performance-and-reporting/horizontal-priorities/green-budgeting/climate-mainstreaming_en

European Commission. "The future of European competitiveness." September 2024. https://commission.europa.eu/topics/eu-competitiveness/

European Commission. *The 2021 Ageing Report: Economic and Budgetary Projections for the EU Member States (2019–2070)*. Publications Office of the European Union, 2021.

European Commission. *The 2024 Ageing Report: Economic and Budgetary Projections for the EU Member States (2022–2070)* May 15, 2024. https://economyfinance.ec.europa.eu/publications/2024-ageing-report-economic-andbudgetary-projections-eu-member-states-2022-2070_en.

European Union, Council. "Stability and Growth Pact: Council Launches Excessive Deficit Procedures against Seven Member States." July 26, 2024. https://www.consilium.europa.eu/en/press/press-releases/2024/07/26/stability-and-growth-pact-council-launches-excessive-deficit-procedures-against-seven-member-states/

European Union. *Treaty of Maastricht on European Union.* Publications Office of the European Union, 1992. https://eur-lex.europa.eu/legal-content/EN/TXT/?uri=CELEX:11992M/TXT.

Fabrichnaya, E., and G. Faulconbridge. "What and Where Are Russia's $300 Billion in Reserves Frozen in the West? Reuters." December 28, 2023. https://www.reuters.com/world/europe/what-where-are-russias-300-billion-reserves-frozen-west-2023-12-28/

Fama, E.F. "Stock Returns, Real Activity, Inflation, and Money." *American Economic Review* 71, no. 4 (1981): 545–65. https://www.jstor.org/stable/1806180

Fama, E.F., and K.R. French. "A Five-Factor Asset Pricing Model." *Journal of Financial Economics* 116, no. 1 (2015): 1–22. https://doi.org/10.1016/j.jfineco.2014.10.010

Fama, E.F., and K.R. French. "Common Risk Factors in the Returns on Stocks and Bonds." *Journal of Financial Economics* 33, no. 1 (1993): 3–56. https://doi.org/10.1016/0304-405X(93)90023-5

Federal Reserve Bank of St. Louis. "10-Year Treasury Constant Maturity Rate [DGS10]." FRED, Federal Reserve Bank of St. Louis, 2025. https://fred.stlouisfed.org/series/DGS10

Fisher, I. *The Purchasing Power of Money: Its Determination and Relation to Credit, Interest and Crises.* Macmillan, 1911.

Fisher, I. *The Theory of Interest: As Determined by Impatience to Spend Income and Opportunity to Invest It.* Macmillan, 1930.

Friedman, M. *The Counter-Revolution in Monetary Theory.* Institute of Economic Affairs, 1970.

Friedman, M., and A.J. Schwartz. *A Monetary History of the United States, 1867–1960.* Princeton University Press, 1963.

Fund, International Monetary. "Money, Inflation, and Output in Emerging Markets." *IMF Staff Papers* 55, no. 2 (2008): 215–51. https://www.imf.org/external/pubs/ft/staffp/2008/04/pdf/vol55index.pdf

Gates, B. "The Rise and Fall of American Growth – A Review. GatesNotes." 2016. https://www.gatesnotes.com/the-rise-and-fall-of-american-growth.

Gerlis, M. "New Claimant to €35mn Klimt Emerges." *Financial Times* May 2, 2024. https://www.ft.com/content/78ade088-3ffc-41ff-b072-414c11d1759b

Geske, R., and R. Roll. "The Fiscal and Monetary Linkage between Stock Returns and Inflation." *The Journal of Finance* 38, no. 1 (1983): 1–33. https://www.jstor.org/stable/2327635

Gordon, R.J. *The Rise and Fall of American Growth: The U.S. Standard of Living since the Civil War*. Princeton University Press, 2016.

Gray, A., Rinke, A., and Siebold, S. "Vance Attack on Europe Overshadows Ukraine Talks at Security Conference." *Reuters*, February 14, 2025. https://www.reuters.com/world/europe/zelenskiy-expected-meet-vance-munich-security-conference-begins-2025-02-14/

Gray, D. "The Lightning Network: Expanding Bitcoin Use Cases." *Fidelity Digital Assets*, 2025. https://www.fidelitydigitalassets.com/research-and-insights/lightning-network-expanding-bitcoin-use-cases

Group, Rhodium. "Tapped Out." 2023. https://rhg.com/research/tapped-out/

Hamilton, A. "Letter to Robert Morris." In *The Papers of Alexander Hamilton*, edited by H.C. Syrett, vol. 2. Columbia University Press, 1781.

Harari, Y.N. "Sapiens: A Brief History of Humankind." *Harper. Hasu*, 2014. https://uncommoncore.co/unpacking-bitcoins-social-contract/

Hotelling, H. "The Economics of Exhaustible Resources." *Journal of Political Economy* 39, no. 2 (1931): 137–75. https://www.jstor.org/stable/1822328

Howell, M. *Capital Wars: The Rise of Global Liquidity*. Springer, 2020.

Hume, D. "Of Money." In *Essays, Moral, Political, and Literary*. Liberty Fund, 1752.

International Monetary Fund. "People's Republic of China: 2024 Article IV Consultation-Press Release; Staff Report; and Statement by the Executive Director for the People's Republic of China." 2024. https://www.imf.org/en/publications/cr/issues/2024/08/01/peoples-republic-of-china-2024-article-iv-consultation-press-release-staff-report-and-552803

Ishikawa, T., and K. Hachiya. "Policy Proposals for Fiscal Consolidation: With the Return to 'a World with Interest Rates,' the Formulation and Execution of a Long-Term Plan Cannot Wait." *JRI Research Journal* (Japan) 7, no. 6 (2024). https://www.jri.co.jp/en/MediaLibrary/file/english/periodical/jrirj/2024/06/

Kahneman, D. *Thinking, Fast and Slow*. Farrar, Straus and Giroux, 2011.

Kahneman, D., and A. Tversky. "Prospect Theory: An Analysis of Decision under Risk." In *Handbook of the Fundamentals of Financial Decision Making: Part I*, edited by H.K. Baker and J.R. Nofsinger. 2013. https://doi.org/10.1142/9789814417358_0006

Kantor, A. "Wealthy Europeans Lured by Tax Havens Face Surge in Exit Charges." *Bloomberg News*, June 24, 2025. https://news.bloomberglaw.com/daily-tax-report-international/wealthy-europeans-lured-by-tax-havens-face-surge-in-exit-charges

Kelton, S. *The Deficit Myth: Modern Monetary Theory and the Birth of the People's Economy*. PublicAffairs, 2020.

Kraemer, C. and Martinez, M. "Hopes for German Economic Recovery Vanish as Election Nears." *Reuters*, January 29, 2025. https://www.reuters.com/markets/europe/germany-sees-2025-export-decline-due-growing-trade-tensions-government-report-2025-01-29/

Kristoufek, L. "Bitcoin and Its Mining on the Equilibrium Path." *Energy Economics* 85 (2020): 104588. https://doi.org/10.1016/j.eneco.2019.104588

Labor Statistics, Bureau. *Productivity*. U.S. Department of Labor, 2025. https://www.bls.gov/productivity/

Lopez, L. *Trump Signs Executive Order to Create 'Strategic Reserve' of Crypto*. 2025. https://www.politico.com/news/2025/03/06/trump-executiveorder-create-strategic-reserve-crypto-00217147

Lucas, R.E. "Expectations and the Neutrality of Money." *Journal of Economic Theory* 4, no. 2 (1972): 103–24. https://doi.org/10.1016/0022-0531(72)90142-1

Macleod, H.D., *The Elements of Political Economy*. Longman, 1858.

Maestas, N., K.J. Mullen, and D. Powell. "The Effect of Population Aging on Economic Growth, the Labor Force and Productivity (NBER Working Paper No. 22452.) *National Bureau of Economic Research. Https://*, ahead of print, 2016. https://doi.org/10.3386/w22452

Malthus, T. *An Essay on the Principle of Population*. Oxford University Press, 1798. https://math.uchicago.edu/~shmuel/Modeling/Malthus,%20

Mankiw, N.G. "A Skeptic's Guide to Modern Monetary Theory." *AEA Papers and Proceedings* 110 (2020): 141–44. https://doi.org/10.1257/pandp.20201102

McKinnon, R.I. *Money and Capital in Economic Development*. Brookings Institution, 1973.

McKinsey and Company. "The New Face of Wealth: The Rise of the Female Investor." 2024. https://www.mckinsey.com/capabilities/growth-marketing-and-sales/

McWilliams, D. *Money: A Story of Humanity*. Simon & Schuster, 2024.

Miller, H. "A Stanford Student-Run Fund's Bitcoin ETF Investment Stirs up a Buzz." *Bloomberg*. March 7, 2024. https://www.bloomberg.com/news/newsletters/2024-03-07/a-stanford-student-run-fund-s-bitcoin-etf-investment-stirs-up-a-buzz

Molenaar, R., E. Sénéchal, L. Swinkels, and Z. Wang. "Empirical Evidence on the Stock–Bond Correlation." *Financial Analysts Journal* 80, no. 3 (2024): 17–36. https://doi.org/10.1080/0015198X.2024.2317333.

Moritz, E. "Isaac Newton and the Alchemical Transformation of English Money: Order, Value." In *And the Royal Mint (SSRN Scholarly Paper No. 5281506). SSRN*. 2025. https://doi.org/10.2139/ssrn.5281506

Mosler, W. *Soft Currency Economics*. University Library of Munich, 1995. https://ideas.repec.org/p/wpa/wuwpma/9502007.html

Nakamoto, S. "Bitcoin: A Peer-to-Peer Electronic Cash System." 2008. https://bitcoin.org/bitcoin.pdf

Nieuwenhuijs, Jan. "Why Gold Will Continue to Shine in 2025 and Beyond." 2025. https://www.moneymetals.com/news/2025/01/17/why-gold-will-continue-to-shine-in-2025-and-beyond-003764

O'Donoghue, P. "NEWS: Dutch Finance Minister says AML rules have 'gone too far'." May 19, 2025. https://www.amlintelligence.com/2025/05/news-dutch-finance-minister-says-aml-rules-have-gone-too-far/

OECD *Survey on Drivers of Trust in Public Institutions – 2024 Results: Building Trust in a Complex Policy Environment*. OECD Publishing, 2024. https://doi.org/10.1787/9a20554b-en

One Planet Summit. "€320 Bn for Climate from the European Union." https://oneplanetsummit.fr/en/coalitions-82/eu-320-b-european-union-climate-274

Piketty, T. *Capital in the Twenty-First Century*. Harvard University Press, 2014.

Piketty, T., E. Saez, and S. Stantcheva. "Optimal Taxation of Top Incomes: A Tale of Three Elasticities." *American Economic Journal: Economic Policy* 6, no. 1 (2014): 230–71. https://doi.org/10.1257/pol.6.1.230

Recouso, A. "Norway's Wealth Tax Unchains a Capital Exodus." *CitizenX*, December 17, 2024. https://citizenx.com/insights/norway-wealth-exodus/

Reinhart, C.M., and K.S. Rogoff. "Growth in a Time of Debt." *American Economic Review* 100, no. 2 (2010): 573–78. https://doi.org/10.1257/aer.100.2.573

Reinhart, C.M., M.B. Sbrancia, and E.S. Shaw. "The Liquidation of Government Debt." *Economic Policy* 30, no. 82 (2015): 291–333. https://doi.org/10.1093/epolic/eiv003

Restrepo, M.L. "200 U.K. Companies Have Opted for a Four-Day Workweek, Latest Data Shows." *NPR*, January 27, 2025. https://www.npr.org/2025/01/27/g-s1-44918/

Ricardo, D. *Proposals for an Economical and Secure Currency: With Observations on the Profits of the Bank of England, as They Regard the Public and the Proprietors of Bank Stock*. Cambridge University Press, 1816. https://doi.org/10.1017/CBO9781107589490

River. "What's Driving Bitcoin Adoption in 2025?" 2025. https://river.com/learn/files/river-bitcoin-adoption-report-2025.pdf

Robbins, L. *An Essay on the Nature and Significance of Economic Science*. Macmillan, 1932.

Rogoff, K. "Modern monetary nonsense." *Project Syndicate*. 2019. https://www.project-syndicate.org/commentary/federal-reserve-modern-monetary-theorydangers-by-kenneth-rogoff-2019-03

Rothman, L. "The U.S. Dollar Hasn't Been Linked to Gold for 45 Years." *Here's Why. Time*, Reserve History, August 15, 2016. https://time.com/4444172/gold-standard-history/

Royal Mint. "The Royal Mint Sees Significant Uplift in Female Investors as More Women Look to Gold and Silver to Manage Investment Risk." 2024. https://www.royalmint.com/aboutus/press-centre/the-royal-mint-sees-significant-uplift-in-female-investors-as-more-women-look-to-gold-and-silver-to-manage-investment-risk/

Ryan, J. "Crypto Firm Tether Holds $8 Billion Pile of Gold in a Secret Swiss Vault." *Bloomberg News*, July 8, 2025. https://www.bloomberg.com/news/articles/2025-07-08/crypto-firm-tether-holds-8-billion-pile-of-gold-in-a-secret-swiss-vault

Sanders, F. "A Moneychanger Interview: Mr." *John Exter". The Money Changer*, n.d. https://web.archive.org/web/20041119031856/http://the-moneychanger.com/articles_files/mmm_files/economy/exter.phtml

Sargent, T.J., and N. Wallace. "Some Unpleasant Monetarist Arithmetic." *Federal Reserve Bank of Minneapolis Quarterly Review* 5, no. 3 (1981): 1–17. https://doi.org/10.21034/qr.531.

Siegel, J.J. "Stocks for the Long Run: A Guide to Selecting Markets for Long-Term Growth." Irwin, 1994. https://www.spglobal.com/spdji/en/

Sigma, Two. "Desmoothing and Interpolation: A Deep Dive. Venn by Two Sigma." 2024. https://www.venn.twosigma.com/resources/desmoothing-interpolation-deep-dive

Singh, K. "Yale University Explores Sale of Private Equity Fund Interests." *Reuters*, April 22, 2025. https://www.reuters.com/world/us/yale-university-exploressale-private-equity-fund-interests-2025-04-22/

Smith, H. "Greece Introduces Growth-Oriented Six-Day Working Week." *The Guardian*, July 1, 2024. https://www.theguardian.com/world/article/2024/jul/01/

Solow, R.M. "A Contribution to the Theory of Economic Growth." *The Quarterly Journal of Economics* 70, no. 1 (1956): 65–94. https://doi.org/10.2307/1884513

Stöferle, R.-P., and M. Valek. "The Optimal Gold Allocation: How Much Gold Does Your Portfolio Need?" Incrementum AG. 2024. https://www.incrementum.li/en/journal/the-optimal-gold-allocation-how-much-gold-does-your-portfolio-need/

Swan, T.W. "Economic Growth and Capital Accumulation." *Economic Record* 32, no. 2 (1956): 334–61. https://doi.org/10.1111/j.1475-4932.1956.tb00434.x

Tapscott, D., and A. Tapscott. *Blockchain Revolution: How the Technology behind Bitcoin Is Changing Money, Business, and the World.* Portfolio, 2016.

Taylor, J.B. "Discretion versus Policy Rules in Practice." *Carnegie Rochester Conference Series on Public Policy*, 39 (1993): 195214. https://web.stanford.edu/~johntayl/Onlinepaperscombinedbyyear/1993/Discretion_versus_Policy_Rules_in_Practice.pdf

Thinking Ahead Institute. "Global Pension Assets Study – 2024." *WTW*, 2024. https://www.thinkingaheadinstitute.org/research-papers/global-pensionassets-study-2024/

Toksabay, E., and E. Erkoyun. "Turkey's Erdogan Repeats Call for Citizens to Convert Forex, Gold Holdings." *Reuters*, March 29, 2021. https://www.reuters.com/world/middle-east/turkeys-erdogan-repeats-call-citizens-convert-forex-gold-holdings-2021-03-29/

Trabandt, M., and H. Uhlig. "The Laffer Curve Revisited." *Journal of Monetary Economics* 58, no. 4 (2011): 305–27. https://doi.org/10.1016/j.jmoneco.2011.07.003

Triffin, R. *Gold and the Dollar Crisis: The Future of Convertibility*. Yale University Press, 1960.

UBS. "Global Family Office Report 2024." 2024. https://www.ubs.com/global/en/media/display-page-ndp/en-20240522-global-family-office-report-2024.html

UBS. "UBS Billionaire Ambitions Report 2024." 2024. https://www.ubs.com/global/en/media/display-page-ndp/en-20241205-billionaire-ambitions-report-2024.html

United Nations. "World Population Prospects." *United Nations Department of Economic and Social Affairs, Population Division*, n.d. https://population.un.org/wpp/

University of Michigan. "Surveys of Consumers." 2025. https://www.sca.isr.umich.edu/.

US Congressional Budget Office. "Historical Data on Federal Debt Held by the Public." *U.S. Congress*, July 2010. https://www.cbo.gov/publication/21728

US Congressional Budget Office. "The Longterm Budget Outlook: 2024 to 2054." 2024. https://www.cbo.gov/publication/59711

US Congressional Budget Office. "Effects of Physical Infrastructure Spending on the Economy and the Budget Under Two Illustrative Scenarios." CBO Publication No. 57327. 2021. https://www.cbo.gov/publication/57327

US Department of the Treasury. "An Unsustainable Fiscal Path. In Executive Summary to the FY 2024 Financial Report of the U.S." https://fiscal.treasury.gov/reports-statements/financial-report/unsustainable-fiscal-path.html

US Government Accountability Office. "Corporate Income Tax: Effective Rates before and after 2017 Law Change." GAO-23-105384. December 2022. https://www.gao.gov/assets/gao-23-105384.pdf

US Government Accountability Office. "The Nation's Fiscal Health: Road Map Needed to Address Projected Unsustainable Debt Levels" GAO-24-106987. 2024. https://www.gao.gov/products/gao-24-106987

Walker, F.A. *Money*. Henry Holt and Company, 1878.

World Gold Council. "Gold Demand Trends: Full Year 2024." 2025. https://www.gold.org/goldhub/research/gold-demand-trends/gold-demand-trends-full-year-2024

World Gold Council. "Gold Reserves by Country." *Goldhub*, 2025. https://www.gold.org/goldhub/data/gold-reserves-by-country

World Health Organization. "Global Health Expenditure Database: Country Profiles." *World Health Organization*. https://apps.who.int/nha/database/country_profile/index/en

Zulaica, O. "What Share for Gold? On the Interaction of Gold and Foreign Exchange Reserve Returns." 2020. https://www.bis.org/publ/work906.htm